John Aubrey

Miscellanies upon various subjects

5th ed

John Aubrey

Miscellanies upon various subjects
5th ed

ISBN/EAN: 9783337303587

Printed in Europe, USA, Canada, Australia, Japan

Cover: Foto ©Andreas Hilbeck / pixelio.de

More available books at **www.hansebooks.com**

MISCELLANIES

UPON VARIOUS SUBJECTS.

BY

JOHN AUBREY, F.R.S.

THE FIFTH EDITION.

TO WHICH IS ADDED,

HYDRIOTAPHIA; OR, URN BURIAL.

BY SIR THOMAS BROWNE.

LONDON:
REEVES AND TURNER
196, STRAND.
1890.

CONTENTS.

Lower Easton-Pierse, Wiltshire, the birth-place of John Aubrey.

THE LIFE OF JOHN AUBREY.

JOHN AUBREY, the subject of this brief notice, was born at Easton Pïerse, (Parish of Kington,) in Wiltshire, on the 12th of March, 1626; and not on the 3rd of November in that year, as stated by some of his biographers. He was the eldest son of Richard Aubrey, Esq. of Burleton, Herefordshire, and Broad Chalk, Wiltshire. Being, according to his own statement, "very weak, and like to dye," he was baptized on the day of his birth, as appears by the Register of Kington. At an early age (1633) he was sent to the Grammar School at Yatton Keynel, and in the following year he was placed under the tuition of Mr. Robert Latimer, the preceptor of Hobbes, a man then far advanced in years.

On the 2nd of May, 1642, being then sixteen years of age, Aubrey was entered a gentleman commoner of Trinity College, Oxford, where he appears to have applied himself closely to study. He however cherished a strong predilection for English History and Antiquities, which was fostered and encouraged at this time by the appearance of the "Monasticon Anglicanum," to which he contributed a plate of Osney Abbey, an ancient ruin near Oxford, entirely destroyed in the Civil Wars.

On the 16th of April, 1646, Aubrey was admitted a student of the Middle Temple, but the death of his father shortly after, leaving him heir to estates in Wiltshire, Surrey, Herefordshire, Brecknockshire and Monmouthshire, obliged him to relinquish his studies and look to his inheritance, which was involved in several law suits.

Though separated from his associates in the University, he appears to have kept up a correspondence with several of them, and among others, Anthony Wood, whom he furnished with much valuable information. Wood made an ungrateful return for this assistance, and in his Autobiography thus speaks of him:—"An. 1667, John Aubrey of Easton Piers in the parish of Kingston, Saint Michael in Wiltshire, was in Oxon. with Edward Forest, a Bookseller, living against Alls. Coll. to buy books. He then saw lying on the stall Notitiæ Academiæ Oxoniensis, and asking who the author of that book was? he [Edw. Forest] answered, the report was that one Mr. Anth. Wood, of Merton College was the author, but was not. Whereupon Mr. Aubrey, a pretender to Antiquities, having been contemporary to A. Wood's elder brother in Trin. Coll. and well acquainted with him, he thought, that he might be as well acquainted with A. W. himself. Whereupon repairing to his lodgings, and telling him who he was, he got into his acquaintance, talked to him about his studies, and offered him what assistance he could make, in order to the completion of the work that he was in hand with. Mr. Aubrey was then in sparkish garb, came to town with his man and two horses, spent high, and flung out A. W. in all his recknings. But his estate of 700li per an. being afterwards sold and he reserving nothing of it to himself, liv'd afterwards in very sorry condition, and at length made shift to rub out by hanging on Edm. Wyld, Esq., living in Blomesbury near London, on James Carle of Abendon, whose first wife was related to him, and on Sr Joh. Aubrey his kinsman, living sometimes in Glamorganshire and sometimes at Borstall near Brill in Bucks. He was a shiftless person, roving and magotie-headed, and sometimes little better than crased. And being exceedingly credulous, would stuff his many letters sent to A. W. with folliries and misinformations, which would sometimes guid him into the paths of errour." This example of bad English, and worse taste, was written after twenty-five years acquaintance! In singular contrast to it, is a letter of Aubrey to Wood, charging him, it is true, with an abuse of confidence and detraction, but urging his complaint in terms which sufficiently evince the kindly and affectionate nature of the writer.

Malone, in his "Historical Account of the English Stage," has done Aubrey justice; and his remarks may properly find a place here. "That the greater part of his (Aubrey's) life was devoted to literary pursuits, is ascertained by the works which he has published, the correspondence which he held with many eminent men, and the collections which he left in manuscript and which are now reposited in the Ashmolean Museum. Among these collections is a curious account of our English Poets, and many other writers. While Wood was preparing his

Athenæ Oxonienses, this manuscript was lent to him, as appears from many queries in his handwriting in the margin; and his account of Milton, with whom Aubrey was intimately acquainted, is (as has been observed by Mr. Warton) literally transcribed from thence." After alluding to the quarrel between Wood and Aubrey, he continues, "But whatever Wood in a peevish humour may have said or thought of Mr. Aubrey, by whose labours he has highly profited, or however fantastical Aubrey may have been on the subject of chemistry and ghosts, his character for veracity has never been impeached, and as a very diligent Antiquary, his testimony is worthy of attention. Mr. Toland, who was well acquainted with him, and certainly a better judge of men than Wood, gives this character of him: 'Though he was extremely superstitious, or seemed to be so, yet he was a very honest man, and most accurate in his account of matter of fact. But the facts he knew, not the reflections he made, were what I wanted.'"

Aubrey preserved, amidst all his troubles, an intimacy with the men of Science and Letters of his day, and with them formed the nucleus of the Royal Society. Some of the principal incidents of his life are briefly detailed in the following autobiographical memoranda, entitled

ACCIDENTS OF JOHN AUBREY.

Born at Easton-Piers, March 1625,6, about sun-rising; very weak and like to Dye, & therefore christned that morning before Prayer. I think I have heard my mother say I had an Ague shortly after I was born.

1629. About three or four years old I had a grievous ague, I can remember it. I got not health till eleven or twelve, but had sickness of Vomiting for 12 hours every fortnight for years, then it came monthly for then quarterly & then half yearly, the last was in June 1642. This sickness nipt my strength in the bud.

1633. At eight years old I had an issue (naturall) in the coronall sutor of my head, which continued running till 21.

1634. October, I had a violent fevor, it was like to have carried me off; 'twas the most dangerous sickness that ever I had.

1639. About 1639 or 1643 I had the measills, but that was nothing, I was hardly sick. Monday after Easter week my Uncle's Nag ranne away with me & gave me a very dangerous fall.

1642. May 3. Entered at Trinity College.

1643. April and May, the Small Pox at Oxon; after left that ingeniouse place & for three years led a sad life in the Country.

1646. April—Admitted of the M. Temple, but my fathers sickness and business never permitted me to make any settlement to my study.

1651. About the 16 or 18 of April I saw that incomparable good conditioned gentlewoman M[rs] M. Wiseman, with whom at first sight I was in love.

1652. October the 21. my father died.

1655. (I think) June 14. I had a fall at Epsam & brake one of my ribbes, and was afraid it might cause an apostumation.

1656. Sept. 1655 or rather I think 1656 I began my chargeable & tedious lawe Suite on the Entaile in Brecknockshire and Monmouthshire. This yeare and the last was a strange yeare to me. Several love and lawe suites.

1656 — Decemb ρ morb.

1657. Novemb 27. obiit Dña Kasker Ryves with whom I was to marry, to my great losse.

1659. March or April like to break my neck in Ely Minster; and the next day, riding a gallop there my horse tumbled over and over, and yet I thank God no hurt.

1660. July. Aug. I accompanied A. Ettrick into Ireland for a month & returning were like to be shipwrecked at Holyhead but no hurt done.

1621. }
1662. } About these yeares I sold my Estate in Herefordshire. Janu. I had the honour to be elected
1663. } Fellow of the R. S.

1664. June 11 landed at Calais, in August following had a terrible fit of the spleen and piles at Orleans. I returned in October.

1664 or 1665. Munday after Christmas was in danger to be spoiled by my horse; and the same day received læsio in testiculo, which was like to have been fatal. O. R. Wiseman quod—I believe 1664.

1665. November 1. I made my first address (in an ill hour) to Joane Sumner.

1666. This yeare all my business and affairs ran kim kam, nothing tooke effect, as if I had been under an ill tongue. Treacheries and enmities in abundance against me.

1667. December —— Arrested in Chancery Lane at M[rs] Sumner's suite.

Feb. 24 A.M. about 8 or 9 Triall with her at Sarum; Victory and £600 damaged; through devilish opposition against me.

1668. July 6. was arrested by Peter Gale's malicious contrivance the day before I was to go to Winton for my second triall; but it did not retard me above two hours, but did not then go to triall.

1669. March 5 was my triall at Winton from eight to nine. The Judge being exceedingly made against me by my Lady Hungerford but four of the appearing and much adoe got the moiety of Sarum: Verdict in £300.

1669 and 1670 I sold all my Estate in Wilts. From 1670 to this very day (I thank God) I have enjoyed a happy delitescency.

1671. Danger of Arrests.

1677. Latter end of June an impostume brake in my head. Mdm. S[t] John's night 1673 in danger of being run through with a sword by a young templer at M. Burges' chamber in the M. Temple.

I was in danger of being killed by William Earl of Pembroke then Lord Herbert at the election of Sir William Salkeld for New Sarum. I have been in danger of being drowned twice.

The year that I lay at M. Neve's (for a short time) I was in great danger of being killed by a drunkard in the

Street of Grays Inn Gate by a Gentleman whom I never saw before but (Deo gratias) one of his companions hindred his thrust.

[1754 June 11. transcribed from a MS. in M. Aubrey's own handwriting in the possession of Dr. R. Rawlinson.]

These incidents are so curiously narrated, and afford such interesting glimpses of the times to which they refer, that it is to be regretted they exist in so brief a form.

Several of Aubrey's biographers have given a very loose and unsatisfactory account of him, and it was left for Mr. Britton to prepare a more authentic Life of one who had laboured long and zealously to preserve the records of the past. To that gentleman we owe many particulars regarding the close of Aubrey's career; among others, the entry of his burial at Oxford, in the church of St. Mary Magdalene—"1697. John Aubery a stranger was Buryed Jun. 7th."

To Mr. Britton we are also indebted for the fact that Aubrey was never married; the statement that he had been united to Joan Sumner, resting on no surer foundation than the allusion to that lady in the "Accidents" above quoted. He died intestate, and Letters of Administration were granted on the 18th December, 1697, to his surviving brother William. In that license he is described as "late of Broad Chalk in the County of Wilts, *Batchelor*."

[DEDICATION TO THE FIRST EDITION.]

TO THE RIGHT HONOURABLE,

JAMES EARL OF ABINGDON,

LORD CHIEF-JUSTICE IN EYRE OF ALL HIS MAJESTY'S FORESTS AND CHACES ON THIS SIDE TRENT.

MY LORD,

WHEN I enjoyed the contentment of Solitude in your pleasant walks and gardens at Lavington the last summer, I reviewed several scattered papers which had lain by me for several years; and then presumed to think, that if they were put together, they might be somewhat entertaining: I therefore digested them there in this order, in which I now present them to your Lordship.

The matter of this collection is beyond human reach: we being miserably in the dark, as to the œconomy of the invisible world, which knows what we do, or incline to, and works upon our passions and sometimes is so kind as to afford us a glimpse of its præscience.

My Lord,

It was my intention to have finished my *Description of Wiltshire** (half finished already) and to have dedicated it to your Lordship: but my age is now too far spent for such undertakings: I have therefore devolved that task on my country man, Mr. Thomas Tanner,† who hath youth to go through with it, and a genius proper for such an undertaking.

Wherefore, I humbly beseech your Lordship to accept of this small offering, as a grateful memorial of the profound respect which I have for you, who have for many years taken me into your favour and protection.

My Lord,

May the blessed Angels be your careful guardians: such are the prayers of

Your Lordship's

Most obliged

And humble Servant,

John Aubrey.

1696.

* In the Ashmolean Museum at Oxford.

† Afterwards Bishop of St. Asaph.

DAY-FATALITY:

OR, SOME OBSERVATIONS OF DAYS LUCKY AND UNLUCKY.

LUC. xix. 43.

In hoc die tuo: In this thy day.

THAT there be good and evil times, not only the sacred scriptures, but prophane authors mention: see 1 Sam. 25, 8. Esther 8, 17. and 9, 19, 22. Ecclus. 14. 14.

The fourteenth day of the first month was a memorable and blessed day amongst the children of Israel: see Exod. 12, 18, 40, 41, 42, 51. Levit. 23, 5. Numb. 28, 16. Four hundred and thirty years being expired of their dwelling in Egypt, even in the self same day departed they thence.

A thing something parallel to this we read in the Roman histories: that, that very day four years, that the civil wars were begun by Pompey the father, Cæsar made an end of them with his sons; Cneius Pompeius being then slain, and it being also the last battle Cæsar was ever in. (Heylin in the kingdom of Corduba.) The calendar to Ovid's *Fastorum*, says, *Aprilis erat mensis Græcis auspicatisimus*, a most auspicious month among the Græcians.

As to evil days and times; see Amos 5, 13. and 6, 3. Eccles. 9, 12. Psal. 37, 19. Obad. 12. Jer. 46, 21. And Job hints it, in cursing his birth-day. Cap. 3, v. 1, 10, 11. See *Weever*, p. 458.

Early in a morning
In an evil tyming,
  Went they from Dunbar.

Horace, lib. 2. Ode 13. Cursing the tree that had like to have fallen upon him, says, *Ille nefasto te posuit die;* intimating that it was planted in an unlucky day.

The Romans counted Feb. 13, an unlucky day, and therefore then never attempted any business of importance; for on that day they were overthrown at Allia by the Gauls; and the Fabii attacking the city of the Veii, were all slain, save one. (Heylin, speaking of St. Peter's patrimony.) And see the calendar annext to Ovid's *Fastorum*, as to the last circumstance.

The Jews accounted August 10, an unfortunate day; for on that day the Temple was destroyed by Titus, the son of Vespasian; on which day also the first Temple was consumed with fire by Nebuchadnezzar. (Heylin.) The treasury of the times says the eighth of Loyon (August) the very same day 679 years one after another.

And not only among the Romans and Jews, but also among Christians, a like custom of observing such days is used, especially Childermas or Innocent's day. Comines tells us, that Lewis XI. used not to debate any matter, but accounted it a sign of great misfortune towards him, if any man communed with him of his affairs; and would be very angry with those about him, if they troubled him with any matter whatsoever upon that day.

But I will descend to more particular instances of lucky and unlucky days.

Upon the sixth of April, Alexander the Great was born. Upon the same day he conquered Darius, won a great victory at sea, and died the same day.

Neither was this day less fortunate to his father Philip; for on the same day he took Potidea; Parmenio, his General, gave a great overthrow to the Illyrians; and his horse was victor at the Olympic Games. Therefore, his prophets foretold to him, *Filium cujus natalis*, &c. That a son whose birth-day was accompanied with three victories, should prove invincible. *Pezelius in melificio historico.*

Upon the thirtieth of September, Pompey the Great was born: upon that day he triumphed for his Asian conquest, and on that day he died.

The nineteenth of August was the day of Augustus his adoption: on the same day he began his consulship: he conquered the Triumviri, and on the same day he died. Hitherto out of the memories of King Charles I's. heroes.

If Solomon counts the day of one's death better than the day of one's birth, there can be no objection why that also may not be reckoned amongst one's remarkable and happy days. And therefore I will insert here, that the eleventh of February was the noted day of Elizabeth, wife to Henry VII. who was born and died that day. Weever, p. 476. Brooke, in Henry VII. marriage. Stow, in Anno 1466, 1503.

As also that the twenty-third of November was the observable day of Francis, Duke of Lunenburgh, who was born on that day, and died upon the same, 1549, as says the French author of the Journal History, who adds upon particular remark and observable curiosity.

Ipsa dies vitam contulit, ipsa necem.
The same day life did give,
And made him cease to live.

Sir Kenelm Digby, that renowned knight, great linguist, and magazine of arts, was born and died on the eleventh of June, and also fought fortunately at Scanderoon the same day. Here his epitaph, composed by Mr. Ferrar, and recited in the aforesaid Memoirs:

Under this stone the matchless Digby lies,
Digby the great, the valiant and the wise:
This age's wonder for his noble parts;
Skill'd in six tongues, and learn'd in all the arts.
Born on the day he died, th' eleventh of June,
On which he bravely fought at Scanderoon.
'Tis rare that one and self-same day should be
His day of birth, of death, of victory.

I had a maternal uncle, that died the third of March, 1678, which was the anniversary day of his birth; and (which is a truth exceeding strange) many years ago he foretold the day of his death to be that of his birth; and he also averred the same but about the week before his departure. The third of March is the day of St. Eutropius; and as to my uncle it was significative; it turned well to him, according to that of Rev. 14, 13. Blessed are the dead, &c. and that of Ovid Metam. lib. 3.

——*Dicique beatus,*
Ante obitum nemo supremaque funera debet.——
——None happy call
Before their death, and final funeral.

The sixth of January was five times auspicious to Charles, Duke of Anjou. Ibid. in the life of the Earl of Sunderland.

The twenty-fourth of February was happy to Charles V. four times. (Ibid.) Heylin, speaking of the Temple of Jerusalem, hints three of these four; his birth, taking of

Francis, King of France, prisoner; his receiving the Imperial crown at Bononia. And so doth also the Journal History before mentioned.

Of the family of the Trevors, six successive principal branches have been born the sixth of July. Same memoirs.

Sir Humphrey Davenport was born the 7th of July; and on that day anniversary, his father and mother died, within a quarter of an hour one of another. Same memoirs.

I have seen an old Romish MSS. prayer-book, (and shewed the same to that general scholar, and great astrologer, Elias Ashmole, Esq.;) at the beginning whereof was a Calendar wherein were inserted the unlucky days of each month, set out in verse. I will recite them just as they are, sometimes infringing the rule of grammar, sometimes of Prosodia; a matter of which the old monkish rhymers were no way scrupulous. It was as ancient as Henry the sixth, or Edward the fourth's time.

January. *Prima dies mensis, & septima truncat ut ensis.*
February. *Quarta subit mortem, prosternit tertia fortem.*
March. *Primus mandentem, disrumpit quarta bibentem.*
April. *Denus & undenus est mortis vulnere plenus.*
May. *Tertius occidit, & septimus ora relidit.**
June. *Denus pallescit, quindenus fœdera nescit.*

* Ex re & ledo.

July. *Ter-decimus mactat, Julij denus labefactat.*
August. *Prima necat fortem, prosternit secunda cohortem.*
September. *Tertia Septembris & denus fert mala membris.*
October. *Tertius & denus est, sicut, mors alienus.*
November. *Scorpius est quintus, & tertius è nece cinctus.*
December. *Septimus exanguis, virosus denus & anguis.*

The tenth verse is intolerable, and might be mended thus.

Tertia cum dena sit sicut mors aliena.

If any object and say, *Deni* is only the plural; I excuse my self by that admirable chronogram upon King Charles the martyr.

Ter deno, Jani, Lunæ, Rex (Sole cadente)
Carolus euxtus Solio, Sceptroque, secure.

Neither will I have recourse for refuge to that old terrastich,

Intrat Avaloniam duodena Caterva virorum
Flos Arimathiæ Joseph, &c.

because I have even now blamed the liberty of the ancient rhymers. He means by *Mors aliena,* some strange kind of death; though *aliena* signifies in quite another sense than there used.

I shall take particular notice here of the third of November, both because 'tis my own birth day, and also for that I have observed some remarkable accidents to have happened thereupon.

Constantius, the Emperor, son of Constantine the Great, little inferior to his father, a worthy warrior, and good man, died the third of November: *Ex veteri Calendario penes me.*

Thomas Montacute, Earl of Salisbury, that great man, and famous commander under Henry IV. V. and VI. died this day, by a wound of a cannon-shot he received at Orleans, E MSS. *quodam, & Glovero.*

So also Cardinal Borromeo, famous for his sanctity of life, and therefore canonized, (Heylin in his *Præcognita,* says, he made Milan memorable, by his residence there) died 1584, this day, as Possevinus in his life.

Sir John Perrot, (Stow corruptly calls him Parrat) a man very remarkable in his time, Lord Deputy of Ireland, son to Henry VIII. and extremely like him, died in the tower, the third of November, 1592 (as Stow says). Grief, and the fatality of this day, killed him. See Naunton's *Fragmenta Regalia,* concerning this man.

Stow, in his Annals, says, Anno 1099, November 3, as well in Scotland as England, the sea broke in, over the banks of many rivers, drowning divers towns, and much people, with an innumerable number of oxen and sheep, at which time the lands in Kent, sometimes belonging to Earl Godwin, were covered with sands, and drowned, and to this day are called Godwin's Sands.

I had an estate left me in Kent, of which between thirty

and forty acres was marsh-land, very conveniently flanking its up-land; and in those days this marsh-land was usually let for four nobles an acre. My father died, 1643. Within a year and half after his decease, such charges and water-schots came upon this marsh-land, by the influence of the sea, that it was never worth one farthing to me, but very often eat into the rents of the up-land: so that I often think, this day being my birth-day, hath the same influence upon me, that it had 580 years since upon Earl Godwin, and others concerned in low-lands.

The Parliament, so fatal to Rome's concerns here, in Henry VIII's. time, began the third of November (26 of his reign;) in which the Pope, with all his authority, was clean banished the realm; he no more to be called otherwise than Bishop of Rome; the King to be taken and reputed as supreme head of the church of England, having full authority to reform all errors, heresies and abuses of the same: also the first-fruits and tenths of all spiritual promotions and dignities were granted to the King. See Stow's Annals, and Weever, page 80.

Not long after which, followed the visitation of abbies, priories, and nunneries; and after that, their final suppression: this Parliament being the door, or entrance thereto.

The third of November 1640, began that Parliament so direfully fatal to England, in its peace, its wealth, its religion, its gentry, its nobility; nay, its King. So verifying the former verse of the calendar.

Scorpius est quintus, & tertius è nece cinctus.
A killing day to some or other.

On the third of November 1703, was the remarkable storm.

The third of September was a remarkable day to the English Attila, Oliver, 1650. He obtained a memorable victory at Dunbar; another at Worcester, 1651, and that day he died, 1658.

The first two occurrences wonderfully accord to the preceding verses.

Tertia Septembris, & denus fert mala membris.

Being fatal to the two members of great Britain, Scotland and England. The third, as happy to them both, as the same day, 1666, was dismal and unhappy to the city of London, and consequently to the whole kingdom, with its immediate preceding and two succeeding days, viz. the second, fourth, and fifth of September.

I come now to the days of the week.

Tuesday *(Dies Martis)* was a most remarkable day with Thomas Becket, Arch Bishop of Canterbury, as Weever, 201, observes from Mat. Paris: *Mars Secundum Poetas, Deus Belli nuncupatur. Vita Sancti Thomæ (secundum illud Job, Vita hominis militia est super terram) tota fuit contra hostem bellicosa, &c.* The life of St. Thomas (according to that of Job, the life of a man is a warfare upon earth) was a continual conflict against the enemy. Upon a Tuesday he suffered; upon Tuesday he was translated; upon Tuesday the Peers of the land sat against him at Northampton; upon Tuesday he was banished; upon Tuesday the Lord appeared to him at Pontiniac, saying, Thomas, Thomas, my church shall be glorified in thy blood; upon Tuesday he returned from exile; upon Tuesday he got the palm or reward of martyrdom; upon Tuesday 1220, his venerable body received the glory and renown of translation, fifty years after his passion. Thus my author.

One thing I make bold to gloss upon. His translation is here mentioned twice.

Note, this is no tautology of the historian; but the latter paragraph is a mere recitation of the first, viz. reference to the time when he was translated into the number of Saints and Martyrs: *quando in divorum numerum relatus*, as Camden.

Wednesday is said to have been the fortunate day of Sixtus Quintus, that Pope of renowned merit, that did so great and excellent things in the time of his government. See the just weight of the scarlet robe, (page 101, his desired praises.) On a Wednesday he was born; on that day he was made Monk; on the same he was made General of his order; on that also, was he successively created Cardinal, elected Pope, and also inaugurated. See *Heylin*, speaking of the Temple of Jerusalem.

Friday was observed to be very fortunate to the great

renowned Captain Gonsalvo, he having on that day given the French many memorable defeats.

Saturday was a lucky day to Henry VII. upon that day he atchieved the victory upon Richard III. being August 22, 1485. On that day he entered the city, being August 29 (correct Stow, who mistakes the day) and he himself always acknowledged, he had experienced it fortunate. See *Bacon* in his Life.

Thursday was a fatal day to Henry VIII. (as Stow, 812) and so also to his posterity. He died on Thursday, Jan. 28. King Edward VI. on Thursday, July 6. Queen Mary on Thursday, November 17. Queen Elizabeth on Thursday, March 24.

Saturday (or the Jewish Sabbath) was fatal to Jerusalem Temple; for on that day it was taken by Pompey, Herod and Titus, successively. *Heylin.*

Hitherto by way of prologue. And be pleased to take notice, as to the days of the month, I have taken such care, that all are according to the Julian or old account, used by us here in England. (See Partridge's almanack, preface to the reader) Pope Gregory XIII. brought in his new stile (generally used beyond sea) *anno* 1585, in October, as asserts the Journal History before recited.

An old proverb.

When Easter falls in our lady's lap,
Then let England beware a rap.

Easter falls on March 25, when the Sunday letter is G, and the golden number 5, 13, or 16. As in the late years, 1459, 1638, 1649.

1459, King Henry VI. was deposed and murdered.

1638, The Scottish troubles began, on which ensued the great rebellion.

1648-9, King Charles I. murdered.

I think it will not happen so again till the year 1991.

Now for epilogue and remarkable reflection.

Turning over our annals, I chanced upon a two-fold circumstance: I will not say, that none else hath observed the same; but I protest, *(Ita me Deus amet, ut verum loquor)* I do not know of any that have; and therefore must justly claim to be acquitted from the least suspicion of plagiarism, or plowing with others heifers.

The first is, of William the Conqueror. The second, of Edward III. (I need not say any thing of the eminency of these two; every one knows what great things they did.) And making reflection upon the auspicious birth-day of His Royal Highness the Duke of York, I adventured upon the following composure. (I cannot be proud of my poetry; but I cannot but be glad of my Bon Heur, *d'avoir (en lisant) tombé si fortuemènt sur les evenements d'un si* Bon Jour.)

Ad Illustrissimum & Celsissimum Principem, Jacobum *Ducem* Eboracensem, *de Natali suo Auspicatissimo Octobris* XIV. *Anno* 1633.

——————*Deus*
Anne nefasto te posuit die? Hor. lib. 2. ode 13.

Oct. *Decimo quarto Normannus Haraldum*
Dux superavit, & Hinc Regia sceptra tulit.
Tertius Edwardus, capto pernice Caleto,
(Gallica quo Regna sunt resarata sibi)
Ire domum tentans, diris turbinibus actus
In pelago, Vitæ magna pericla subit.
Oct. *Decimo quarto, tamen appulit Oras*
Nativas. (His quàm prosperus ille dies!)
Natali lætare tuo, quàm Maxime Princeps;
Fausta velut sunt hæc, Omnia semper habe.

October's fourteenth gave the Norman Duke
That victory, whence he Englands sceptre took.*
Third Edward, after he had Calais won,
(The mean whereby he France did over-run)
Returning home, by raging tempests tost,
(And near his life (so fortunes) to have lost)†
Arrived safe on shore the self-same date.
(This day to them afforded so fair fate.)
Great Duke, rejoice in this your day of birth;
And may such omens still encrease your mirth.

The Verses I presented in *anno* 1672, to a most honourable Peer of the land, and of great place near his Royal Highness.

Since which time, old Fabian's chronicle coming into my hands, from him I got knowledge, that that advantagi-

* Stow, in *anno* 1066. † Stow, in *anno* 1347.

ous peace, mentioned by Stow, *anno* 1360, (concluded between the forementioned King Edward III. and the French King) was acted upon the fourteenth of October, with grand solemnity.

The two former circumstances must needs fall out providentially: whether this last of *anno* 1360, was designed by Edward III. or no, (as remembering his former good hap) may be some question: I am of opinion not.

Where things are under a man's peculiar concern, he may fix a time; but here was the French King concerned equally with the English, and many other great personages interested. To have tied them up to his own auspicious conceit of the day, had been an unkind oppression, and would have brought the judgment of so wise a Prince into question: we may conclude then, it was meerly fortuitous. And therefore to the former observation concerning this famous Edward, give me leave to add,

Insuper hoc ipso die (sibi commoda) Grandis
Rex cum Galligenis, fœdera fecit idem,

An advantageous peace, on day self-same,
This mighty Prince did with the Frenchmen frame.

A memorable peace (foretold by Nostradamus) much conducing to the saving of Christian blood, was made upon the fourteenth of October 1557, between Pope Paul IV. Henry II. of France, and Philip II. of Spain. Nostradamus says, these great Princes were *frappèz du Ciel*, moved from Heaven to make this peace. See *Garencier's* Comment on *Nostradamus*, p. 76.

A lucky day this, not only to the Princes of England, but auspicious to the welfare of Europe. *John Gibbon,* 1678.

Thus far Mr. John Gibbon. The Latin verses of the twelve months quoted by him out of an old manuscript, I have seen in several mass-books; and they are printed in the calendar to the works of the Venerable Bede. 'Tis to be presumed, that they were grounded upon experience; but we have no instances left us of the memorables of those days.

As for the third and tenth of September, I have here set down some extractions from a little book called The Historian's Guide: or, Britain's Remembrancer; which was carefully collected by a club. It begins at the year 1600, and is continued to 1690. There cannot be found in all the time aforesaid, the like instances.

Tertia Septembris, & denus fere mala membris.

September 3, 1641. The Parliament adjourned to the 20th of October next, and the Irish rebellion broke out, where were 20,000 persons barbarously murdered.

September 3, 1643. Biddeford, Appleford, and Barnstable surrendered to the King.

September 3, 1650. Dunbar fight.

September 3, 1651. Worcester fight.

September 3, 1651. Earl of Derby defeated at Preston.

September 3, 1654. A third Parliament at Westminster.

September 3, 1658. Oliver, Protector died.

September 3, 1675. The town of Northampton near burnt down to the ground by accidental fire.

September 3, 1662. William Lenthal, Speaker of the House of Commons, died.

September 3, 4, 1665. Four Dutch men of war, two East-India ships, and several merchant-men taken by the Earl of Sandwich, with the loss only of the Hector.

September 2, 1644. The Earl of Essex fled to Plymouth, and the army submitted to the King.

September 2, 1645. The Scots raised the siege from before Hereford.

September 2, 1653. The Londoners petition the Parliament to continue tythes.

September 2, 1685. The Lady Lisle beheaded at Winchester, for harbouring Hicks, a rebel.

September 4, 1643. Exeter taken by Prince Maurice.

September 4, 1653. General Blake buried at Westminster.

September 5, 1652. The French fleet beaten by the English.

Memorables on September the tenth.

September 10, 1643. The siege of Gloucester raised. I remember over that gate which leads to Nymphs-field was this following inscription in free-stone: the walls are now pulled down.

Always remember,
The tenth of September,
One thousand six hundred forty three,
And give God the glory.

September 10, 1645. Bristol surrendered to the Parliament.

September 10, 1649. Drogheda taken, as appears by Cromwell's letter to the Speaker Lenthal.

September 10, 1660. Peace with Spain proclaimed.

September 10, 1670. Peace concluded between England and Spain in America, was this day ratified at Madrid.

September 10, 1673. This day his majesty commanded the Earl of Ossory to take the command of the fleet at the Buoy in the Nore, in the absence of Prince Rupert.

September 12, 1679. The King takes from the Duke of Monmouth his commission of General.

September 12, 1680. Mrs. Cellier tried at the Old Bailey, for publishing a book called Malice Defeated, &c. and found guilty.

September 12, 1683. The siege of Vienna raised (after the besieged had lost 10,000 men, and the besiegers 70,000) by the King of Poland, and the Duke of Lorrain.

May 29, 1630. King Charles II. born.

May 29, 1660. Restored.

May 29, 1672. The fleet beaten by the Dutch.

May 29, 1679. A rebellion broke out in the west of Scotland, where they proclaimed the covenant, and put forth a declaration.

The Emperor Charles V. was born on February 24, 1500.

He won the battle of Pavia, February 24, 1525.

Clement VII. crowned him Emperor, February 24, 1530.

Raphael d'Urbino (the famous painter) was born on Good-Friday, and died on Good-Friday.

At Feltwell in Norfolk (which lies east and west) a fire happened to break out at the west end, which the west wind blew and burned all the street: on that day twenty years, another fire happened there, which began at the east end, and burned it to the ground again. This I had from a reverend divine. *Quære de hoc.*

Colonel Hugh Grove of Wiltshire, was beheaded at Exeter (together with Colonel John Penruddock) on the ninth day of May 1655. On that very day three years, his son and heir died at London of a malignant fever, and about the same hour of the day.

A very good friend of mine and old acquaintance was born on the 15th of November: his eldest son was born on the 15th of November, and his second son's first son on the 15th of November.

At the hour of prime, April 6, 1327, Petrarch first saw his mistress Laura in the Church of Saint Clara in Avignon. In the same city, same month, same hour, 1348, she died. 'Tis his own remark. *Petrarcha Redivivus*, 242.

DAY-FATALITY OF ROME,

Written by Mr. John Pell, D.D. *from whom I had it.*

THEY that called the city of Rome, *Urbs Æterna*, seemed to believe that Rome could never be destroyed. But there have been great numbers of men, that did verily believe, that it shall have an irrecoverable overthrow. Writers have proceeded so far, as to foretell the time of Rome's final ruin. Some said that Rome's perdition should happen in the year of Christ 1670, they have now been decried nine whole years: so that few take care to know what reasons moved them to pitch upon that number.

A Lutheran historian, *anno* 1656, wrote thus, *Finem Jubileorum Ecclesiasticorum omniumque tempòrum in Scriptura revelatorum, desinere in Annum Christi Millesimum sexcentesimum & septuagesimum, antehac observavit Beatus Gerhardus cum Philippo Nicolao.* But all men are not of Dr. Gerhard's opinion. Many men believe, that some of the prophecies in the Revelations do reach far beyond our times, and that the events of future times will unclasp and unseal a considerable portion of the Apocalypse.

One of the reasons, that recommended the number of 1670, was because it is the sum of 410, and 1260.

Historians agree, that in the year of Christ 410, in the month of August, Rome was trampled under foot, and her heathen inhabitants were miserably slaughtered by the victorious army of Alaric, a Christian King of the Goths. Paulus Diaconus saith, August the 24th was the day of King Alaric's taking Rome. Kedrenus saith, it was August the 26th, perhaps the army first entered the 24th, and the King followed not till two days after.

As for the other number 1260. It is twice found in the Revelations of St. John, ch. 11, 3. "My two witnesses shall prophesy a thousand two hundred and sixty days." And chap. 12, 6. "Should feed the woman in the Wilderness, a thousand two hundred and threescore days." And it is there expressed in another form, (42 times 30) chap. 11, 2. "The Gentiles shall tread the holy city under foot forty and two months." Chap. 13, 5. "Power was given to the blasphemous beast to continue forty and two months." Chap. 12, 14. "The woman is nourished in the Wilderness for (*Καιρὸν καὶ καιροὺς καὶ ἥμισυ καιροῦ*) a season and seasons, and half a season." See Act. 1, 7. 360 and 720, and 180 are equal to 1260. So it seems every *καιρὸ* hath 360 days, or twelve months at thirty days to a month. No doubt Daniel had given occasion to this expression, chap. 7, 25. "A time, and times, and the dividing of time." No man can ground any distinct reasoning upon such general words. But yet it is not tied to a just number of days, (as 360) but is capable of various interpretations in several prophecies. Daniel useth a plural in both places, and not a dual, (two times and two seasons) nor doth John say, two seasons: but by his Numeral Illustration, he teaches us to understand him, as if he had said, (chap. 12, 14). "For three seasons and half a season:" I say Numeral Illustration. For I take it to be no other than an easy example (12 and 24 and 6 are 42) to direct the sons of the prophets not yet arrived to the skill of dealing with difficult supputations of numbers not then discoverable. As Revel. 13, 18. "Here is wisdom, let him that hath understanding count the number of the beast."

By 1260 days, almost all the interpreters understand so many years, but not a year of 360 days; because they find no nation that hath so short a year. The Egyptians had a year of just 365 days; but before St. John was born, the Romans had forced them to allow $365\frac{1}{4}$ as we use now in England.

In an enquiry concerning Rome, it is fit to consider the length of a Roman year. (I may justly say a Roman-Moyed; for no city ever had their year's length and form of a calendar determined, settled, and commanded with so much absolute authority as Rome had) Julius Cæsar by an edict commanded that number of $365\frac{1}{4}$ to be observed, and therefore it is called a Julian year. Three Julians and an half have days $1278\frac{3}{8}$, but Julian years $1378\frac{3}{8}$ are 1278 Julian years, and days $136\frac{31}{32}$; or almost 137 days.

Almost 100 years ago, Pope Gregory the XIII. by a papal bull introduced a calendar wherein the year's length is supposed to have days $365\frac{97}{500}$. Then three Gregorian years and an half have days $1278\frac{279}{800}$. But Gregorian years $1278\frac{279}{800}$ are 1278 Julian years, and days almost 118. Wherefore instead of adding 1260, add 1278, add 137 days to the year of our Lord 410, August 26. The sum shews the year of our Lord 1688, August 163, that is, ten days after the end of December 1688 old stile. This is the utmost, or farthest day, beyond which no Apocalypse account (reckoning from Alaric) can point out a time for the final destruction of the city of Rome.

Again (instead of adding 1260) add 1278 years, and days 118 to the year of our Lord 410, August 24. The sum shews the year of our Lord 1688, August 142, that is, eleven days before the end of December 1688 old stile. This (December 20) is the nearest or soonest day that can be gathered by Apocalyptic account (reckoning from Alaric) to point out the time of Rome's final ruin. But if it happens not before the eleventh of January, men will make no more reckoning of Alaric; but begin a new account from Attila, in the year of Christ, 453.

Calculation to a day (when we can do it) may be defended by a great example. Exod. 12, 41. "At the end of 430 "years, even the self-same day, &c." *John Pell.*

Dr. Pell told me, that St. Augustin writes somewhere, to this purpose, viz. "That it were to be wished, that "some skilful mathematician would take the pains to examine and consider the mathematical parts of the holy "scripture."

OF FATALITIES OF FAMILIES AND PLACES.

THE Lord Chancellor Bacon says,* "As for "nobility in particular persons, it is a reverend thing to see an antient castle or "building not in decay: or to see a fair "timber tree sound and perfect; how much more to behold an antient noble family, which hath stood against "the waves and weathers of time: for new nobility is but "the act of power; but antient nobility is the act of time."

But *Omnium rerum est vicissitudo:* families and places have their fatalities, according to that of *Ovid.*

Fors sua cuique loco est. Fast. lib. 4.

This piece of a verse puts me in mind of several places in Wiltshire, and elsewhere, that are, or have been fortunate to their owners: and *è contra.*

* Essay XIV. of Nobility.

Stourton, (the seat of the Lord Stourton) was belonging to this family before the conquest. They say, that after the victory at Battaile, William the Conqueror came in person into the west, to receive their rendition; that the Lord Abbot of Glastonbury, and the rest of the Lords and Grandees of the western parts waited upon the Conqueror at Stourton-house; where the family continue to this day.

The honourable family of the Hungerfords, is probably of as great antiquity as any in the county of Wilts. Hungerford, (the place of the barony) was sold but lately by Sir Edward Hungerford, Knight of the Bath; as also the noble and ancient seat of Farleigh-Castle, about *anno* 167. But that this estate should so long continue is not very strange; for it being so vast, 'twas able to make several with-standings against the shock of fortune.

The family of Gawen, have been long at Norington, in the parish of Alvideston in Wiltshire. It was sold by —— Gawen, Esq. to Sir Wadham Wyndham, one of the Judges of the King's Bench, about 1665. They continued in this place four hundred fifty and odd years. Then also was sold their estate in Broad-Chalk, which they had as long, or perhaps longer. On the south down of the farm of Broad-Chalk, is a little barrow, called Gawen's Barrow (which must be before ecclesiastical canons were constituted; for since, burials are only in consecrated ground). King Edgar gave the manor and farm of Broad-Chalk to the nuns of Wilton-Abby, which is 900 years ago.

Mr. Thynne, in his explanation of the hard words in Chaucer, writes thus, Gawen, fol. 23, p. 1. This Gawyn was sisters son to Arthur the Great, King of the Britains, a famous man in war, and in all manner of civility ; as in the acts of the Britains we may read. In the year 1082, in a province of Wales, called Rose, was his sepulchre found. *Chaucer*, in the Squire's Tale.

This straunger night that came thus sodenly
All armed, save his head, full royally
Salued the King, and Queen, and Lordes all
By order as they sitten in the Hall
With so high Reverence and Obeisaunce
As well in Speech as in Countenaunce,
That Gawain with his old Courtesie,
Though he came again out of Fairie,
He could him not amend of no word.

Sir William Button of Tockenham, Baronet, (the father) told me that his ancestors had the lease of Alton-farm (400*l. per annum*) in Wilts, (which anciently belonged to Hyde-Abby *juxta Winton*) four hundred years. Sir William's lease expired about 1652, and so fell into the hands of the Earl of Pembroke.

Clavel, of Smedmore, in the Isle of Purbec, in the county of Dorset, was in that place before the conquest, as appears by Dooms-day book. The like is said of Hampden, of Hampden in Bucks : their pedigree says, that one of that family had the conduct of that county in two invasions of the Danes. Also Pen of Pen, in that county, was before the conquest, as by Dooms-day book.

Contrariwise, there are several places unlucky to their possessors, *e. g.* Charter-house, on Mendip in Somersetshire, never passed yet to the third generation. The manor of Butleigh near Glastonbury, never went yet to the third generation.

Bletchington, in Oxfordshire, continued in the family of the Panures, for about 300 years: it was alienated by —— Panure, to Sir John Lenthal, about the year 1630, who sold it again to Sir Thomas Coghill, about 1635. He sold it to William Lewis, Esq. whose relict made it over to the Duke of Richmond and Lenox, about the year 166. His Grace sold it to Arthur, Earl of Anglesey, about the year 166.

Fatality of proper names of Princes, *e. g.* Augustus, the first Roman Emperor, and Augustulus the last. Constantine, the first Grecian Emperor, and Constantine the last. The like is observed of the first and last Mexican Emperors. And the Turks have a prophesy that the last Emperor will be a Mahomet.

John hath been an unfortunate name to Kings. All the second Kings since the conquest have been unfortunate.

London-Derry was the first town in Ireland that declared for the Parliament against King Charles I. and for the Prince of Orange against King James II. It was closely besieged both times without effect. The King's party were once masters of all the kingdom, except London-Derry and Dublin, and King James had all in his power but London-Derry and Inniskilling. One Taylor, a minister, was as famous for his martial feats in the first siege, as Walker in the last.

'Tis certain, that there are some houses unlucky to their inhabitants, which the reverend and pious Dr. Nepier could acknowledge. See *Tobit*, chap. 3, v. 8. "That she "had been married to seven husbands, whom Asmodæus, "the evil spirit, had killed, before they had lain with her."

The Fleece-tavern, in Covent-garden, (in York-street) was very unfortunate for Homicides:* there have been several killed, three in my time. It is now (1692) a private house.

A handsome brick house on the south side of Clerkenwell church-yard had been so unlucky for at least forty years, that it was seldom tenanted; and at last, no body would adventure to take it. Also a handsome house in Holborn, that looked towards the fields; the tenants of it did not prosper, several, about six.

At the sign of —— over against Northumberland house,

* "Clifton the master of the house, hanged himself, having perjured himself." MS. Note in a copy of the Miscellanies in the Library of the Royal Society.

near Charing-Cross, died the Lady Baynton, (eldest daughter of Sir John Danvers of Dansey.) Some years after in the same house, died my Lady Hobbey (her sister) of the small-pox, and about twenty years after, died their nephew Henry Danvers, Esq. of the small-pox, aged twenty-one, wanting two weeks. He was nephew and heir to the Right Honourable Henry Danvers, Earl of Danby.

Edmund Wild, Esq. hath had more Deodands from his manor of Totham in Essex, than from all his estate besides : two mischiefs happened in one ground there.

Disinheriting the eldest son is forbid in the holy scripture, and estates disinherited are observed to be unfortunate ; of which one might make a large catalogue. See Dr. *Saunderson's* Sermon, where he discourses of this subject.

Periodical Small-Poxes.

The small-pox is usually in all great towns :* but it is observed at Taunton in Somersetshire, and at Sherborne in Dorsetshire, that at one of them at every seventh year, and at the other at every ninth year comes a small-pox, which the physicians cannot master, *e. g.*

Small-pox in Sherborne † during the year 1626.

---

* This account I had from Mr. Thomas Ax.

† Extracted out of the register-book.

And during the year 1634.

From Michaelmas 1642, to Mich. 1643.

From Michaelmas 1649, to Mich. 1650.

From Michaelmas 1657, to Mich. 1658.

In the year 1667, from Jan. to Sept. 1667.

Mr. Ax promised me to enquire the years it happened there after 1670, and 1680; but death prevented him.

Small-pox in Taunton all the year 1658.*

Likewise in the year 1670.

Again in the year 1677.

Again very mortal in the year 1684.

Mr. Ax also promised me to enquire at Taunton the years it happened there after 1660.

It were to be wished that more such observations were made in other great towns.

Platerus makes the like observations in the second book of his Practice, p. 323. He practised at Basil, fifty-

---

* Out of the register-book.

six years, and did observe, that every tenth year they died of the plague there.

See Captain J. Graunt's observations on the bills of mortality at London, (indeed written by Sir William Petty, which in a late transaction he confessed) for the periodical plagues at London, which (as I remember) are every twenty-fifth year.

OSTENTA; OR, PORTENTS.

"HOW it comes to pass, I know not;* but "by ancient and modern example it is "evident, that no great accident befalls a "city or province, but it is presaged by "divination, or prodigy, or astrology, or some way or "other. I shall here set down a few instances."

A Rainbow appeared about the sun before the battle of Pharsalia. See *Appian*, and Mr. *T. May's* 5th book of his Continuation of Lucan.

"*Ex Chronico Saxonico*, p. 112, *Anno* 1104, *fuit* "*primus Pentecostes dies Nonis Junii, & die Martis se* "*quente, conjuncti sunt quatuor Circuli circa Solem, albi* "*coloris, & quisque sub alio collocatus, quasi picti essent.* "*Omnes qui videbant obstupuerunt, propterea quod nun-* "*quam ante tales meminerant. Post hæc facta est Pax*

---

* Discourses of Nicholas Machiavel, book 1. chap. 56.

"*inter Comitem Robertum de Normanniâ, & Robertum* "*de Bœlœsme i. e.*"

In the year 1104, on the first day of Pentecost, the sixth of June, and on the day following being Tuesday, four circles of a white colour, were seen to roll in conjunction round the sun, each under the other regularly placed, as if they had been drawn by the hand of a painter. All who beheld it were struck with astonishment, because they could not learn that any such spectacles had ever happened in the memory of man. After these things it is remarkable, that a peace was immediately set on foot, and concluded between Robert, Earl of Normandy, and Robert de Bœlœsme.

The Duke of York (afterwards Edward IV.) met with his enemies near to Mortimer's Cross, on Candlemas day in the morning, at which time the Sun (as some write) appeared to him like three Suns, and suddenly joined altogether in one, and that upon the sight thereof, he took such courage, that he fiercely set on his enemies, and them shortly discomfited: for which cause, men imagined that he gave Sun in his full brightness for his cognisance or badge. *Halle*, F. 183, b. 4.

Our Chronicles tell us, that *Anno Secundo Reginæ Mariæ*, 15th of February, two suns appeared, and a rainbow reversed: see the bow turned downwards, and the two ends standing upwards, before the coming in of King Philip.

The phænomenon, fig. 1, was seen at Broad-Chalk in

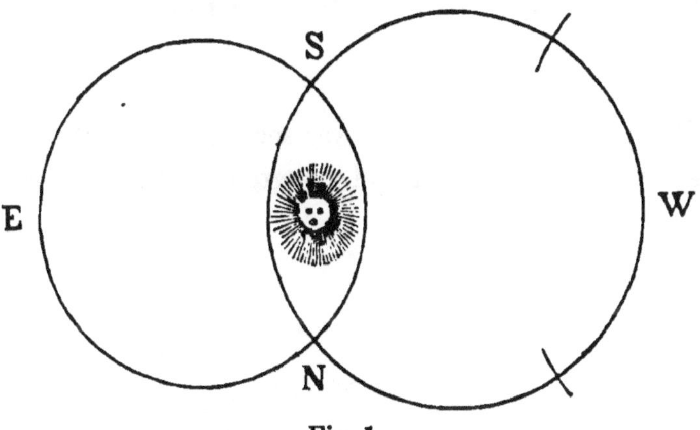

Fig. 1.

Wiltshire, on the first day of May, 1647. It continued from about eleven o'clock (or before) till twelve. It was a very clear day; but few did take notice of it, because it was so near the sun-beams. My mother happened to espy it, going to see what o'clock it was by an horizontal dial; and then all the servants saw it. Upon the like occasion, Mr. J. Sloper, B.D. vicar there, saw it, and all his family; and the servants of Sir George Vaughan, (then of Falston) who were hunting on the downs, saw it. The circles were of rainbow colour; the two filots, which cross the greater circle, (I presume they were segments of a third circle) were of a pale colour. The sun was within the intersections of the circles.

The next remarkable thing that followed was, that on the third of June following;* Cornet Joyce carried King

* See Sir W. Dugdale's hist. of the Civil Wars.

Charles I. prisoner from Holdenby to the Isle of Wight. The Isle of Wight lieth directly from Broad-Chalk, at the 10 o'clock point.

The phænomenon, fig. 2, was seen in the north side of the church-yard of Bishop-Lavington in Wiltshire, about

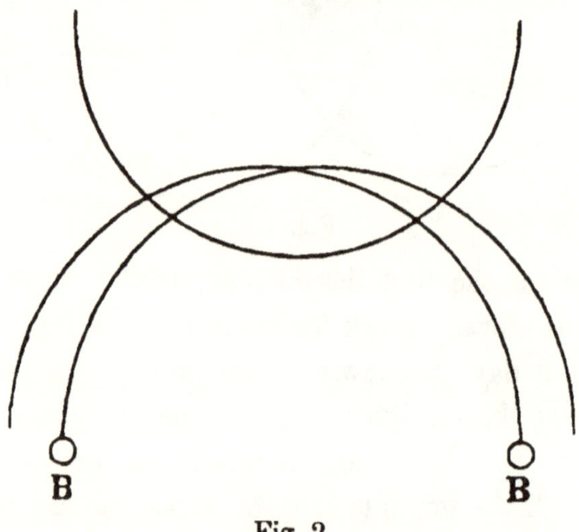

Fig. 2.

the latter end of September 1688, about three o'clock in the afternoon. This was more than a semicircle.

B. B. two balls of light. They were about eleven degrees above the Horizon by the quadrant; observed by Mr. Robert Blea, one of the Earl of Abingdon's gentlemen.

"*Cicero de Natura Deorum*, lib. 2. *Multa prætere*
"*Ostentis, multa ex eis admonemur, multisque rebus aliis,*
"*quas diuturnus usus ita notarit, ut artem Divinationis*
"*efficeret. i. e.*"

Besides, we learn a world of things from these Portents and Prodigies, and many are the warnings and admonitions we receive from them, and not only from them indeed, but from a number of extraordinary accidents, upon which daily use and constant observation has fixed such marks, that from thence the whole art of divination has been compounded.

OMENS.

BEFORE the battle at Philippi began, two eagles fought in the air between the two armies: both the armies stood still and beheld them, and the army was beaten that was under the vanquished eagle. See *Appian's* Hist. part 2, lib. 4, §. 2.

It is worthy of notice, that, at the time the cities of Jerusalem and Antioch were taken from the Pagans, the Pope that then was, was called *Urban*, and the Patriarch of Jerusalem was called *Eraclius*, and the Roman Emperor was called *Frederick;* in like manner when Jerusalem was taken from the Christians by the siege of Saladin, the Pope was called *Urban;* the Patriarch of Jerusalem, *Eraclius;* and the Emperor, *Frederick:* and it is remarkable, that fourscore and seven years passed between these two events. *Hoveden*, f. 363.

Mathew Parker, *seventieth* Arch-Bishop of Canterbury, in the *seventieth* year of his age, feasted Queen Elizabeth on her birth day, 1559, in his palace at Canterbury. *Parker. Vitæ*, 556.

It is a matter of notable consideration, says a Spanish historian, that the royal throne of the Morish Kings of Granada, began and ended in the times of the *Fernandos* of Castille: beginning in the time of Saint *Fernando*, the third of that name, and ending in that of the Catholic King, Don *Fernando* the fifth, his successor in the ninth descent. In the same manner, it is observable that the first Morish King was called *Mahomad*, and the last had the same name of *Mahomad:* which resembles what passed in the empire of Constantinople, where the first and last Emperors were called *Constantines. Garibay*, l. 40, c. 43.

The same author mentions it as an extraordinary circumstance that, at one time lived in Castille, Arragon, and Portugal, three Kings called *Pedros*, and whose fathers were named *Alonfos*, who were also Kings at the same time. L. 14, c. 35.

While Edward, Duke of York,* was declaring his title, in the Chamber of the Peers, there happened a strange chance, in the very same time, amongst the Commons in the nether house, then there assembled: for a *Crown*, which did hang in the middle of the same, to garnish a branch to set lights upon, without touch of any creature, or rigor of wind, suddenly fell down, and at the same time also, fell down the *Crown*, which stood on the top of the Castle of Dover: as a sign and prognostication, that the

* Father of Edward IV.

Crown of the realm should be divided and changed from one line to another. *Halle's* Chronicle, H. 6. F. 181.

Anno 1506. Through great tempest of wind in January, Philip, King of Castille and his wife, were weather-driven and landed at Falmouth. This tempest blew down the *Eagle of Brass* from the spire of St. Paul's church in London, and in the falling, the same eagle broke and battered the *black Eagle*,* which hung for a sign in St. Paul's Church-yard. *Stow's* Annals, 484.

The silver cross that was wont to be carried before Cardinal Wolsey, fell out of its socket, and was like to have knocked out the brains of one of the Bishop's servants. A very little while after, came in a messenger, and arrested the Cardinal, before he could get out of the house. See *Stow's* Chronicle.

'Tis commonly reported, that before an heir of the Cliftons, of Clifton in Nottinghamshire, dies, that a Sturgeon is taken in the river Trent, by that place.

Thomas Flud, Esq. in Kent, told me that it is an old observation which was pressed earnestly to King James I. that he should not remove the Queen of Scots body from Northamptonshire, where she was beheaded and interred: for that it always bodes ill to the family when bodies are

* The black Eagle is the cognizance of the house of Austria, of which Philip was head.

removed from their graves. For some of the family will die shortly after, as did Prince Henry, and I think Queen Ann.

A little before the death of Oliver, the Protector, a Whale came into the river Thames, and was taken at Greenwich, —— feet long. 'Tis said Oliver was troubled at it.

When I was a freshman at Oxford, 1642, I was wont to go to Christ Church, to see King Charles I. at supper; where I once heard him say, "That as he was hawking in "Scotland, he rode into the quarry, and found the covey "of partridges falling upon the hawk; and I do remember "this expression further, viz. and I will swear upon the "book 'tis true." When I came to my chamber, I told this story to my tutor; said he, *that covey was* London.

The bust of King Charles I. carved by Bernini, as it was brought in a boat upon the Thames, a strange bird (the like whereof the bargemen had never seen) dropped a drop of blood, or blood-like, upon it; which left a stain not to be wiped off. This bust was carved from a picture of Sir Anthony Van Dyke's drawing: the sculptor found great fault with the fore-head as most unfortunate. There was a seam in the middle of his fore-head, (downwards) which is a very ill sign in Metoposcopie.

Colenel Sharington Talbot was at Nottingham, when King Charles I. did set up his standard upon the top of the tower there. He told me, that the first night, the wind blew it so, that it hung down almost horizontal; which some did take to be an ill omen.

The day that the long Parliament began, 1641, the Sceptre fell out of the figure of King Charles in wood, in Sir Thomas Trenchard's hall at Wullich, in Dorset, as they were at dinner in the parlour: Justice Hunt then dined there.

The picture of Arch-Bishop Laud, in his closet, fell down (the string broke) the day of the sitting of that Parliament. This is mentioned in Canterbury's doom by W. Prynne.

The psalms for the eleventh day of the month, are 56, 57, 58, &c. On the eleventh day of one of the months in the summer time, the citizens came tumultuously in great numbers in boats and barges over against Whitehall, to shew they would take the Parliament's part. The psalms aforesaid, both for morning and evening service, are as prophecies of the troubles that did ensue.

When the high court of justice was voted in the parliament house, as Berkenhead (the mace bearer) took up the mace to carry it before the Speaker, the top of the mace fell off. This was avowed to me by an eye witness then in the house.

The head of King Charles I's. staff did fall off at his trial: that is commonly known.

The second lesson for the 30th of January in the calendar before the common prayer, is concerning the trial of Christ: which, when Bishop Duppa read, the King was displeased with him, thinking he had done it of choice; but the Bishop cleared himself by the calendar, as is to be seen.

King Charles II. was crowned at the very conjunction of the sun and Mercury; Mercury being then in *Corde Solis.* As the King was at dinner in Westminster Hall, it thundered and lightened extremely. The cannons and the thunder played together.

King Charles II. went by long sea to Portsmouth or Plymouth, or both; an extraordinary storm arose, which carried him almost to France. Sir Jonas Moor (who was then with his Majesty) gave me this account, and said, that when they came to Portsmouth to refresh themselves, they had not been there above half an hour, but the weather was calm, and the sun shone: his Majesty put to sea again, and in a little time they had the like tempestuous weather as before.

Not long before the death of King Charles II. a Sparrow-hawk escaped from the perch, and pitched on one of the iron crowns of the white tower, and entangling its string in the crown, hung by the heels and died. Not long after, another hawk pitched on one of the crowns. From Sir *Edward Sherborne*, Knight.

The Gloucester frigate cast away at the Lemanore, and

most of the men in it; the Duke of York escaping in a cock boat, *anno* 1682, May the 5th, on a Friday.

When King James II. was crowned, (according to the ancient custom, the Peers go to the throne, and kiss the king) the Crown was almost kissed off his head. An Earl did set it right; and as he came from the Abbey to Westminster Hall, the Crown tottered extremely.

The canopy (of cloth of gold) carried over the head of King James II. by the Wardens of the Cinque Ports, was torn by a puff of wind as he came to Westminster Hall; it hung down very lamentably: I saw it.

When King James II. was crowned, a signal was given from Westminster Abbey to the Tower, where it was Sir Edward Sherborne's post to stand to give order for firing the cannons, and to hoist up the great flag with the King's arms. It was a windy day, and the wind presently took the flag half off, and carried it away into the Thames. From Sir *Edward Sherborne.*

The top of his sceptre (Flower de Lys) did then fall.

Upon Saint Mark's Day, after the coronation of King James II. were prepared stately fire works on the Thames: it hapened, that they took fire all together, and it was so dreadful, that several spectators leaped into the river, choosing rather to be drowned than burned. In a yard by the Thames, was my Lord Powys's coach and horses; the horses were so frightened by the fire works, that the coach man was not able to stop them, but ran away over one, who with great difficulty recovered.

When King James II. was at Salisbury, *anno* 1688, the Iron Crown upon the turret of the council house, was blown off.—This has often been confidently asserted by persons who were then living.

In February, March, and April, two ravens built their nests on the weather cock of the high steeple at Bakewell in Derbyshire.

I did see Mr. Christopher Love beheaded on Tower Hill, in a delicate clear day; about half an hour after his head was struck off, the clouds gathered blacker and blacker; and such terrible claps of thunder came that I never heard greater.

'Tis reported, that the like happened after the execution of Alderman Cornish, in Cheapside, October 23, 1685.

Anno 1643. As Major John Morgan of Wells, was marching with the King's army into the west, he fell sick of a malignant fever at Salisbury, and was brought dangerously ill to my father's at Broad-Chalk, where he was lodged secretly in a garret. There came a sparrow to the chamber window, which pecked the lead of a certain pannel only, and only one side of the lead of the lozenge, and made one small hole in it. He continued this pecking and biting the lead, during the whole time of his sickness; (which was not less than a month) when the major went away, the sparrow desisted, and came thither no more. Two of the servants that attended the Major, and sober persons, declared this for a certainty.

Sir Walter Long's (of Draycot in Wilts) widow, did make a solemn promise to him on his death-bed, that she would not marry after his decease, but not long after, one Sir —— Fox, a very beautiful young gentleman, did win her love; so that notwithstanding her promise aforesaid, she married him: she married at South-Wraxhall, where the picture of Sir Walter hung over the parlour door, as it doth now at Draycot. As Sir ——Fox led his bride by the hand from the church, (which is near to the house) into the parlour, the string of the picture broke, and the picture fell on her shoulder, and cracked in the fall. (It was painted on wood, as the fashion was in those days.) This made her ladyship reflect on her promise, and drew some tears from her eyes.*

See Sir Walter Raleigh's history, book 4, chap. 2, §. 7. The dogs of the French army, the night before the battle of Novara, ran all to the Swisses army: the next day, the Swisses obtained a glorious victory of the French. Sir Walter Raleigh affirms it to be certainly true.

The last battle fought in the north of Ireland, between the Protestants and the Papists, was in Glinsuly near

* This story may be true in all its details, except the name of the lady, who was a daughter of Sir W. Long; she married Somerset Fox, Esq. See Sandford's Geneal. Hist. of the Kings of England, p. 344.

Letterkenny in the county of Donegall. Veneras, the Bishop of Clogher, was General of the Irish army; and that of the Parliament army, Sir Charles Coot. They pitched their tents on each side the river Suly, and the Papists constantly persist in it to this very day, that the night before the action,* a woman of uncommon stature, all in white, appearing to the said Bishop, admonished him not to cross the river first, to assault the enemy, but suffer them to do it, whereby he should obtain the victory. That if the Irish took the water first to move towards the English, they should be put to a total rout, which came to pass. Ocahan, and Sir Henry O'Neal, who were both killed there, saw severally the same apparition, and dissuaded the Bishop from giving the first onset, but could not prevail upon him. In the mean time, I find nothing in this revelation, that any common soldier might not conclude without extraordinary means.

Near the same place, a party of the Protestants had been surprized sleeping by the Popish Irish, were it not for several wrens that just wakened them by dancing and pecking on the drums as the enemy were approaching. For this reason the wild Irish mortally hate these birds, to this day, calling them the Devil's servants, and killing them wherever they catch them; they teach their children

---

* So an apparition of a woman greater than ordinary, beckoned to Julius Cæsar to pass over the Rubicon, L. Flor. lib. 4. Satyres appeared to Alexander when he besieged Tyrus; Alexander asked the divines, what was the signification of it; they told him the meaning is plain, Σὰ τυρος (*i.e.*) Tyre is thine. Alexander took the town. *Q. Curtius.*

to thrust them full of thorns: you will see sometimes on holidays, a whole parish running like mad men from hedge to hedge a wren-hunting.

Anno 1679. After the discovery of the Popish plot, the penal laws were put in execution against the Roman Catholics; so that, if they did not receive the sacrament according to the church of England, in their parish church, they were to be severely proceeded against according to law: Mr. Ploydeu, to avoid the penalty, went to his parish church at Lasham, near Alton, in Hampshire: when Mr. Laurence (the minister) had put the chalice into Mr. Ployden's hand, the cup of it (wherein the wine was) fell off. 'Tis true, it was out of order before; and he had a tremor in his hand. The communion was stopt by this accident. This was attested to me by two neighbouring ministers, as also by several gentlemen of the neighbourhood.

When King James II. first entered Dublin, after his arrival from France, 1689, one of the gentlemen that bore the mace before him, stumbled without any rub in his way, or other visible occasion. The mace fell out of his hands, and the little cross upon the crown thereof stuck fast between two stones in the street. This is very well known all over Ireland, and did much trouble King James himself, with many of his chief attendants.

The first Moors that were expelled Spain, were in number five thousand five hundred and fifty-five. They sailed from Denia, October 2, 1609. *H. Bleda.* Expulsion de Moriscos, p. 1000.

DREAMS.

——"Οναρ και Διος ἐστι. Homer Iliad A.

Dreams proceed from Jove.

HE that has a mind to read of dreams, may peruse *Cicero de Divinatione*, *Hier. Cardani Somniorum Synesiorum*, lib. 4, and *Moldinarius de Insomniis*, &c. I shall here mention but little out of them, my purpose being chiefly to set down some remarkable and divine dreams of some that I have had the honour to be intimately acquainted with, persons worthy of belief.

Cicero *de Divinatione*, lib. 1. Hannibalem, Cælius *scribit, cùm Columnam auream, quæ esset in fano Junonis Laciniæ, auferre vellet, dubitaretque utrum ea solida esset, an extrinsecus inaurata, perterebravisse; cumque solidam invenisset, statuissetque tollere: secundum quietem visam esse ei Junonem prædicere, ne id faceret; minarique, si id fecisset se curaturam, ut eum quoque oculum, quo bene videret, amitteret; idque ab homine acuto non esse neglectum; itaque ex eo auro quod exterebratum esset, buculam curasse faciendam, & eam in summa columna collocavisse.* i. e.

Cœlius writes, that Hannibal, when he had a mighty mind to take away a gold pillar, that was in the Temple of Juno Lacinia, being in doubt with himself, whether it was solid massive gold, or only gilt, or thinly plated over on the out side, bored it through. When he had found it to be solid, and fully designed to have it carried off; Juno appeared to him in his sleep, and forewarned him against what he was about, threatening him withal, that if he persisted and did it, she would take care that he should lose the eye, that he saw perfectly well with, as he had done the other.

The great man, it seems, was too wise to slight and neglect this warning; nay, he even took care to have a ring made of the very gold, that had been bored out of it, and placed it on the top of the pillar.

——*Cum duo quidam Arcades familiares iter unà facerent, & Megaram venissent, alterum ad cauponem divertisse; ad hospitem alterum. Qui, ut cœnati quiescerent, concubia nocte visum esse in somnis ei qui erat in hospitio, illum alterum orare ut subveniret, quòd sibi à caupone interitus pararetur; eum primò perterritum somnio surrexisse; deinde cùm se colligisset, idque visum pro nihilo habendum esse duxisset, recubuisse; tum ei dormienti eundem illum visum esse rogare, ut quoniam sibi vivo non subvenisset, mortem suam ne inultam esse pateretur; se interfectum in plaustrum à caupone esse conjectum, & supra stercus injectum; petere, ut manè ad portum adesset, priusquam plaustrum ex oppido exiret. Hoc verò somnio commotum manè bubulco prestò ad portam fuisse, quæsisse ex eo, quid esset in plaustro; illum perterritum fugisse, mortuum erutum esse, cauponem re patefactâ pœnas dedisse. Quid hoc somnio dici divinius potest?* i. e.

As two certain Arcadians, intimate companions, were travelling together, it so happened, that, when they came to Megara, one of them went to an inn, and the other to a friend's house. Both had supped at their respective places, and were gone to bed; when lo! he, that was at his friend's house, dreamt, that his companion came to him, and begged of him for Heaven's sake to assist him, for that the inn-keeper had contrived a way to murder him: frightened at first out of his sleep, he rose up; but soon afterward coming a little better to himself, he thought, upon recollection, there was no heed to be given to the vision, and went very quietly to bed again. But as soon as he was got into his second sleep, the same vision repeated the visit, but the form of his petition was quite altered. He beseeched him, that, since he had not come to his assistance, while he was among the living, he would not suffer his death, however, to go unrevenged. Told him that as soon as he was murdered, he was tossed by the inn-keeper into a waggon, and had a little straw thrown over his corpse. He entreated him to be ready very early at the door before the waggon was to go out of town. This dream truly disturbed him it seems very much, and made him get up very early: he nicked the time, and met with the waggoner just at the very door, and asked him what he had in his cart. The fellow run away frightened and confounded. The dead body was pulled out of it, and the whole matter coming plainly to light, the inn-keeper suffered for the crime.—What is there that one can call more divine than a dream like this?

——*Somnium de* Simonide, *qui, cum ignotum quendam projectum mortuum vidisset, eumque humavisset, haberetque in animo navem conscendere, moneri visus est, ne id faceret, ab eo, quem sepultum affecerat: si navigasset, eam naufragio esse perituram: itaque Simondem rediisse periisse cæteros, qui tum navigassent.*

——The dream of Simonides. This person, when he saw a certain body thrown dead upon the shore, though a stranger, caused him to be buried. Much about that time he had it in his head to go on ship-board, but dreamt that he had warning given him by the man he had got to be interred, not to go; that if he went, the ship would infallibly be cast away. Upon this Simonides returned, and every soul of them besides that went on board was lost.

Cicero *de Divinatione*, lib. 2. *Somnium*, Alexandri. *Qui, cùm* Ptolomæus *familiaris ejus, in prælio, telo venenato ictus esset, eóque vulnere summo cum dolore moreretur,* Alexander *assidèns somno est consopitus; tum secundùm quietem visus ei dicitur draco is, quem mater* Olympias *alebat, radiculam ore ferre & simul dicere quo illa loci nasceretur neque is longe aberat ab eo loco: ejus autem esse vim tantam, ut* Ptolomæum *facile sanaret. Cúm* Alexander *experrectus narrasset amicis somnium, emisisse qui illam radiculam quærerent. Quâ inventâ, &* Ptolomæus *sanatus dicitur, & multi milites, qui erant eodem genere teli vulnerati.*

(*i. e.*) The dream of Alexander, when his friend Ptolemy was wounded in battle, by an envenomed dart, and died of the wound, in all the extremities of pain and anguish; Alexander sitting by him, and wearied out and quite fatigued, fell into a profound sleep. In this sleep, that dragon is reported to have appeared to him, which was bred up by his mother Olympias, carrying a little root in his mouth and to have told him in what spot of ground it grew, (nor was it far from that very place) and told him withal it seems, that such was the force, efficacy, and virtue of it, that it would work an easy cure upon Ptolomy. When Alexander waked, he told his friends the dream, and sent some out in quest of this little root. The root (as story says) was found, and Ptolomy was healed, so were many soldiers likewise, that had been wounded with the same kind of darts.

Cardanus Somniorum Synesiorum, lib. 4, chap. 2. *Narrat Plinius* 35 lib. *Nat. Hist. vir ab omnia superstitione alienissimus, Historiam hujusmodi.* "Nuper cujus-"dam militantis in Prætorio mater vidit in quiete, ut "radicem sylvestris Rosæ (quam *Cynorrhodon* vocant)

" blanditam sibi aspectu pridie in Fruteto, mitteret filio " bibendam : In Lusitaniâ res gerebatur, Hispaniæ, prox- " imâ parte : casuque accidit, ut milite à morsu Canis " incipiente aquas expavescere superveniret epistola orantis " ut parêtet religioni ; servatusque est ex insperato, & " posteà quisquis auxilium simile tentavit."

i. e. In his natural history, Pliny, a man the most averse to superstition, relates to us the following passage. Lately, the mother of one of the guards, who attended upon the General, was admonished by a vision in her sleep, to send her son a draught composed of the decoction of the root of a wild rose, (which they call Cynorrhodon) with the agreeable look whereof she had been mightily taken the day before, as she was passing through a coppice. The seat of the war at that time lay in Portugal, in that part of it next adjoining to Spain, that a soldier, beginning to apprehend mighty dangerous consequences from the bite of a dog, the letter came unexpectedly from her, entreating him to pay a blind obedience to this superstition. He did so, and was preserved beyond all expectation; and everybody afterwards had recourse to the same remedy.

Ibid. Galeni *tria Somnia.——Tertium magis dignum miraculo, cum bis per somnium admonitus, ut arteriam secaret, quæ inter pollicem & indicem est, idque agens liberatus sit à diuturno dolore, quo infestabatur eâ in parte, quâ septo transverso jecur jungitur, idque in libri de sectione venæ fine testatus est. Magno certè exemplo, quod tantus vir in medicina eam adhibuerit somnio fidem, ut in seipso periculum vitæ subierit, in arte propriâ. Deinde probitatem admiror, ut quò potuerit solertia ingenii sibi inventum ascribere, Deo cui debebatur, rediderit. Dignus vel hoc solo vir immortalitate nominis, & librorum suorum.*

Galen's three dreams. The third more worthy of being called a miracle, was, when being twice admonished in his sleep, to cut the artery that lies between the fore finger and the thumb, and doing it accordingly, he was freed from a continual daily pain with which he was afflicted in that part where the liver is joined to the midriff; and this he has testified at the end of his book of Venesection. 'Tis certainly a very great example, when a man so great as he was in the medicinal art, put so much confidence in a dream as to try experiments upon himself; where he was to run the risque of his life, in his own very art. I cannot help but admire his probity in the next place, that where he might have arrogated the merit of the invention to himself, and placed it wholly to the account of the subtility and penetration of his own genius, he attributed it to God, to whom it was due. In this alone did the man well deserve to purchase an immortality to his name and his writings.

In his fourth book, chap. 4. *De Exemplis propriis*, he owns the solution of some difficult problems in Algebra to his dreams.

Plinii, Nat. Hist. lib. 22, chap. 17. "Verna carus "Pericli Atheniensium Principi, cùm is in arce templum

" ædificaret, repsissetque super altitudinem fastigii, & inde " cecidisset, hâc herbâ (*Parthenio*) dicitur sanatus, mon- " strata *Pericli* somnio à *Minerva.* Quare Parthenium " vocari cœpta est, assignaturque ei Deæ."

Pliny's Natural History, book 22, chap. 17. "A little Home-bred Slave, that was a darling favourite to Pericles, Prince of the Athenians, and who, while a temple was building in the Prince's palace, had climbed up to the very top of the pinnacle, and tumbled down from that prodigious height; is said to have been cured of his fall by the herb *Parthenium*, or mug-wort, which was shown to Pericles in a dream, by Minerva. From hence it originally took the name of *Parthenium*, and is attributed to that Goddess."

Augustinus, Cui etiam præter sanctitatem, plena fides adhiberi potest, duo narrat inter reliqua somnia admiranda. Primum, quod cum quidam mortuo nuper patre venaretur tanquam de pecuniâ quam pater illi ex chirographo debuisset, dum incastus viveret, hâc causâ nocte quâdam umbram patris videt, quæ illum admonuit de persolutâ pecuniâ & ubi chirographum esset repositum. Cum surrexisset, invenit chirographum loco eo quem umbra paterna docuerat, liberatusque est ab injusto petitore.

Saint Austin, to whom even, besides his sanctity, we owe an entire credit, tells among others, two very wonderful dreams. The first is, when a person was arrested by one, as for a certain sum of money, which his father had owed him by a note under his own hand, while he led a lewd debauched life, saw the ghost of his father one night, upon this very account, which told him of the money being paid, and where the acquittance lay. When he got up in the morning, he went and found the acquittance in that very place that his father's ghost had directed him to, and so was freed from the litigious suit of one that made unjust demands upon him.

Alterum adhuc magis mirum.

Præstantius, vir quidam à Philosopho petierat dubitationem quandam solvi; quod ille pernegavit. Nocte sequente, tametsi vigilaret Præstantius, vidit sibi Philosophum assistere, ac dubitationem solvere, moxque abire. Cùm die sequenti obviam Præstantius eundem habuisset Philosophum, rogat, Cur cùm pridie rogatus nolluisset solvere illam questionem, intempestâ nocte, non rogatus, & venisset ad se & dubitationem aperuisset. Cui Philosophus. Non quidem ego adveni sed somnians visus sum tibi hoc Officium præstare.

The other is much more wonderful still.

A certain gentleman named Prestantius, had been entreating a Philosopher to solve him a doubt, which he absolutely refused to do. The night following, although Prestantius was broad awake, he saw the Philosopher standing full before him, who just explained his doubts to him, and went away the moment after he had done. When Prestantius met the Philosopher the next day, he asks him why, since no entreaties could prevail with him the day before, to answer his question, he came to him unasked, and at an unseasonable time of night, and opened every point to his satisfaction. To whom thus the Philosopher. "Upon my word it was not me that came to you; but in a dream I thought my own self that I was doing you such a service."

The plague raging in the army of the Emperor Charles V. he dreamt that the decoction of the root of the dwarf-thistle (a mountain plant since called the caroline thistle) would cure that disease. See *Gerrard's* Herbal, who tells us this.

In Queen Mary's time, there was only one congregation of Protestants in London, to the number of about three-hundred, one was the deacon to them, and kept the list of their names: one of that congregation did dream, that a messenger, (Queen's Officer) had seized on this deacon, and taken his list; the fright of the dream awaked him: he fell asleep and dreamt the same perfect dream again. In the morning before he went out of his chamber, the deacon came to him and then he told him his dream, and said, 'twas a warning from God; the deacon slighted his advice, as savouring of superstition; but——was so urgent with him that he prevailed with him to deposite the list in some other hand, which he did that day. The next day, the Queen's officer attacked him, and searched (in vain) for the list, which had it been found, would have brought them all to the flame. *Foxe's* Martyrology.

When Arch Bishop Abbot's mother (a poor clothworker's

wife in Guilford) was with child of him, she did long for a Jack, and she dreamt that if she should eat a Jack, her son in her belly should be a great man. She arose early the next morning and went with her pail to the river-side (which runneth by the house, now an ale-house, the sign of the three mariners) to take up some water, and in the water in the pail she found a good jack, which she dressed, and eat it all, or very near. Several of the best inhabitants of Guilford were invited (or invited themselves) to the christening of the child; it was bred up a scholar in the town, and by degrees, came to be Arch Bishop of Canterbury.

In the life of Monsieur Periesk, writ by Gassendus, it is said, that Monsieur Periesk, who had never been at London, did dream that he was there, and as he was walking in a great street there, espied in a goldsmith's glass desk, an antique coin, he could never meet with. (I think an Otho.) When he came to London, walking in (I think) Cheap-side, he saw such a shop, and remembered the countenance of the goldsmith in his dream, and found the coin desired, in his desk. ' See his life.

When Doctor Hamey (one of the physicians college in London) being a young man, went to travel towards Padoa, he went to Dover (with several others) and shewed his pass, as the rest did, to the Governor there. The Governor told him, that he must not go, but must keep him prisoner. The Doctor desired to know for what reason? how he had transgrest? well it was his will to have it so. The pacquet-boat hoisted sail in the evening (which was very clear), and the Doctor's companions in it. There ensued a terrible storm, and the pacquet-boat and all the passengers were drowned: the next day the sad news was brought to Dover. The Doctor was unknown to the Governor, both by name and face; but the night before, the Governor had the perfect vision in a dream, of Doctor Hamey, who came to pass over to Calais; and that he had a warning to stop him. This the Governor told the Doctor the next day. The Doctor was a pious, good man, and has several times related this story to some of my acquaintance.

My Lady Seymour dreamt, that she found a nest, with nine finches in it. And so many children she had by the Earl of Winchelsea, whose name is Finch.

The Countess of Cork (now Burlington) being at Dublin, dreamt, that her father, (the Earl of Cumberland) who was then at York, was dead. He died at that time.

'Tis certain, that several had monitory dreams of the conflagration of London.

Sir Christopher Wren, being at his father's house, *anno* 1651, at Knahill in Wilts (a young Oxford scholar) dreamt, that he saw a fight in a great market-place, which he knew not; where some were flying, and others pursuing; and among those that fled, he saw a kinsman of his, who went into Scotland to the King's army. They heard in the country, that the King was come into England, but whereabouts he was they could not tell. The next night his kinsman came to his father at Knahill, and was the first that brought the news of the fight at Worcester.

When Sir Christopher Wren was at Paris, about 1671, he was ill and feverish, made but little water, and had a pain in his reins. He sent for a physician, who advised him to be let blood, thinking he had a plurisy: but bleeding much disagreeing with his constitution, he would defer it a day longer: that night he dreamt, that he was in a place where palm-trees grew, (suppose Ægypt) and that a woman in a romantic habit, reached him dates. The next day he sent for dates, which cured him of the pain of his reins.

Since, I have learned that dates are an admirable medicine for the stone, from old Captain Tooke of K——. Take six or ten date-stones, dry them in an oven, pulverize and searce them; take as much as will lie on a six-pence, in a quarter of a pint of white wine fasting, and at four in the afternoon: walk or ride an hour after: in a week's time it will give ease, and in a month cure. If you are at the Bath, the Bath water is better than white wine to take it in.

Sir John Hoskin's Lady, when she lay in of her eldest son, had a swelling on one side of her belly, the third day when the milk came, and obstructions: she dreamt that syrup of elderberries and distilled water of wormwood would do her good, and it did so; she found ease in a quarter of an hour after she had taken it. I had this account from her Ladyship's own mouth.

Captain —— Wingate told me, that Mr. Edmund Gunter, of Gresham College, did cast his nativity, when about seventeen or eighteen years old; by which he did prognosticate that he should be in danger to lose his life for treason. Several years before the civil wars broke out, he had dreamt that he was to be put to death before a great castle, which he had never seen; which made a strong impression in his memory. In *anno* 1642, he did oppose the church ceremonies, and was chosen a member of Parliament, then was made a Captain, and was taken prisoner at Edge Hill, by Prince Rupert, and carried to Kenilworth Castle, where he was tried by a council of war, and condemned to die: but they did better consider of it, and spared his life; for that he being so considerable a person, might make an exchange for some of the King's party:* and he was exchanged for the right Honourable Montague, Earl of Lindsey (heir of the General.) Since the restoration, he was made one of the commissioners of the excise office in London. He did protest that Kenilworth castle was the very castle he saw in his dream.

Sir Roger L'Estrange was wont to divertise himself with cocking in his father's (Sir Hammond L'Estrange's) park; he dreamt that there came to him in such a place

---

* Captain Wingate was a prisoner in Oxford, after Edgehill fight, 1642.

of the park, a servant, who brought him news, that his father was taken very ill. The next day going to his usual recreation, he was resolved for his dream sake to avoid that way.; but his game led him to it, and in that very place the servant came and brought him the ill news according to his dream.

Mr. Edmund Halley, R. S. S. was carried on with a strong impulse to take a voyage to St. Hellens, to make observations of the southern constellations, being then about twenty-four years old. Before he undertook his voyage, he dreamt that he was at sea, sailing towards that place, and saw the prospect of it from the ship in his dream, which he declared to the Royal Society, to be the perfect representation of that island, even as he had it really when he approached to it.

A Gentlewoman dreamt that a pultess of blew corants would cure her sore throat; and it did so. She was a pious woman, and affirmed it to be true.

Anno 1690. One, in Ireland, dreamed of a brother or near relation of his, (who lived at Amesbury in Wiltshire) that he saw him riding on the downs, and that two thieves robbed him and murdered him. The dream awaked him, he fell asleep again and had the like dream. He wrote to his relation an account of it, and described the thieves complexion, stature and cloaths; and advised him to take care of himself. Not long after he had received this monitory letter, he rode towards Salisbury, and was robbed and murdered; and the murderers were discovered by this very letter, and were executed. They hang in chains on the road to London.

'Twas revealed to a King of Scots, that if he drank of the water of Muswell, he would be cured. After great enquiry they heard of such a place, not far from Hornsey in Middlesex. See *Weever's* Funeral Monuments of the Well. *John Norden's* Description of Middlesex. Here was afterwards founded a religious house for Austin Monks: since it belonged to Sir Thomas Row, and in 1677, was pulled down and the materials sold. Anciently the Kings of Scotland were feudatory to the Kings of England, and did their homage every Christmas day. They had several lodges belonging to them for their reception in their journey; as at Huntingdon, &c. See *Caxton's* Chronicle concerning this.

The water of this spring is drank for some distempers still.

Somnium ex Eubernea portâ.

Mrs. Cl——, of S——, in the county of S——, had a beloved daughter, who had been a long time ill, and received no benefit from her physicians. She dreamed that a friend of hers deceased, told her, that if she gave her daughter a drench of yew pounded, that she would recover; she gave her the drench, and it killed her. Whereupon she grew almost distracted: her chamber maid to complement her, and mitigate her grief, said surely that could not kill her, she would adventure to take the same herself; she did so, and died also. This was about the year 1670, or 1671. I knew the family.

A Gentlewoman, of my acquaintance, dreamed, that if she slept again, the house would be in danger to be robbed. She kept awake, and anon thieves came to break open the house, but were prevented.

J. H. Esq.* being at West-Lavington with the Earl of Abbingdon, dreamed, December the 9th, his mother rose up in mourning: and anon the Queen appeared in mourning. He told his dream the next morning to my Lord, and his Lordship imparted it to me (then there) Tuesday, December 11. In the evening came a messenger, post from London, to acquaint Mr. H. that his mother was dangerously ill: he went to London the next day; his mother lived but about eight days longer. On Saturday, December 15, the Queen was taken ill, which turned to the small pox, of which she died, December 28, about two o'clock in the morning.

Sir Thomas White, Alderman of London, was a very rich man, charitable and public spirited. He dreamt that he had founded a college at a place where three elms grow out of one root. He went to Oxford, probably with that intention, and discovering some such tree near Gloucester

* J. H. Against these initials there is a note in the copy of the first edition already referred to, in these words,—"James Herbert: He saies he was never there."

Hall, he began to repair it, with a design to endow it. But walking afterwards by the Convent where the Bernardines formerly lived, he plainly saw an elm with three large bodies rising out of the same root: he forthwith purchased the ground, and endowed his college there, as it is at this day, except the additions which Arch-bishop Laud made, near the outside of which building in the garden belonging to the president, the tree is still to be seen. He made this discovery about the year 1557.

There are millions of such dreams too little taken notice of, but they have the truest dreams whose IXth house is well dignified, which mine is not: but must have some monitory dreams. The Germans are great observers of them. It is said in the life of Vavasor Powell, that he was a great observer of dreams, (p. 17 and 114, of his life) that he had many warnings from them, that God had spoken to himself and others by them; for warning, instruction, or reproof. And it is also there averred, that Angels had appeared to him. See p. 8, of his life.

In Mr. Walton's life of Sir Hen. Wotton, there is a remarkable story of the discovery of stolen plate in Oxford, by a dream which his father had at Bocton-Malherbe, in Kent. See in *Ath. & Fasti. Oxon.* vol. 1, p. 351.

William Penn, proprietor of Pensylvania, told me, that he went with his mother on a visit to Admiral Dean's wife, who lived then in Petty-France; the Admiral was then at sea. She told them, that, the night before, she had a perfect dream of her husband, whom she saw walking on the deck, and giving directions, and that a cannon bullet struck his arm into his side. This dream did much discompose her, and within forty-eight hours she received news of the fight at sea, and that her husband was killed in the very manner aforesaid.

Sir Berkley Lucy sold the fabric of the chapel of Netley Abbey, to one Taylor, a carpenter of Southampton, who took off the roof, and pulled down great part of the walls. During the time that this Taylor was in treaty for the chapel, he was much disturbed in his sleep with frightful dreams, and as some say, apparitions; and one night he dreamt that a large stone, out of one of the windows of the chapel, fell upon him and killed him. The undertaker, though staggered with these intimations, finished his agreement, and soon after fell to work on pulling down the chapel; but he was not far advanced in it, when, endeavouring with a pickax to get out some stones at the bottom of the west wall, in which there was a large window, the whole body of the window fell down suddenly upon him, and crushed him to pieces. *Willis's* Mitred Abbeys, vol. 2, p. 205, 6.

Jan. 1774. One Daniel Healy, of Donaghmore, in Ireland, having three different times dreamed that money lay concealed under a large stone in a field near where he lived, procured some workmen to assist him in removing it, and when they had dug as far as the foundation, it fell suddenly and killed Healy on the spot.

March 25, 1779. This morning A. B. dreamt that he saw his friend C. D. throw himself from a bridge into a river, and that he could not be found. The same evening, reading Dr. Geddes's account of *Ignatius Loyola*, p. 105, 5th tract. v. 3, he met with the following particular of him; as he was going into Bononia, he tumbled off a bridge into a moat full of mud; this circumstance was quite new. Every tittle of the above is strictly true, as the writer will answer it to God.—To what can be attributed so singular an impression upon the imagination when sleeping?

Comical History of three Dreamers.

Three companions, of whom two were Tradesmen and Townsmen, and the third a Villager, on the score of devotion, went on pilgrimage to a noted sanctuary; and as they went on their way, their provision began to fail them, insomuch that they had nothing to eat, but a little flour, barely sufficient to make of it a very small loaf of bread. The tricking townsmen seeing this, said between themselves, we have but little bread, and this companion of ours is a great eater; on which account it is necessary we should think how we may eat this little bread without him. When they had made it and set it to bake, the tradesmen seeing in what manner to cheat the countryman, said: let us all sleep, and let him that shall have the most marvellous dream betwixt all three of us, eat the bread. This bargain being agreed upon, and settled between them, they laid down to sleep. The countryman, discovering the trick of his companions, drew out the bread half baked, eat it by himself, and turned again to sleep. In a while, one of the tradesmen, as frightened by a marvellous dream, began to get up, and was asked by his companion, why he was so frightened? he answered, I am frightened and dreadfully surprized by a marvellous dream: it seemed to me that two Angels, opening the gates of Heaven, carried me before the throne of God with great joy: his companion said: this is a marvellous dream, but I have seen another more marvellous, for I saw two Angels, who carried me over the earth to Hell. The countryman hearing this, made as if he slept; but the townsmen, desirous to finish their trick, awoke him; and the countryman, artfully as one surprised, answered: Who are these that call me? They told him, we are thy companions. He asked them: How did you return? They answered: We never went hence; why d'ye talk of our return? The countryman replied: It appeared to me that two Angels, opening the gates of Heaven, carried one of you before our Lord God, and dragged the other over the earth to Hell, and I thought you never would return hither, as I have never heard that any had returned from Paradise, nor from Hell, and so I arose and eat the bread by myself.—From an old edition of *Lazarillo de Tormes.*

APPARITIONS.

CYNTHIA, Propertius's mistress, did appear to him after her death, with the beryl-ring on her finger. See *Propertius*, eleg. 7. lib. 4.

Sunt aliquid manes, letum non omnia finit,
Luridaque evictos effugit umbra rogos.
Cynthia *namque meo visa est incumbere fulcro,*
Murmur ad extremæ nuper humata viæ:
Quum mihi ab exequiis somnus penderet amaris.
Et quererer lecti frigida regna mei.
Eosdem habuit secum, quibus est elata, capillos,
Eosdem oculos. Lateri vestis adusta fuit.
Et solitum digito beryllon adederat ignis,
Summaque Lethæus triverat ora liquor:
Spirantisque animos, & vocem misit, at illi
Pollicibus fragiles increpuere manus.

Thus translated by Mr. DART.

Manes exist, when we in death expire,
And the pale shades escape the funeral fire;
For Cynthia's form beside my curtain's stood,
Lately interr'd near Aniens' murm'ring flood.

Thoughts of her funeral would not let me close
These eyes, nor seek the realms of still repose;
Around her shoulders wav'd her flowing hair,
As living Cynthia's tresses soft and fair:
Beauteous her eyes as those once fir'd my breast,
Her snowy bosom bare, and sing'd her breast.
Her beryl-ring retain'd the fiery rays,
Spread the pale flame, and shot the funeral blaze;
As late stretch'd out the bloodless spectre stood,
And her dead lips were wet with Lethe's flood.
She breath'd her soul, sent forth her voice aloud,
And chaf'd her hands as in some angry mood.

St. Augustin affirms that he did once see a satyr or dæmon.

The antiquities of Oxford tell us, that St. Edmund, Arch-Bishop of Canterbury, did sometimes converse with an angel or nymph, at a spring without St. Clement's parish near Oxford; as Numa Pompilius did with the nymph Egeria. This well was stopped up since Oxford was a garrison.

Charles the Simple, King of France, as he was hunting in a forest, and lost his company, was frighted to simplicity by an apparition.

Philip Melancthon writes that the apparition of a venerable person came to him in his study, and bade him to warn his friend Grynæus to depart from him as soon as he could, or else the inquisitors would seize on him; which monitory dream saved Grynæus's life.

Mr. Fynes Moryson, in his travels, saith, that when he was at Prague, the apparition of his father came to him; and at that very time his father died.

In the life of JOHN DONNE, Dean of St. Paul's, London, writ by Isaak Walton.

At this time of Mr. Donne's, and his wife's living in Sir Robert Drury's house in Drury-Lane, the Lord Haye was by King James sent upon a glorious embassy, to the then French King Henry the IV. and Sir Robert put on a sudden resolution to accompany him to the French Court, and to be present at his audience there. And Sir Robert put on as sudden a resolution, to subject Mr. Donne to be his companion in that journey; and this desire was suddenly made known to his wife, who was then with child, and otherwise under so dangerous a habit of body, as to her health, that she protested an unwillingness to allow him any absence from her; saying her divining soul boded her some ill in his absence, and therefore desired him not to leave her. This made Mr. Donne lay aside all thoughts of his journey, and really to resolve against it. But Sir Robert became restless in his persuasions for it, and Mr. Donne was so generous as to think he had sold his liberty, when he had received so many charitable kindnesses from him, and told his wife so; who, therefore, with an unwilling willingness, did give a faint consent to the journey, which was proposed to be but for two months: within a few days after this resolve, the Ambassador, Sir Robert, and Mr. Donne, left London, and were the twelfth day got safe to Paris. Two days after their arrival there, Mr. Donne was left alone in the room, where Sir Robert and he, with some others, had dined: to this place Sir Robert returned within half an hour, and as he left, so he found Mr. Donne alone, but in such an extacy, and so altered as to his looks, as amazed Sir Robert to behold him, insomuch as he earnestly desired Mr. Donne to declare what had befallen him in the short time of his absence? to which Mr. Donne was not able to make a present answer, but after a long and perplexed pause, said, "I have seen "a dreadful vision since I saw you: I have seen my dear "wife pass twice by me through this room, with her "hair hanging about her shoulders, and a dead child "in her arms; this I have seen since I saw you." To which Sir Robert replied, "Sure Sir, you have slept since "I saw you, and this is the result of some melancholy "dream, which I desire you to forget, for you are now "awake." To which Mr. Donne's reply was, "I cannot "be surer that I now live, than that I have not slept since "I saw you, and am sure that at her second appearing, she "stopt and lookt me in the face and vanished."—Rest and sleep had not altered Mr. Donne's opinion the next day, for he then affirmed this vision with a more deliberate, and so confirmed a confidence, that he inclined Sir Robert to a faint belief, that the vision was true. It is truly said, that desire and doubt have no rest, and it proved so with Sir

Robert, for he immediately sent a servant to Drury-House, with a charge to hasten back and bring him word whether Mrs. Donne were alive? and if alive, in what condition she was as to her health. The twelfth day the messenger returned with this account—that he found and left Mrs. Donne very sad, sick in her bed, and that, after a long and dangerous labour, she had been delivered of a dead child: and upon examination, the abortion proved to be the same day, and about the very hour, that Mr. Donne affirmed he saw her pass by him in his chamber.

Henry IV. King of France, not long before he was stabbed by Ravillac, as he was hunting in the forest (I think of Fontaine-Bleau), met in a thicket, the Gros Venure, who said to him, *Demandez vous?* or *Entendez vous?* He could not tell whether of the two.

There is a tradition (which I have heard from persons of honour), that as the Protector Seymour and his Dutchess were walking in the gallery at Sheen (in Surrey), both of them did see a hand with a bloody sword come out of the wall. He was afterwards beheaded.

Sir John Burroughes being sent envoy to the Emperor by King Charles I. did take his eldest son Caisho Burroughes along with him, and taking his journey through Italy, left his son at Florence, to learn the language; where he having an intrigue with a beautiful courtisan (mistress of the Grand Duke), their familiarity became so public, that it came to the Duke's ear, who took a resolution to have him murdered; but Caisho having had timely notice of the Duke's design, by some of the English there, immediately left the city without acquainting his mistress with it, and came to England; whereupon the Duke being disappointed of his revenge, fell upon his mistress in most reproachful language; she on the other side, resenting the sudden departure of her gallant, of whom she was most passionately enamoured, killed herself. At the same moment that she expired, she did appear to Caisho, at his lodgings in London; Colonel Remes* was then in bed with him, who saw her as well as he; giving him an account of her resentments of his ingratitude to her, in leaving her so suddenly, and exposing her to the fury of the Duke, not omitting her own tragical exit, adding withal, that he should be slain in a duel, which accordingly happened; and thus she appeared to him frequently, even when his younger brother (who afterwards was Sir John) was in bed with him. As often as she did appear, he would cry out with great shrieking, and trembling of his body, as anguish of mind, saying, O God! here she comes, she comes, and at this rate she appeared till he was killed; she appeared to him the morning before he was killed. Some of my acquaintance have told me, that he was one of the most beautiful men in England, and very valiant, but proud and blood-thirsty.

This story was so common, that King Charles I. sent

* This Colonel Remes was a Parliament man, and did belong to the wardrobe, *tempore Caroli* II.

for Caisho Burroughes's father, whom he examined as to the truth of the matter; who did (together with Colonel Remes) aver the matter of fact to be true, so that the King thought it worth his while to send to Florence, to enquire at what time this unhappy lady killed herself; it was found to be the same minute that she first appeared to Caisho, being in bed with Colonel Remes. This relation I had from my worthy friend Mr. Monson, who had it from Sir John's own mouth, brother of Caisho; he had also the same account from his own father, who was intimately acquainted with old Sir John Burroughes, and both his sons, and says, as often as Caisho related this, he wept bitterly.

Anno 1647, the Lord Mohun's son and heir (a gallant gentleman, valiant, and a great master of fencing and horsemanship), had a quarrel with Prince Griffin; there was a challenge, and they were to fight on horse-back in Chelsea-fields in the morning: Mr. Mohun went accordingly to meet him; but about Ebury-Farm, he was met by some who quarrelled with him and pistoled him; it was believed, by the order of Prince Griffin; for he was sure, that Mr. Mohun, being so much the better horseman, &c. would have killed him, had they fought.

In James-street, in Covent-Garden, did then lodge a gentlewoman, a handsome woman, but common, who was Mr. Mohun's sweet heart. Mr. Mohun was murdered about ten o'clock in the morning; and at that very time, his mistress being in bed, saw Mr. Mahon come to her bed-side, draw the curtain, look upon her and go away; she called after him, but no answer: she knocked for her maid, asked her for Mr. Mohun; she said she did not see him, and had the key of her chamber-door in her pocket. This account my friend aforesaid, had from the gentlewoman's own mouth, and her maid's.

A parallel story to this, is, that Mr. Brown, (brother-in-law to the Lord Coningsby) discovered his being murdered to several. His phantom appeared to his sister and her maid in Fleet-street, about the time he was killed in Herefordshire, which was about a year since, 1693.

Sir Walter Long of Draycot, (grandfather of Sir James Long) had two wives; the first a daughter of Sir Thomas Packington in Worcestershire; by whom he had a son: his second wife was a daughter of Sir John Thynne of Long-Leat; by whom he had several sons and daughters. The second wife did use much artifice to render the son by the first wife, (who had not much Promethean fire) odious to his father; she would get her acquaintance to make him drunk, and then expose him in that condition to his father; in fine, she never left off her attempts, till she got Sir Walter to disinherit him. She laid the scene for doing this at Bath, at the assizes, where was her brother Sir Egrimond Thynne, an eminent serjeant at law, who drew the writing; and his clerk was to sit up all night to engross it; as he was writing, he perceived a shadow on the parchment, from the candle; he looked up, and there appeared a hand, which immediately vanished; he was startled at it, but thought it might be only his fancy, being sleepy; so he writ on; by and by a fine white hand interposed between the writing and the candle (he could discern it was a woman's hand) but vanished as before; I have forgot, it appeared a third time. But with that the clerk threw down his pen, and would engross no more, but goes and tells his master of it, and absolutely refused to do it. But it was done by somebody, and Sir Walter Long was prevailed with to seal and sign it. He lived not long after; and his body did not go quiet to the grave, it being arrested at the church porch by the trustees of the first lady. The heir's relations took his part, and commenced a suit against Sir Walter (the second son) and compelled him to accept of a moiety of the estate; so the eldest son kept South-Wraxhall, and Sir Walter, the second son, Draycot-Cernes, &c. This was about the middle of the reign of King James I.

I must not forget an apparition in my country, which appeared several times to Doctor Turbervile's sister, at Salisbury; which is much talked of. One married a second wife, and contrary to the agreement and settlement at the first wife's marriage, did wrong the children by the first venter. The settlement was hid behind a wainscot in the chamber where the Doctor's sister did lie: and the apparition of the first wife did discover it to her. By which means right was done to the first wife's children. The apparition told her that she wandered in the air, and was now going to God. Dr. Turbervile (oculist) did affirm this to be true. See Mr. Glanvill's *Sadducismus Triumphatus.*

To one Mr. Towes, who had been schoolfellow with Sir George Villers, the father of the first Duke of Buckingham, (and was his friend and neighbour) as he lay in his bed awake, (and it was day-light) came into his chamber, the phantom of his dear friend Sir George Villers : said Mr. Towes to him, why, you are dead, what make you here? said the Knight, I am dead, but cannot rest in peace for the wickedness and abomination of my son George, at Court. I do appear to you, to tell him of it, and to advise and dehort him from his evil ways. Said Mr. Towes, the Duke will not believe me, but will say that I am mad, or doat. Said Sir George, go to him from me, and tell him by such a token (a mole) that he had in some secret place, which none but himself knew of. Accordingly Mr. Towes went to the Duke, who laughed at his message. At his return home the phantom appeared again, and told him that the Duke would be stabbed (he drew out a dagger) a quarter of a year after : and you shall outlive him half a year ; and the warning that you shall have of your death, will be, that your nose will fall a bleeding. All which accordingly fell out so. This account I have had (in the main) from two or three ; but Sir William Dugdale affirms what I have here taken from him to be true, and that the apparition told him of several things to come, which proved true, *e. g.* of a prisoner in the Tower, that shall be honourably delivered. This Mr. Towes had so often the ghost of his old friend appear to him, that it was not at all terrible to him. He was surveyor of the works at Windsor, (by the favour of the Duke) being then sitting in the hall, he cried out, the Duke of Buckingham is stabbed: he was stabbed that very moment.

This relation Sir William Dugdale had from Mr. Pine, (neighbour to Mr. Towes without Bishops-gate) they were both great lovers of music, and sworn brothers. Mr. W. Lilly, astrologer, did print this story false, which made Sir Edmund Wyndham (who married Mr. Pine's daughter) give to Sir George Hollis this true account contrary to Mr. Lilly.

Mr. Thomas Ellyot, Groom of the bedchamber, married Sir Edmund Wyndham's daughter, and had the roll (of near a quire of paper) of the conferences of the apparition and Mr. Towes. Mr. Ellyot was wont to say, that Mr. Towes was (not a bigot, or did trouble himself much about a religion, but was) a man of great morals.

Sir William Dugdale did farther inform me that Major General Middleton (since Lord) went into the Highlands of Scotland, to endeavour to make a party for King Charles I. An old gentleman (that was second-sighted) came and told him, that his endeavour was good, but he would be unsuccessful: and moreover, "that they would put the King to death: And that several other attempts would be made, but all in vain: but that his son would come in, but not reign; but at last would be restored." This Lord Middleton had a great friendship with the Laird

Bocconi, and they had made an agreement, that the first of them that died should appear to the other in extremity. The Lord Middleton was taken prisoner at Worcester fight, and was prisoner in the Tower of London, under three locks. Lying in his bed pensive, Bocconi appeared to him; my Lord Middleton asked him if he were dead or alive? he said, dead, and that he was a ghost; and told him, that within three days he should escape, and he did so, in his wife's cloaths. When he had done his message, he gave a frisk, and said,

Givenni Givanni 'tis very strange,
In the world to see so sudden a change.

And then gathered up and vanished. This account Sir William Dugdale had from the Bishop of Edinburgh. And this, and the former account he hath writ in a book of miscellanies, which I have seen, and is now reposited with other books of his in the Musæum at Oxford.

Anno 1670, not far from Cirencester, was an apparition: being demanded, whether a good spirit, or a bad? returned no answer, but disappeared with a curious perfume and most melodious twang. Mr. W. Lilly believes it was a fairy. So *Propertius.*

Omnia finierat; tenues secessit in auras:
Mansit odor; posses scire fuisse Deam.

Here, her speech ending, fled the beauteous fair,
Melting th' embodied form to thinner air,
Whom the remaining scent a goddess did declare.

The learned Henry Jacob, fellow of Merton college in Oxford, died at Dr. Jacob's, M. D. house in Canterbury. About a week after his death, the doctor being in bed and awake, and the moon shining bright, saw his cousin Henry standing by his bed, in his shirt, with a white cap on his head and his beard-mustachoes turning up, as when he was alive. The doctor pinched himself, and was sure he was awaked: he turned to the other side from him; and, after some time, took courage to turn the other way again towards him, and Henry Jacob stood there still; he should have spoken to him, but he did not; for which he has been ever since sorry. About half an hour after, he vanished. Not long after this, the cook-maid, going to the wood-pile to fetch wood to dress supper, saw him standing in his shirt upon the wood-pile.* This account I had in a letter from Doctor Jacob, 1673, relating to his life, for Mr. Anthony Wood; which is now in his hands.

When Henry Jacob died, he would fain have spoken to the Doctor, but could not, his tongue faltered.† 'Tis imagined he would have told Doctor Jacob, with what person he had deposited his manuscripts of his own writing; they were all the riches he had, 'tis suspected that one had them and printed them under his own name. —— See there in the said *Athenæ*, vol. or part 2. p. 90.

---

* See the whole story in *Ath. & Fasti Oxon.* Part 2, p. 91.

† This very story Dr. Jacob told me himself, being then at Lord Teynham's, in Kent, where he was then physician to my eldest son; whom he recovered from a fever. (*A. Wood's* note.)

T. M. Esq., an old acquaintance of mine, hath assured me that about a quarter of a year after his first wife's death, as he lay in bed awake with his grand-child, his wife opened the closet-door, and came into the chamber by the bedside, and looked upon him and stooped down and kissed him; her lips were warm, he fancied they would have been cold. He was about to have embraced her, but was afraid it might have done him hurt. When she went from him, he asked her when he should see her again? she turned about and smiled, but said nothing. The closet door striked as it used to do, both at her coming in and going out. He had every night a great coal fire in his chamber, which gave a light as clear almost as a candle. He was hypochondriacal; he married two wives since, the latter end of his life was uneasy.

Anno 165*.—At——in the Moorlands in Staffordshire, lived a poor old man, who had been a long time lame. One Sunday, in the afternoon, he being alone, one knocked at his door: he bade him open it, and come in. The Stranger desired a cup of beer; the lame man desired him to take a dish and draw some, for he was not able to do it himself. The Stranger asked the poor old man how long he had been ill? the poor man told him. Said the Stranger, "I can cure you. Take two or three balm leaves steeped in your beer for a fortnight or three weeks, and you will be restored to your health; but constantly and zealously serve God." The poor man did so, and became perfectly well. This Stranger was in a purple-shag gown, such as was not seen or known in those parts. And no body in the street after even song did see any one in such a coloured habit. Doctor Gilbert Sheldon, since Archbishop of Canterbury, was then in the Moorlands, and justified the truth of this to Elias Ashmole, Esq., from whom I had this account, and he hath inserted it in some of his memoirs, which are in the Musæum at Oxford.

MR. J. LYDAL *of Trinity College*, Soc. Oxon. *March* 11, 1649, 50, *attests the ensuing relation, in a letter to Mr. Aubrey, thus,*

MR. AUBREY,

CONCERNING that which happened at Woodstock, I was told by Mr. William Hawes, (who now lives with Sir William Fleetwood in the park) that the committee which sat in the manor-house for selling the king's lands, were frighted by strange apparitions; and that the four surveyors which were sent to measure the park, and lodged themselves with some other companions in the manor, were pelted out of their chambers by stones thrown in at the windows; but from what hands the stones came they could not see; that their candles were continually put out, as fast as they lighted them; and that one with his sword drawn to defend a candle, was with his own scabbard in the mean time well cudgelled; so that for the blow, or for fear, he fell sick; and the others were forced to remove, some of them to Sir William Fleetwood's house, and the rest to some other places. But concerning the cutting of the oak, in particular, I have nothing.

Your Friend,

To be commanded to my power,

JOHN LYDALL.

One Lambert, a gun-smith at Hereford, was at Caermarthen, to mend and put in order the ammunition of that county, before the expedition to Scotland, which was in 1639. He was then a young man, and walking on the sand by the sea side, a man came to him (he did verily believe it was a man) and asked him if he knew Hereford? yes, quoth he, I am a Hereford man. Do you know it well, quoth the other; perfectly well, quoth Lambert. "That city shall be begirt" (he told me he did not know what the word begirt meant then) "by a foreign nation, "that will come and pitch their camp in the Haywood, "and they shall batter such gate," which they did, (I have forgot the name of it) "and shall go away and not "take it."

The Scots came in 1645, and encamped before Hereford in the Hay-wood, and stormed the —— gate, and raised the siege. Lambert did well remember this discourse, but did not heed it till they came to the Hay-wood. Many of the city had heard of this story, but when the —— gate was stormed, Lambert went to all the guards of the town, and encouraged them with more than ordinary confidence: and contrary to all human expectation, when the besieged had no hope of relief, the Scots raised the siege, September 2, 1645, and went back into Scotland, *re infecta.* I knew this Lambert, and took this account from his own mouth; he is a modest poor man, of a very innocent life, lives poor, and cares not to be rich.

—— A minister, who lived by Sir John Warre in

Somersetshire, about 1665, walking over the Park to give Sir John a visit, was rencountered by a venerable old man, who said to him, "prepare yourself, for such a day" (which was about three days after) "you shall die." The minister told Sir John Warre and my Lady this story, who heeded it not. On the morning forewarned, Sir John called upon the Parson early to ride a hunting, and to laugh at his prediction: his maid went up to call him, and found him stark dead. This from my Lady Katherine Henley, who had it from my Lady Warre. But Dr. Burnet, in the life of the Earl of Rochester, makes it a dream.

This put me in mind of a story in the Legend, &c. of King Edward the Confessor, being forewarned of his death by a Pilgrim, to whom St. John the Evangelist revealed it, for which the King gave the Pilgrim a rich ring off his finger: and the event answered. The story is well painted on glass, in a window of the south isle of Westminster-Abbey, (the next window from that over the door that opens into the west walk of the cloyster) it is the best window in the church. Underneath the two figures, viz. of the King and the Pilgrim, are these following verses, viz.

Rex cui nil aliud præsto fuit, accipe, dixit.
Annulum, & ex digito detrahit ille suo.
—— *Evangelistæ* —— *villa Johannis.*
—————— *gratia petit.*

The verses under the Pilgrim are not legible. This story is in *Caxton's* Chronicle.

Dr. —— Twiss, minister of the new church at Westminster, told me, that his father, (Dr. Twiss, prolocutor of the assembly of divines, and author of *Vindiciæ Gratiæ*) when he was a school-boy at Winchester, saw the phantom of a school-fellow of his, deceased, a (rakehell) who said to him "I am damned." This was the occasion of Dr. Twiss's (the father's) conversion, who had been before that time, as he told his son, a very wicked boy; he was hypochondriacal. There is a story like this, of the conversion of St. Bruno, by an apparition: upon which he became mighty devout, and founded the order of the Carthusians.

John Evelyn, Esq., R.S.S., showed us at the Royal-Society, a note under Mr. Smith's hand, the curate of Deptford, that in November, 1679, as he was in bed sick of an ague, came to him the vision of a master of arts, with a white wand in his hand, and told him that if he did lie on his back three hours, viz. from ten to one, that he should be rid of his ague. He lay a good while on his back, but at last being weary he turned, and immediately the ague attacked him; afterwards he strictly followed the directions, and was perfectly cured. He was awake, and it was in the day-time.

This puts me in mind of a dream of old Farmer Good, a neighbour of mine at Broad-Chalk, who being ill, dreamt that he met with an old friend of his, (long since deceased) by Knighton Ashes (in that parish) who told him, that if he rose out of his bed, that he would die. He awaked, and rose to make water, and was immediately seized with a shivering fit, and died of an ague, aged 84.

The Lady Viscountess Maidstone told me she saw (as it were) a fly of fire, fly round about her in the dark, half an hour before her lord died: he was killed at sea, and the like before her mother-in-law the Countess of Winchelsea died, (she was then with child).

A Dutch prisoner at Wood-bridge, in Suffolk, in the reign of K. Charles II. could discern Spirits; but others that stood by could not. The bell tolled for a man newly deceased. The prisoner saw his phantom, and did describe him to the Parson of the parish,* who was with him; exactly agreeing with the man for whom the bell tolled. Says the prisoner, now he is coming near to you, and now he is between you and the wall; the Parson was resolved to try it, and went to take the wall of him, and was thrown down; he could see nothing. This story is credibly told by several persons of belief.

There is a very remarkable story of an apparition, which Martin Luther did see. Mentioned in his *Commensalia or Table-Talk*, which see.

Those that are delirious in high fevers, see (waking, men, and things that are not there). I knew one Mr. M. L. that took opium, and he did see (being awake) men and things that were not present, (or perhaps) not in being. Those whose spleens are ill affected have the like phantasies. The power of imagination is wonderful.

---

* Dr. Hooke, the Parson of the parish, has often told this story.

De seipso duplicato.

Cardanus, Synes. Somniorum, lib. ii. cap. 12. *In somniis mortis est signum, quia duo fiunt, cum anima separatur à corpore. Est & signum morbi in ipsis ægrotantibus, nec tum aliud quicquam significat.*

Of One's being divided into a Two-fold person.

In dreams it is a sign of death, because out of one are then made two, when the soul is separated from the body. And it is a sign of the disease in sick men, nor signifies it any thing else at that time.

As concerning apparitions of a man's own self, there are sundry instances, some whereof, I shall here set down.

The Countess of Thanet (Earl John's Lady) saw as she was in bed with her Lord in London, her daughter my Lady Hatton, who was then in Northamptonshire, at Horton Kirby; the candle was burning in her chamber. Since, viz. *anno* 1675, this Lady Hatton was blown up with gunpowder set on fire by lightning, in the castle at Guernsey, where her Lord was Governor.*

The beautiful Lady Diana Rich, daughter to the Earl of Holland, as she was walking in her father's garden at Kensington, to take the fresh air before dinner, about eleven o'clock, being then very well, met with her own apparition, habit, and every thing, as in a looking-glass. About a month after, she died of the small-pox. And it

* See Mr. Baxter's Treatise of Spirits.

is said that her sister, the Lady Isabella Thynne, saw the like of herself also, before she died. This account I had from a person of honour.

Mrs. E. W. daughter of Sir W. W. affirms that Mrs. J. (her father's sister) saw herself, *i. e.* her phantom, half a year before she died, for a quarter of an hour together. She said further, that her aunt was sickly fourteen years before she died, and that she walked living, *i. e.* her apparition, and that she was seen by several at the same time. The like is reported of others.

Mr. Trahern, B.D. (chaplain to Sir Orlando Bridgman, Lord Keeper) a learned and sober person, was son of a shoe-maker in Hereford: one night as he lay in bed, the moon shining very bright, he saw the phantom of one of the apprentices, sitting in a chair in his red waistcoat, and head-band about his head, and strap upon his knee; which apprentice was really in bed and asleep with another fellow-apprentice, in the same chamber, and saw him. The fellow was living, 1671. Another time, as he was in bed, he saw a basket come sailing in the air, along by the valence of his bed; I think he said there was fruit in the basket: it was a phantom. From himself.

When Sir Richard Nepier, M.D. of London, was upon the road coming from Bedfordshire, the chamberlain of the inn, shewed him his chamber, the doctor saw a dead man lying upon the bed; he looked more wistly and saw it was himself: he was then well enough in health. He went forward on his journey to Mr. Steward's in Berkshire, and there died. This account I have in a letter from Elias Ashmole, Esq. They were intimate friends.

" In the Desarts of Africk, you shall meet oftentimes "with fairies appearing in the shape of men and women, "but they vanish quite away like phantastical delusions."*

I Captain Henry Bell, do hereby declare both to the present age and to posterity, that being employed beyond the seas, in state affairs, divers years together, both by King James, and also by the late King Charles in Germany. I did hear and understand in all places great bewailing and lamentation made, by reason of destroying and burning of above fourscore thousand of Martin Luther's books, entituled, His last Divine Discourses.†

Upon which divine work or discourses, the reformation, begun before in Germany, was wonderfully promoted and spread in other countries.

But afterwards it so fell out, that the Pope then living, viz. Gregory XIII. understanding what great hurt and prejudice he and his religion had already received by reason of the said Luther's discourses, and also fearing that the same might bring further contempt and mischief upon himself and his church, he therefore to prevent the same,

---

* Pliny's Natural Hist. lib. 7, chap. 2.

† This narrative is in the Preface of the translation of Mr. Luther's Table-Talk.

did fiercely stir up and instigate the Emperor then in being, viz. Rodolphus III. to make an edict through the whole empire, that all the foresaid printed books should be burned, and also that it should be death for any person to have or keep a copy thereof, but to burn the same, which edict was speedily put in execution accordingly ; insomuch that not one of all the said printed books, nor any one copy of the same, could be found out, or heard of in any place.

Yet it pleased God, that in *anno* 1626, a German gentleman, named Casparus Van Sparr, with whom, in my stay in Germany, about King James's business, I became familiarly known and acquainted, having occasion to build upon an old foundation of a house, wherein his grand-father dwelt at that time, when the said edict was published in Germany, for the burning the said books, and digging deep under the said old foundation, one of the said original printed books was there happily found, lying in a deep obscure hole, being wrapped in a strong linen cloth, which was waxed all over with bees wax within and without, whereby the said book was preserved fair without any blemish.

And at the same time Ferdinandus II. being Emperor of Germany, who was a severe enemy and persecutor of the Protestant religion, the foresaid gentleman, and grandchild to him, that had hidden the said book in that obscure hole, fearing that if the said Emperor should get knowledge that one of the said books were yet forthcoming, and in his custody, whereby not only himself might be brought into trouble, but also the book be in danger to be destroyed, as all the rest were long before; and also calling to mind, that I had the High-Dutch tongue very perfect, did send the said original book over hither into England unto me: related to me the passages of the preserving and finding the said book; and earnestly moved me in his letter, to translate the said book into English.

Whereupon, I took the said book before me, and many times began to translate the same, but always I was hindered therein, being called upon about other business, insomuch that by no possible means I could remain by that work. Then about six weeks after I had received the said book, it fell out, that being in bed with my wife, one night between twelve and one o'clock, she being asleep, but myself yet awake, there appeared unto me an antient man, standing at my bed-side, arrayed in white, having a long and broad white beard, hanging down to his girdle steed, who taking me by the right ear, spake these words following unto me; "Sirrah, will not you take time to translate "that book which is sent unto you out of Germany? I "will provide for you both place and time to do it:" and then he vanished out of my sight.

Whereupon being much affrighted, I fell into an extream sweat, insomuch that my wife awaking, and finding me all over wet, she asked me what I ailed; I told her what I had seen and heard; but I never did heed or regard visions nor dreams. And so the same fell soon out of my mind.

Then about a fortnight after I had seen the vision, on a Sunday I went to Whitehall to hear the sermon, after which ended, I returned to my lodging which was then in King-street, Westminster, and sitting down to dinner with my wife, two messengers were sent from the council-board with a warrant to carry me to the keeper of the gate-house at Westminster, there to be safely kept, until farther order from the Lords of the Council; which was done without shewing any cause* at all, wherefore I was committed; upon which said warrant I was kept there ten whole years close prisoner; where I spent five years thereof about translating of the said book: Insomuch as I found the words very true which the old man in the aforesaid vision said unto me, "I will shortly provide you both place "and time to translate it."

Then after I had finished the translation, Dr. Laud, Arch-Bishop of Canterbury, sent to me in the prison, by Dr. Bray his chaplain, ten pounds, and desired to peruse the book; he afterwards sent me by Dr. Bray forty pounds. There was a committee of the House of Commons for the printing of this translation, which was in 1652.

A full and true relation of the examination and confession of William Barwick and Edward Mangall, of two horrid

---

* Whatsoever was pretended, yet the true cause of the Captain's commitment was, because he was urgent with the Lord Treasurer for his arrears, which amounted to a great sum, he was not willing to pay, and to be freed from his clamours, clapt him up into prison.

murders; one committed by William Barwick, upon his wife being with child, near Cawood in Yorkshire, upon the 14th of April last: as likewise a full account how it came to be discovered by an apparition of the person murdered.

The second was committed by Edward Mangall, upon Elizabeth Johnson, alias Ringrose, and her bastard child, on the 4th of September last, who said he was tempted thereto by the Devil.

Also their trials and convictions before the Honourable Sir John Powel, Knight, one their Majesties Justices, at the assizes holden at York, on the 16th of September, 1690.

As murder is one of the greatest crimes that man can be guilty of, so it is no less strangely and providentially discovered, when privately committed. The foul criminal believes himself secure, because there was no witness of the fact. Not considering that the all-seeing eye of Heaven beholds his concealed iniquity, and by some means or other bringing it to light, never permits it to go unpunished. And indeed so certainly does the revenge of God pursue the abominated murderer, that, when witnesses are wanting of the fact, the very ghosts of the murdered parties cannot rest quiet in their graves, till they have made the detection themselves. Of this we are now to give the reader two remarkable examples that lately happened in Yorkshire; and no less signal for the truth of both tragedies, as being confirmed by the trial of the offenders, at the last assizes held for that county.

The first of these murders was committed by William Barwick, upon the body of Mary Barwick, his wife, at the same time big with child. What were the motives, that induced the man to do this horrid fact, does not appear by the examination of the evidence, or the confession of the party: only it appeared upon the trial, that he had got her with child before he married her: and 'tis very probable, that, being then constrained to marry her, he grew weary of her, which was the reason he was so willing to be rid of her, though he ventured body and soul to accomplish his design.

The murder was committed on Palm-Monday, being the fourteenth of April, about two of the clock in the afternoon, at which time the said Barwick having drilled his wife along 'till he came to a certain close, within sight of Cawood-Castle, where he found the conveniency of a pond, he threw her by force into the water, and when she was drowned, and drawn forth again by himself upon the bank of the pond, had the cruelty to behold the motion of the infant, yet warm in her womb. This done, he concealed the body, as it may readily be supposed, among the bushes, that usually encompass a pond, and the next night, when it grew duskish, fetching a hay-spade from a rick that stood in a close, he made a hole by the side of the pond, and there slightly buried the woman in her cloaths.

Having thus despatched two at once, and thinking himself secure, (because unseen) he went the same day to his brother-in-law, one Thomas Lofthouse of Rufforth, within three miles of York, who had married his drowned wife's sister, and told him he had carried his wife to one Richard Harrison's house in Selby, who was his uncle, and would take care of her. But Heaven would not be so deluded, but raised up the ghost of the murdered woman to make the discovery. And therefore it was upon the Easter Tuesday following, about two of the clock in the afternoon, the forementioned Lofthouse having occasion to water a quickset hedge, not far from his house; as he was going for the second pail full, an apparition went before him in the shape of a woman, and soon after sat down upon a rising green grass-plat, right over against the pond: he walked by her as he went to the pond; and as he returned with the pail from the pond, looking sideways to see whether she continued in the same place, he found she did; and that she seemed to dandle something in her lap, that looked like a white bag (as he thought) which he did not observe before. So soon as he had emptied his pail, he went into his yard, and stood still to try whether he could see her again, but she was vanished.

In this information he says, that the woman seemed to be habited in a brown coloured petticoat, waistcoat, and a white hood; such a one as his wife's sister usually wore, and that her countenance looked extreamly pale and wan, with her teeth in sight, but no gums appearing, and that her physiognomy was like to that of his wife's sister, who was wife to William Barwick.

But notwithstanding the ghastliness of the apparition,

it seems it made so little impression in Lofthouse's mind, that he thought no more of it, neither did he speak to any body concerning it, 'till the same night as he was at his family duty of prayer, that that apparition returned again to his thoughts, and discomposed his devotion; so that after he had made an end of his prayers, he told the whole story of what he had seen to his wife, who laying circumstances together, immediately inferred, that her sister was either drowned, or otherwise murdered, and desired her husband to look after her the next day, which was Wednesday in Easter week. Upon this, Lofthouse recollecting what Barwick had told him of his carrying his wife to his uncle at Selby, repaired to Harrison beforementioned, but found all that Barwick had said to be false; for that Harrison had neither heard of Barwick, nor his wife, neither did he know anything of them. Which notable circumstance, together with that other of the apparition, encreased his suspicions to that degree, that now concluding his wife's sister was murdered, he went to the Lord Mayor of York; and having obtained his warrant, got Barwick apprehended, who was no sooner brought before the Lord Mayor, but his own conscience then accusing him, he acknowledged the whole matter, as it has been already related, as it appears by his examination and confession herewith printed: to which are also annexed the informations of Lofthouse, in like manner taken before the Lord Mayor of York, for a further testimony and confirmation of what is here set down.

On Wednesday the sixteenth of September, 1690, the criminal, William Barwick, was brought to his trial, before the Honourable Sir John Powel, Knight, one of the judges of the northern circuit, at the assizes holden at York, where the prisoner pleaded not guilty to his indictment: but upon the evidence of Thomas Lofthouse, and his wife, and a third person, that the woman was found buried in her cloaths in the Close by the pond side, agreeable to the prisoner's confession, and that she had several bruises on her head, occasioned by the blows the murderer had given her, to keep her under water: and upon reading the prisoner's confession before the Lord Mayor of York, attested by the clerk, who wrote the confession, and who swore the prisoner's owning and signing it for truth, he was found guilty, and sentenced to death, and afterwards ordered to be hanged in chains.

All the defence which the prisoner made, was only this, that he was threatened into the confession that he had made, and was in such a consternation, that he did not know what he said or did. But then it was sworn by two witnesses, that there was no such thing as any threatening made use of; but that he made a free and voluntary confession, only with this addition at first; that he told the Lord Mayor, he had sold his wife for five shillings; but not being able to name either the person or the place where she might be produced, that was looked upon as too frivolous to outweigh circumstances, that were proofs to apparent.

The information of Thomas Lofthouse, of Rufforth, taken upon oath the twenty-fourth day of April, 1690,

Who sayeth and deposeth, that one William Barwick,

who lately married this informant's wife's sister, came to this informant's house, about the fourteenth instant, and told this informant, he had carried his wife to one Richard Harrison's house in Selby, who was uncle to him, and would take care of her; and this informant hearing nothing of the said Barwick's wife, his said sister-in-law, imagined he had done her some mischief, did yesterday go to the said Harrison's house in Selby, where he said he had carried her to; and the said Harrison told this informant, he knew nothing of the said Barwick, or his wife, and this informant doth verily believe the said Barwick to have murdered her.

THOMAS LOFTHOUSE.

Jurat die & Anno
super dicto coram me,

S. DAWSON, Mayor.

The examination of the said William Barwick, taken the day and year abovesaid,

WHO sayeth and confesseth, that he, this examinant, on Monday was seventh night, about two of the clock in the afternoon, this examinant was walking in a Close, betwixt Cawood and Wistow; and he farther sayeth, that he threw his said wife into the pond, where she was drowned, and the day following, towards the evening, got a hay-spade at a hay-stake in the said Close, and made a grave beside the said pond, and buried her.

WILLIAM BARWICK.

Exam. capt. die & Anno
super dict. coram me,

S. DAWSON, Mayor.

The examination of William Barwick, taken the twenty-fifth day of April, 1690,

WHO sayeth and confesseth, that he carried his wife over a certain wain-bridge, called Bishopdike-bridge, betwixt Cawood and Sherborne, and within a lane about one hundred yards from the said bridge, and on the left hand of the said bridge, he and his wife went over a stile, on the left hand of a certain gate, entering into a certain close, on the left hand of the said lane; and in a pond in the said close, adjoining to a quick-wood-hedge, did drown his wife, and upon the bank of the said pond, did bury her: and further, that he was within sight of Cawood Castle, on the left hand; and that there was but one hedge betwixt the said close, where he drowned his said wife, and the Bishop-slates belonging to the said castle.

WILLIAM BARWICK.

Exam. capt. die & Anno super dict. coram me,

S. DAWSON, Mayor.

On Tuesday, September the seventeenth, 1690, *at York assizes.*

THOMAS LOFTHOUSE of Rufforth, within three miles of York city, sayeth, that on Easter Tuesday last, about half an hour after twelve of the clock, in the day time, he was watering quickwood, and as he was going for the second pail, there appeared walking before him, an apparition in the shape of a woman, soon after she sat down over against the pond, on a green hill, he walked by her as he went to the pond, and as he came with the pail of water from the pond, looking side-ways to see if she sat in the same place, which he saw she did; and had on her lap something like a white bag, a dandling of it (as he thought) which he did not observe before: after he had emptied his pail of water, he stood in his yard, to see if he could see her again; but could not: he says her apparel was brown cloaths, waistcoat and petticoat, a white hood, such as his wife's sister usually wore, and her face looked extream pale, her teeth in sight, no gums appearing, her visage being like his wife's sister and wife to William Barwick.

Signed,

THOMAS LOFTHOUSE.

THE second was a murder committed by one Edward Mangall, upon the body of Elizabeth Johnson alias Ringrose, the fourth of September last past, at a place called King's Causey, near Adling-street, in the county of York. He had got her with child, at least as she pretended; and was brought to bed of a boy, which she called William, and laid him to Mangall's charge, and required him to marry her: which he refused at first to do; but afterwards pretending to make her his wife, bid her go before him down King's Causey, towards the church, and he would follow her, as he did; but knocked out her brains in a close by the way, and at the same time, as was shrewdly suspected, killed the child.

This Mangall being examined by Mr. William Mauleverer, the coroner, confessed that he had murdered the woman; but denied that he meddled with the boy. And being asked why he murdered the woman, he made answer that the Devil put him upon it; appearing to him in a flash of lightning, and directing him where to find the club, wherewith he committed the murder. So ready is the Devil with his temptations, when he finds a temper easy to work upon.

He was convicted and found guilty upon the evidence of Anne Hinde, and his own confession to the coroner, as may be seen by the information annexed; and was thereupon sentenced to death, and ordered to be hanged in chains, as Barwick was before him, he making no defence for himself for so foul and horrid a murder, but that he was tempted thereto by the Devil.

Informations taken upon oath, September the 10*th*, 1690.

The information of Anne Hinde, wife of James Hinde, of Adling-street, in the County of York, husband-man, upon her oath saith;

THAT on Monday, the first of September, one Elizabeth Johnson, alias Ringrose, came to her house in the evening, with a child she called William; and the said Elizabeth the next day told this deponent, that the said Elizabeth was going to Gawthrope, in the county of Lincoln, to seek for one Edward Mangall, who had got her with that child, to see if he would marry her: upon which this deponent went with the said Elizabeth, to persuade him to marry her; but he denied having any dealings with her. But this deponent doth further depose, that on the fourth of September, the said Edward came to this deponent's house, and asked for the said Elizabeth; if she were there she might serve a warrant on him, if she had one, for he was going to Rawclyff, to consult his friends about it; and after some private discourse had betwixt the said Edward and the said Elizabeth, the said Elizabeth told this deponent, that he said, the said Elizabeth might go down King's-Causey; and he would follow her, and marry her: and this deponent did see the said Elizabeth go down King's-Causey; and a little after this deponent saw the said Edward also go down the King's-Causey; and after that, this deponent did not see the said Elizabeth, nor the said child till she saw them lie dead.

ANNE HINDE.

Capt. 10. *die*
Septembris 1690.

By me

W. MAULEVERER.

Un. Coron. Commit. prædict.

THE examination of Edward Mangall, upon the murder of Elizabeth Johnson alias Ringrose, taken before me William Mauleverer, Gent. one of the Coroners of our Sovereign Lord and Lady King William and Queen Mary, &c.

THE said Edward Mangall did confess, that he did murder the said Elizabeth Johnson, alias Ringrose upon the fourth day of September instant, in a close nigh to King's-Causey, he being asked the reason, said the Devil put him upon it, appearing to him in a flash of lightning; but denied that he medled with William Johnson alias Ringrose, the child.

Taken the 10th of Sept. 1690,

By me

W. MAULEVERER, Coroner.

VOICES.

SÆPE etiam & in prœliis Fauni auditi, & in rebus turbidis veridicæ voces ex occulto missæ esse dicuntur. Cujus generis duo sunt ex multis exempla, sed maxima. Nam non multo ante Urbem captam exaudita vox est à Luco Vestæ, qui à Palatii radice in novam viam devexus est, ut muri & portæ reficerentur: futurum esse, nisi provisum esset, ut Roma caperetur. Quod neglectum cùm caveri poterat, post acceptam illam maximam cladem explicatum est. Ara enim Aio loquenti, quam septam videmus, & adversus eum locum consecrata est.

i. e. Often even in battles have the Gods of the woods been heard to speak, and in troublesome times, when the affairs of governments have gone wrong, and been in disorder and turmoil, voices have been known to steal upon the ears of persons, that came as it were from a corner, but they knew not whence, and told them important truths. Of which kind there are out of a great many, two examples, and those indeed very rare and extraordinary. For not long before the city was taken, a voice was heard from the grove of Vesta, which went from the foot, and basis of the palace, sloping and bending into a new road, that the city walls and gates should be repaired: and that unless care was taken of it, the consequence would be, that Rome would be taken. This being omitted, when provision might have been made, was explained after that most signal and dreadful overthrow. For the altar, which we see enclosed, and that fronts that place, was a consecrated altar.

—— *Neque solum deorum voces Pythagorei observaverunt, sed etiam hominum, quæ vocant omina* ——.

i. e. Neither did the Pythagoræan Philosophers observe the voices of Gods only, but also those of men, which they called Omens.

"*Nero* —— *& lo'n dit qu'on entendoit un son de* "*trumpette dans les collines d'alentour, des gemissemens* "*sur le tombeau de sa mere.*"

Nero, they say, heard the sound of a trumpet among the hills and the rocks round about him, and groans over the tomb of his mother.

In the life of King Henry IV. of France, written by the Arch-Bishop of Paris, it is recorded, that Charles IX. (who caused the massacre) was wont to hear screaches, like those of the persons massacred.

St. Augustin heard a voice, saying, Tolle, Lege, take,

read. He took up his bible, and dipt on Rom. 13. 13. "Not in rioting and drunkenness, not in chambering and "wantonness," &c. And reformed his manners upon it.

One Mr. Smith, a practitioner of physic at Tamworth in Warwickshire, an understanding sober person, reading in *Hollinshead's* Chronicle, found a relation of a great fight between Vortigern and Hengest, about those parts, at a place called Colemore: a little time after, as he lay awake in his bed, he heard a voice, that said unto him, "You "shall shortly see some of the bones of those men and "horses slain, that you read of:" he was surprized at the voice, and asked in the name of God, who it was that spoke to him. The voice made answer, that he should not trouble himself about that; but what he told him should come to pass. Shortly after, as he went to see Colonel Archer (whose servants were digging for marle) he saw a great many bones of men and horses; and also pot-sherds; and upon the view it appeared to be according to the description in *Hollinshead's* Chronicle; and it was the place where the fight was; but it is now called Blackmore.

This was about the year 1685, and I had the account from my worthy friend and old acquaintance Thomas Marriet of Warwickshire, Esq., who is very well acquainted with Mr. Smith aforesaid.

Extracts out of the book entitled *Relation de la-Nouvelle France*, 1662, and 1663, 12.

"*Les Sauvages avoient eu de presentiments aussi bien*

"*que les Francois, et de cet horrible Tremble-terre. Voicy "la deposition d'une sauvage agé 20. fort innocente, "simple, & sincere. La nuict du* 4 *ou* 5 *de Febr.* 1663 "*estant entirement èveillèe, & en plein jugement, assise "comme sur mon seant, j'ay entender une voix distincte "& intelligible, qui m'a dit, Il doit arrive aujourdhuy "de choses extrangees, la Terre doit tremble. Je me "trouveray pour lors saisie d'une grand frageur, parce "que je ne voyois personne d'ou peut provinir cette voix: "Remplie de crainte, ja taschay à m'en dormir auec assez "de peine: Et le jour estant venu, je dis a mon mary "cequi m' estoit arrivè. Sur le* 9, *ou le* 10 *heure de "mesme jour, allant au bois pour buscher, à peine j'estois "entrée en la Forest que la mesme voix se fit —— en "tendre, me disent mesme chose, & de la mesme facon que "la nuicte precedente: La peur fuit bien plus grande, "moy estant tout seule.*"

i. e. The wild inhabitants, as well as the French, had presages of that dreadful earthquake. See here the depositions of a wild Indian, about twenty-six years of age, who was very innocent, simple, and sincere. On the night of the 4th or 5th of February, in the year 1663, being perfectly awake, and in sound judgment, and setting up as it were in my bed, I heard a distinct and intelligible voice, that said to me, There will happen to day many strange things. The earth will quake and tremble. I found myself seized with an extraordinary fear, because I saw no person from whom the voice could proceed. I, full of terror, with great difficulty, endeavoured to compose myself to sleep.

And as soon as it was day I told my husband what had happened to me. About nine or ten of the clock the same day, going to a forest a wood-gathering, I was scarce got into the brow of the forest, but I heard the same voice again, which told me the same thing, and in the same manner as it had done the night before. My fear was much greater this time, because I was all alone. She got her burden of wood, and met her sister who comforted her, to whom she told this story, and when she came to her father's caben, she told the same story there; but they heard it without any reflections.

"—— *La chose en demeure là, jusquez à* 5. *ou* 6 *heures* "*du soir du mesme jour, où un tremblement de Terre* "*survenant, ils reconnurent par experience, que cequ'ils* "*m'auoient intendu dire avant Midy, n'estoit que trop* "*uray.*"

i. e.——The matter rested there, till about five or six of the clock in the evening of the same day, when an earthquake coming suddenly upon us; experience made them recollect and acknowledge that, what they had heard me say before noon, was but too true.

"*Envoyée au R. P. André Castillon Provincial de la* "*Province de* France *par les Missioners de Peres de la* "*Compagnie de Jesu. Imprimé à* Paris, 1664."

i. e. Sent to the reverend father Andrew Castillon, provincial of the province of France, by the missioners of the fathers of the Society of Jesus. Printed at Paris, 1664.

"Livy makes mention, that before the coming of the "Gauls to Rome, Marcus Ceditius, a Plebeian, acquainted "the Senate, that passing one night about twelve o'clock "through the Via Nova, he heard a voice (bigger than a "man's) which advised him to let the Senate know, the "Gauls were on their march to Rome. How those things "could be, it is to be discoursed by persons well versed in "the causes of natural and supernatural events: for my "part I will not pretend to understand them, unless (ac- "cording to the opinion of some Philosophers) we may "believe that the air being full of intelligences and spirits, "who foreseeing future events, and commiserating the "condition of mankind, give them warning by these kind "of intimations, that they may the more timely provide "and defend themselves against their calamities. But "whatever is the cause, experience assures us, that after "such denunciations, some extraordinary thing or other "does constantly happen."

IMPULSES.

Cicero de Natura Deorum, lib. 2.

PRÆTEREA ipsorum Deorum sæpe præsentiæ, quales supra commemoravi, —— declarant, ut ab his, & Civitatibus, & singulis Hominibus consuli. Quod quidem intelligitur etiam significationibus rerum futurarum, quæ tum dormientibus, tum Vigilantibus portentantur.—— Nemo vir magnus sine aliquo afflatu divino unquam fuit.

i. e. Moreover the frequent presence of the Gods themselves, as I have above mentioned, plainly manifest, that they preside, with their good advice, as guardians, not only over cities, but particular men. This may be likewise certainly understood by the several significations of future events, which are predicted to men both sleeping and waking——there was never any one single great man, but what has, in some measure, partaken of this divine inspiration.

Testor Deum me olim ante plures menses melancolia ex adverso casu conceptam, Domini patris mei præsentisse, ac pronunciasse mortem, cum tamen ipso valdè incolumi, nulla ejus mihi ratio probabilis afferretur: & sic ipse postea momentum sui obitus, septem circiter horas antea pronunciavit.

i. e. I call God to witness, that formerly some months before, having conceived it in a fit of melancholy, from an unlucky event, that I foreknew, and foretold my father's death, when he being quite in health, no probable account of it offered itself to me: and in like manner he himself afterwards pronounced the moment of his departure near seven hours before. *Imperialis Musæum Physicum.* 104.

Oliver Cromwell had certainly this afflatus. One that I knew, that was at the battle of Dunbar, told me that Oliver was carried on with a divine impulse; he did laugh so excessively as if he had been drunk; his eyes sparkled with spirits. He obtained a great victory; but the action was said to be contrary to human prudence. The same fit of laughter seized Oliver Cromwell, just before the battle of Naseby; as a kinsman of mine, and a great favourite of his, Colonel J. P. then present, testified. Cardinal Mazarine said, that he was a lucky fool.

In one of the great fields at Warminster in Wiltshire, in the harvest, at the very time of the fight at Bosworth field, between King Richard III. and Henry VII. there was one of the parish took two sheaves, crying (with some intervals) now for Richard, now for Henry; at last lets fall the sheaf that did represent Richard and cried, now for King Henry, Richard is slain. This action did agree with the very time, day and hour. When I was a schoolboy I have heard this confidently delivered by tradition by some old men of our country.

Monsieur de Scudery in his Poem, entituled *Rome Vaincue*, fancies an angel to be sent to Alaric, to impel him to over-run the Roman empire with his swarms of northern people. The like may be fancied upon all changes of government; when providence destines the ends, it orders the means.

By way of parallel to this, the Pope by the like instinct, being at Rome in the consistory, did speak of the engagement in the famous battle of Lepanto, and that the Christians were victors. The fight at sea being two hundred miles or more distant from them.

King Charles I. after he was condemned, did tell Colonel Tomlinson, that he believed, that the English monarchy was now at an end: about half an hour after, he told the Colonel, "that now he had assurance by a strong impulse "on his spirit, that his son should reign after him." This information I had from Fabian Philips, Esq. of the Inner-temple, who had good authority for the truth of it: I have forgot who it was.

The Lord Roscomon, being a boy of ten years of age at Caen in Normandy, one day was (as it were) madly extravagant in playing, leaping, getting over the table-boards, &c.

He was wont to be sober enough: they said, God grant this bodes no ill luck to him; in the heat of this extravagant fit, he cries out, my father is dead. A fortnight after news came from Ireland, that his father was dead. This account I had from Mr. Knolles, who was his governor, and then with him; since Secretary to the Earl of Stafford, and I have heard his Lordship's relations confirm the same.

A very good friend of mine and old acquaintance, hath had frequent impulses; when he was a commoner at Trinity College, Oxford, he had several. When he rode towards the West one time in the stage coach, he told the company, "We shall certainly be robbed," and they were so. When a brother of his, a merchant, died, he left him with other effects, a share of a ship, which was returning from Spain, and of which news was brought to the Exchange at London of her good condition; he had such an impulse upon his spirit, that he must needs sell his share, though to loss; and he did sell it. The ship came safe to Cornwall, (or Devon) and somewhere afterwards fell upon the rocks and sunk: not a man perished; but all the goods were lost except some parrots, which were brought for Queen Katherine.

The good genius of Socrates is much remembered, which gave him warning. The Ethnick Genij are painted like our Angels; strong impulses are to be referred to them.

The learned Dr. John Pell, hath told me, that he did

verily believe, that some of his solutions of difficult problems were not done *Sine Divino auxilio.*

Mr. J. N. a very understanding gentleman, and not superstitious, protested to me, that when he hath been over-persuaded by friends to act contrary to a strong impulse, that he never succeeded.

KNOCKINGS.

MR. BAXTER'S Certainty of the World of Spirits. "A gentleman, formerly seemingly "pious, of late years hath fallen into the sin "of drunkenness; and when he has been "drunk, and slept himself sober, something knocks at his "beds-head, as if one knocked on a wainscot; when they "remove the bed, it follows him, besides loud noises on "other parts where he is, that all the house heareth.

"It poseth me to think what kind of spirit this is, that "hath such a care of this man's soul, (which makes me "hope he will recover). Do good spirits dwell so near us? "or, are they sent on such messages? or, is it his guardian "Angel? or, is it the soul of some dead friend, that suffereth "and yet retaining love to him, as Dives did to his brethren, "would have him saved? God keepeth yet such things "from us in the dark."

Major John Morgan of Wells, did aver, that as he lay in bed with Mr. —— Barlow (son of the Dean of Wells) they heard three distinct knocks on the bed; Mr. Barlow shortly after fell sick and died.

Three or four days before my father died, as I was in my bed about nine o'clock in the morning perfectly awake, I did hear three distinct knocks on the beds-head, as if it had been with a ruler or ferula.

Mr. Hierome Banks, as he lay on his death bed, in Bell-yard, said, three days before he died, that Mr. Jennings of the Inner-temple, (his great acquaintance, dead a year or two before) gave three knocks, looked in, and said, come away. He was as far from believing such things as any man.

Mr. George Ent of the Middle-temple, told me, some days before he died, that he had such a *Deceptio Visus*, he called it.

"In Germany when one is to die out of one's family, or "some friends, there will sometimes likewise happen some "token that signifieth the death of one, *e. g.* some (or "one) in the house heareth the noise, as if a meal-sack "fell down from on high upon the boards of the chamber; "they presently go up thither, where they thought it was "done, and find nothing; but all things in order.

"Also at Berlin, when one shall die out of the electoral "house of Brandenburgh, a woman drest in white linen "appears always to several, without speaking, or doing any "harm, for several weeks before." This from Jasper Belshazer Cranmer, a Saxon gentleman.

BLOWS INVISIBLE.

MR. BROGRAVE, of Hamel, near Puckridge in Hertfordshire, when he was a young man, riding in a lane in that county, had a blow given him on his cheek: (or head) he looked back and saw that nobody was near behind him; anon he had such another blow, I have forgot if a third. He turned back, and fell to the study of the law; and was afterwards a Judge. This account I had from Sir John Penruddocke of Compton-Chamberlain, (our neighbour) whose Lady was Judge Brograve's niece.

Newark (Sir G. L.'s) has knockings before death. And there is a house near Covent Garden that has warnings. The Papists are full of these observations.

The like stories are reported of others.

PROPHESIES.

CICERO *de Divinatione*, Lib. I.—— *gentem quidem nullam video, neque tam humanam atque doctam: neque tam immanem tam; barbaram, quæ non significari futura, & à quibusdam intelligi, prædicique posse censeat.*

i. e. I know of no country, either so polished and learned, or so rude, barbarous and uncivilized, but what always allowed that some particular persons are gifted with an insight into futurity, and are endued with a talent of prediction.

To pass by the prophesies of holy writ, the prophesies of Nostradamus do foretel very strangely; but not easily understood till they are fulfilled. The book is now common.

Peter Martyr, in his Decades, tells us, that there was a prophet among the Salvages in America, that did foretel the coming in of strangers in ships, which they had not known.

The prophesies of St. Malachi, are exceeding strange. He describes the Popes by their coats of arms, or their names, or manners: if his prophesies be true, there will be but fifteen Popes more. It is printed in a book in Octavo, entituled *Bucelini Historiæ Nucleus*, 1654, *in calce Libri* thus, *Prophetia Malachiæ Monachi Bangorensis, & A. Episcopi Ardinensis, Hiberniæ Primatis.* 1665, in two leaves.

Mr. Lancelot Morehouse, in the time of the civil wars, rescued a sheet of parchment in quarto, most delicately writ, from a taylor's sheers. It was a part of a book, and was a prophecy concerning England in Latin Hexameters; I saw it, 1649. It pointed at our late troubles: he gave it to Seth Ward, Bishop of Salisbury, and is lost among other good papers.

In a book* of Mr. William Lilly's, are hieroglyphick prophecies, viz. of the great plague of London, expressed by graves and dead corpses; and a scheme with ascending (the sign of London) and no planets in the twelve houses. Also there is a picture of London all on fire, also moles creeping, &c. Perhaps Mr. Lilly might be contented to have people believe that this was from himself. But Mr. Thomas Flatman (poet) did affirm, that he had seen those hieroglyphicks in an old parchment manuscript, writ in the time of the monks.

---

* Monarchy: or, No Monarchy, 4to.

In the nave of the cathedral church at Wells, above the capitals of two pillars, are the head of the King, and the head of a Bishop : it was foretold, that when a King should be like that King, and a Bishop like that Bishop, that Abbots should be put down, and Nuns should marry : above the arch, is an abbot or monk, with his head hanging downwards; and a nun with children about her. The inside of the arch is painted blue, and adorned with stars, to signify the power and influence of the stars. This prophecy was writ in parchment, and hung in a table on one of those pillars, before the civil wars. Dr. Duck (who was chancellor of Wells) said, that he had seen a copy of it among the records of the tower at London. It was prophesied 300 years before the reformation. Bishop Knight was Bishop here at the reformation, and the picture (they say) did resemble him.

In the Spanish history, it is mentioned, that a vault being opened in Spain, they found there Moors' heads, and some writings that did express, when people resembling those heads should come into Spain, they would conquer that country : and it was so. See this story more at large in *James Howell's* Letters.

There is a prophecy of William Tyndal, poor vicar of Welling, in the county of Hertford, made in the beginning of Queen Elizabeth's reign. I have seen it : it is in English verse, two pages and an half in folio. It foretold our late wars. I know one that read it forty years since.

A Prophecy.

Sexte verere Deos; vitæ tibi terminus instat,
Cum tuus in medio ardebit Carbunculus igne.

O thou sixth King to God due honours pay,
Remember Prince soon after thou'lt expire,
When thou behold'st thy carbuncle display,
Blaze against blaze amidst the red'ning fire.

These verses were made by George Buchanan; but (perhaps) the prediction was made by some second-sighted person. King James, of Scotland, the sixth, was taken with an ague, at Trinity-College in Cambridge; he removed to Theobald's; (where he died) sitting by the fire, the carbuncle fell out of his ring into the fire, according to the prediction. This distich is printed in the life of King James.

Before the civil wars, there was much talk of the Lady Anne Davys's prophesies; for which she was kept prisoner in the tower of London. She was sister to the Earl of Castle-heaven, and wife to Sir John Davys, Lord Chief Justice in Ireland; I have heard his kinsman (Counsellor Davys of Shaftesbury) say, that she being in London, (I think in the tower) did tell the very time of her husband's death in Ireland.

MIRANDA.

OUR English chronicles do record, that in the reign of King Henry III. a child was born in Kent, that at two years old cured all diseases. Several persons have been cured of the King's-evil by the touching, or handling of a seventh son. It must be a seventh son, and no daughter between, and in pure wedlock.

Samuel Scot, seventh son of Mr. William Scot of Hedington in Wiltshire, did when a child wonderful cures by touching only, viz. as to the King's-evil, wens, &c. but as he grew to be a man, the virtue did decrease, and had he lived longer, perhaps might have been spent. A servant boy of his father's was also a seventh son, but he could do no cures at all. I am very well satisfied of the truth of this relation, for I knew him very well, and his mother was my kinswoman.

'Tis certain, the touch of a dead hand, hath wrought wonderful effects, *e. g.* —— One (a painter) of Stowel in

Somersetshire, near Bridgewater, had a wen in the inside of his cheek, as big as a pullet's egg, which by the advice of one was cured by once or twice touching or rubbing with a dead woman's hand, (*è contra*, to cure a woman, a dead man's hand) he was directed first to say the Lord's prayer, and to beg a blessing. He was perfectly cured in a few weeks. I was at the man's house who attested it to me, as also to the reverend Mr. Andrew Paschal, who went with me.

Mr. Davys Mell, (the famous violinist and clock-maker) had a child crook-backed, that was cured after the manner aforesaid, which Dr. Ridgley, M.D. of the college of physicians, averred in my hearing.

The curing of the King's-evil by the touch of the King, does much puzzle our philosophers: for whether our Kings were of the house of York, or Lancaster, it did the cure (*i. e.*) for the most part. 'Tis true indeed at the touching there are prayers read, but perhaps, neither the King attends them nor his chaplains.

In Somersetshire, 'tis confidently reported, that some were cured of the King's-evil, by the touch of the Duke of Monmouth: the Lord Chancellor Bacon saith, "That "imagination is next kin to miracle-working faith."

When King Charles I. was prisoner at Carisbrook Castle, there was a woman touched by him, who had the King's-evil in her eye, and had not seen in a fortnight before, her eye-lids being glued together: as they were at prayers, (after the touching) the woman's eyes opened. Mr Seymer Bowman, with many others, were eye-witnesses of this.

At Stretton in Hertfordshire, in *anno* 1648, when King Charles I. was prisoner, the tenant of the Manor-House there sold excellent cyder to gentlemen of the neighbourhood; where they met privately, and could discourse freely, and be merry, in those days so troublesome to the loyal party. Among others that met, there was old Mr. Hill. B. D. parson of the parish, Quondam Fellow of Brazen-Nose college in Oxford. This venerable good old man, one day (after his accustomed fashion) standing up, with his head uncovered to drink his majesty's health, saying, "God bless our Gracious Sovereign," as he was going to put the cup to his lips, a swallow flew in at the window, and pitched on the brim of the little earthen cup (not half a pint) and sipt, and so flew out again. This was in the presence of the aforesaid parson Hill, Major Gwillim, and two or three more, that I knew very well then, my neighbours, and whose joint testimony of it I have had more than once, in that very room. It was in the bay-window in the parlour there; Mr. Hill's back was next to the window. I cannot doubt of the veracity of the witnesses. This is printed in some book that I have seen, I think in Dr. Fuller's Worthies. The cup is preserved there still as a rarity.

In Dr. Bolton's Sermons, is an account of the Lady

Honywood, who despaired of her salvation. Dr. Bolton endeavoured to comfort her: said she, (holding a Venice-glass in her hand) I shall as certainly be damned, as this glass will be broken: and at that word, threw it hard on the ground; and the glass remained sound; which did give her great comfort. The glass is yet preserved among the Cimelia of the family. This lady lived to see descended from her (I think) ninety, which is mentioned by Dr. Bolton.

William Backhouse, of Swallowfield in Berkshire, Esq. had an ugly scab that grew on the middle of his forehead, which had been there for some years, and he could not be cured; it became so nauseous, that he would see none but his intimate friends: he was a learned gentleman, a chymist, and antiquary: his custom was, once every summer to travel to see Cathedrals, Abbeys, Castles, &c. In his journey, being come to Peterborough, he dreamt there, that he was in a church and saw a hearse, and that one did bid him wet his scab, with the drops of the marble. The next day he went to morning-service, and afterwards going about the church, he saw the very hearse (which was of black say, for Queen Katherine, wife to King Henry VIII.) and the marble grave-stone by. He found drops on the marble, and there were some cavities, wherein he dipt his finger, and wetted the scab: in seven days it was perfectly cured. This accurate and certain information, I had from my worthy friend Elias Ashmole, Esq. who called Mr. Backhouse father, and had this account from his own mouth. May-Dew is a great dissolvent.

Arise Evans had a fungous nose, and said, it was revealed to him, that the King's hand would cure him, and at the first coming of King Charles II. into St. James's Park, he kissed the King's hand, and rubbed his nose with it; which disturbed the King, but cured him. Mr. Ashmole told it me.

In the year 1694, *there was published,*

A true Relation of the wonderful Cure of Mary Mallard, (lame almost ever since she was born) on Sunday the 26th of November 1693.

With the affidavits and certificates of the girl, and several other credible and worthy persons, who knew her both before and since her being cured. To which is added, a letter from Dr. Welwood, to the Right Honourable the Lady Mayoress, upon that subject. London: printed for Richard Baldwin, near the Oxford Arms in Warwick Lane, 1694.

A narrative of the late extraordinary cure, wrought in an instant upon Mrs. Elizabeth Savage, (lame from her birth) without using of any natural means.

With the affidavits which were made before the Right Honourable the Lord Mayor; and the certificates of several credible persons, who knew her both before and since her cure.

Enquired into with all its circumstances, by noted

divines both of the church of England, and others: and by eminent physicians of the college: and many persons of quality, who have expressed their full satisfaction.

With an appendix, attempting to prove, that miracles are not ceased. London, printed for John Dunton at the Raven, and John Harris at the Harrow, in the Poultry. The London divines would have my annotations of these two maids expunged.*

* "This Eliza Savage is still lame. It seems my Lord Mayor of London and Ministers may be imposed on." MS. Note in a copy of the first edition in the Library of the Royal Society.

MAGICK.

IN Barbary are wizards, who do smear their hands with some black ointment, and then do hold them up to the sun, and in a short time you shall see delineated in that black stuff, the likeness of what you desire to have an answer of. It was desired to know, whether a ship was in safety, or no? there appeared in the woman's hand the perfect lineaments of a ship under sail. This Mr. W. Cl. a merchant of London, who was factor there several years, protested to me, that he did see. He is a person worthy of belief.

A parallel method to this is used in England, by putting the white of a new laid egg in a beer glass, and expose it to the sun in hot weather, as August, when the sun is in Leo, and they will perceive their husband's profession.

There are wonderful stories of the Bannians in India, viz. of their predictions, cures, &c. of their charming crocodiles, and serpents: and that one of them walked over an arm of the sea, he was seen in the middle, and never heard of afterwards.

The last summer, on the day of St. John the Baptist, 1694, I accidentally was walking in the pasture behind Montague house, it was 12 o'clock. I saw there about two or three and twenty young women, most of them well habited, on their knees very busy, as if they had been weeding. I could not presently learn what the matter was; at last a young man told me, that they were looking for a coal under the root of a plantain, to put under their head that night, and they should dream who would be their husbands: It was to be sought for that day and hour.

The women have several magical secrets handed down to them by tradition, for this purpose, as, on St. *Agnes'* night, 21st day of Jannary, take a row of pins, and pull out every one, one after another, saying a *Pater Noster*, or (Our Father) sticking a pin in your sleeve, and you will dream of him, or her, you shall marry. Ben Jonson in one of his Masques make some mention of this.

And on sweet Saint *Agnes* night
Please you with the promis'd sight,
Some of husbands, some of lovers,
Which an empty dream discovers.

Another. *To know whom one shall marry.*

You must lie in another county, and knit the left garter about the right legged stocking (let the other garter and stocking alone) and as you rehearse these following verses, at every comma, knit a knot.

This knot I knit,
To know the thing, I know not yet,
That I may see,
The man (woman) that shall my husband (wife) be,
How he goes, and what he wears,
And what he does, all days, and years.

Accordingly in your dream you will see him: if a musician, with a lute or other instrument; if a scholar, with a book or papers.

A gentlewoman that I knew, confessed in my hearing, that she used this method, and dreamt of her husband whom she had never seen: about two or three years after, as she was on Sunday at church, (at our Lady's church in Sarum) up pops a young Oxonian in the pulpit: she cries out presently to her sister, this is the very face of the man that I saw in my dream. Sir William Soames's Lady did the like.

Another way, is, to charm the moon thus: at the first appearance of the new moon* after new year's day, go out in the evening, and stand over the spars of a gate or stile, looking on the moon and say,†

All hail to the moon, all hail to thee,

* Some say any other new moon is as good.

† In Yorkshire they kneel on a ground-fast stone.

I prithee good moon reveal to me,
This night, who my husband (wife) must be.

You must presently after go to bed.

I knew two gentlewomen that did thus when they were young maids, and they had dreams of those that married them.

Alexander Tralianus, of curing diseases by spells, charms, &c. is cited by Casaubon, before John Dee's Book of Spirits: it is now translated out of the Greek into English.

Moreri's Great Historical, Geographical, and Poetical Dictionary. *Abracadabra*, a mysterious word, to which the superstitious in former times attributed a magical power to expel diseases, especially the tertian-ague, worn about their neck in this manner.

Some think, that Basilides, the inventor, intends the name of God by it. The method of the cure was prescribed in these verses.

Inscribes Chartæ quod dicitur Abracadabra
Sæpius, & subter repetes, sed detrahe summam
Et magis atque magis desint elementa figuris
Singula quæ semper capies & cætera figes,
Donec in angustum redigatur Litera Conum,
His lina nexis collo redimire memento.
Talia languentis conducent Vincula collo,
Lethalesque abigent (miranda potentia) morbos.

Abracadabra, strange mysterious word,
In order writ, can wond'rous cures afford.
This be the rule :—a strip of parchment take,
Cut like a pyramid revers'd in make.
Abracadabra, first at length you name,
Line under line, repeating still the same:
Cut at its end, each line, one letter less,
Must then its predecessor line express;
'Till less'ning by degrees the charm descends
With conic form, and in a letter ends.
Round the sick neck the finish'd wonder tie,
And pale disease must from the patient fly.

Mr. Schoot, a German, hath an excellent book of magick: it is prohibited in that country. I have here set down three spells, which are much approved.

To cure an Ague.

Write this following spell in parchment, and wear it about your neck. It must be writ triangularly.

ABRACADABRA
ABRACADABR
ABRACADAB
ABRACADA
ABRACAD
ABRACA
ABRAC
ABRA
ABR
AB
A

With this spell, one of Wells, hath cured above a hundred of the ague.

To cure the biting of a Mad-Dog, write these words in paper, viz.

Rebus Rubus Epitepscum, and give it to the party, or beast bit, to eat in bread, &c. A Gentleman of good quality, and a sober grave person, did affirm, that this receipt never fails.

To cure the Tooth-Ach: out of Mr. Ashmole's manuscript writ with his own hand.

Mars, hur, abursa, aburse.
Jesu Christ for Mary's sake,
Take away this Tooth-Ach.

Write the words three times; and as you say the words, let the party burn one paper, then another, and then the last. "He says, he saw it experimented, and the party "immediately cured."

Mr. Ashmole told me, that a woman made use of a spell to cure an ague, by the advice of Dr. Nepier; a minister came to her, and severely repremanded her, for making use of a diabolical help, and told her, she was in danger of damnation for it, and commanded her to burn it. She did so, and her distemper returned severely; insomuch that she was importunate with the Doctor to use the same again; she used it, and had ease. But the parson hearing of it, came to her again, and thundered hell and damnation, and frighted her so, that she burnt it again. Whereupon she fell extremely ill, and would have had it a third time; but the Doctor refused, saying, that she had contemned and slighted the power and goodness of the blessed spirits (or Angels) and so she died. The cause of the Lady Honywood's Desparation was, that she had used a spell to cure her.

Jamblicus de *Mysteriis* de *nominibus Divinis.*

Porphyrius querit, cur Sacerdotes utantur nominibus quibusdam nihil significantibus? Jamblicus *respondet, omnia ejusmodi nomina significare aliquid apud deos: quamvis in quibusdam significata nobis sint ignota, esse tamen nota quædam, quorum interpretationem divinitus accepimus, omnino verò modum ineis significandi ineffabilem esse. Neque secundum imaginationes humanas, sed secundum intellectum qui in nobis est, divinus, vel potius simpliciore præstantioriequе modo secundum intellectum diis unitum. Auferendum igitur omnes excogitationes & rationales discursus, atque assimulationes naturalis vocis ipsius congenitas, ad res positas innatum. Et quemadmodum character symbolicus divinæ similitudinis in se intellectualis est, atque divinus, ita hunc ipsum in omnibus supponnere, acciperequе debemus, &c.*

Jamblicus, concerning the Mysteries relating to divine names.

Porphyrius asks the question why Priests make use of certain names which carry with them no known import or signification? Jamblicus replies, that all and every of those sort of names have their respective significations among the Gods, and that though the things signified by some of them remain to us unknown, yet there are some which have come to our knowledge, the interpretation of which we have received from above. But that the manner of signifying by them, is altogether ineffable. Not according to human imaginations, but according to that divine intellect which reigns within us, or rather according to an intellect that has an union with the Gods, in a more simple and excellent manner. And whereas the symbolical character of the divine likeness is in it self intellectual and divine, so are we to take and suppose it to be, in all, &c.

To cure an ague, Tertian or Quartan.

Gather Cinquefoil in a good aspect of ♃ to the ☽ and let the Moon be in the Mid-Heaven, if you can, and take —— of the powder of it in white wine: if it be not thus gathered according to the rules of astrology, it hath little or no virtue in it. With this receipt—one Bradley, a quaker at Kingston Wick upon Thames, (near the bridge end) hath cured above an hundred.

To cure the Thrush.

There is a certain piece in the beef, called the mouse-piece, which given to the child, or party so affected to eat, doth certainly cure the thrush. From an experienced midwife.

Another *to cure a Thrush.*

Take a living frog, and hold it in a cloth, that it does not go down into the child's mouth; and put the head into the child's mouth 'till it is dead; and then take another frog, and do the same.

To cure the Tooth-Ach.

Take a new nail, and make the gum bleed with it, and then drive it into an oak. This did cure William Neal's son, a very stout gentleman, when he was almost mad with the pain, and had a mind to have pistolled himself.

For the Jaundice.

The jaundice is cured, by putting the urine after the first sleep, to the ashes of the ash-tree, bark of barberries.

To cure a Bullock, that hath the Whisp, (that is) lame between the Clees.

Take the impression of the bullock's foot in the earth, where he hath trod; then dig it up, and stick therein five or seven thorns on the wrong side, and then hang it on a bush to dry: and as that dries, so the bullock heals. This never fails for wisps. From Mr. *Pacy*, a yeoman in Surry.

To cure a beast that is sprung, (that is) poisoned. It lights mostly upon Sheep.

Take the little red spider, called a tentbob, (not so big as a great pins-head) the first you light upon in the spring of the year, and rub it in the palm of your hand all to pieces: and having so done, piss on it, and rub it in, and let it dry; then come to the beast and make water in your hand, and throw it in his mouth. It cures in a matter of an hour's time. This rubbing serves for a whole year, and it is no danger to the hand. The chiefest skill is to know whether the beast be poisoned or no. From Mr. *Pacy.*

To staunch Bleeding.

Cut an ash of one, two, or three years growth, at the very hour and minute of the sun's entring into Taurus: a chip of this applied will stop it; if it is a shoot, it must be cut from the ground. Mr. Nicholas Mercator, astronomer, told me that he had tried it with effect. Mr. G. W. says the stick must not be bound or holden; but dipped or wetted in the blood. When King James II. was at Salisbury, 1688, his nose bled near two days; and after many essays in vain, was stopped by this sympathetick ash, which Mr. William Nash, a surgeon in Salisbury, applied.

Against an evil Tongue.

Take *Unguentum populeum* and *Vervain*, and *Hypericon*, and put a red hot iron into it; you must anoint the back bone, or wear it on your breast. This is printed in Mr. *W. Lilly's* Astrology. Mr. H. C. hath tried this receipt with good success.

Vervain and dill,
Hinders witches from their will.

A house (or chamber) somewhere in London, was haunted; the curtains would be rashed at night, and awake the gentleman that lay there, who was musical, and a familiar acquaintance of Henry Lawes. Henry Lawes to be satisfied did lie with him; and the curtains were rashed so then. The gentleman grew lean and pale with the frights ; one Dr. —— cured the house of this disturbance, and Mr. Lawes said, that the principal ingredient was *Hypericon* put under his pillow.

In Herefordshire, and other parts, they do put a cold iron bar upon their barrels, to preserve their beer from being soured by thunder. This is a common practice in Kent.

To hinder the night mare, they hang in a string, a flint with a hole in it (naturally) by the manger ; but best of all they say, hung about their necks, and a flint will do it that hath not a hole in it. It is to prevent the night mare, viz. the hag, from riding their horses, who will sometimes sweat all night. The flint thus hung does hinder it.

Mr. Sp. told me that his horse which was bewitched, would break bridles and strong halters, like a Samson. They filled a bottle of the horse's urine, stopped it with a cork and bound it fast in, and then buried it under ground : and the party suspected to be the witch, fell ill, that he could not make water, of which he died. When they took up the bottle, the urine was almost gone ; so, that they did believe, that if the fellow could have lived a little longer, he had recovered.

It is a thing very common to nail horse-shoes on the thresholds of doors : which is to hinder the power of witches that enter into the house. Most houses of the

West end of London, have the horse-shoe on the threshold. It should be a horse-shoe that one finds. In the Bermudas, they use to put an iron into the fire when a witch comes in. Mars is enemy to Saturn. There are very memorable stories of witches in *Gagé's* Survey of the West-Indies of his own Knowledge: which see.

At Paris when it begins to thunder and lighten, they do presently ring out the great bell at the Abbey of St. Germain, which they do believe makes it cease. The like was wont to be done heretofore in Wiltshire; when it thundered and lightened, they did ring St. Aldhelm's bell, at Malmsbury Abbey. The curious do say, that the ringing of bells exceedingly disturbs spirits.

In the Golden Legend by *W. de Worde.* It is said the evill spirytes that ben in the regyon of thayre doubte moche whan they here the belles rongen. And this is the cause why the belles ben rongen whan it thondreth, and whan grete tempeste aud outrages of wether happen to the ende that the feudes and wycked spirytes shold be abasshed, and flee and cease of the movynge of tempeste. Fol. xxiv.

TRANSPORTATION BY AN
INVISIBLE POWER.

A Letter from the Reverend Mr. Andrew Paschal, B.D. Rector of Chedzoy in Somersetshire, to John Aubrey, Esq. at Gresham College, London.

SIR,

LAST week received a letter from a learned friend, the minister of Barnstable in Devon, which I think worthy your perusal. It was dated May 3, 1683, and is as follows. (He was of my time in Queen's College, Cambridge.)

There having been many prodigious things performed lately in a parish adjoining to that which Bishop Sparrow presented me to, called Cheriton-Bishop, by some discontented dæmon, I can easily remember, that I owe you an account thereof, in lieu of that which you desired of me, and which I could not serve you in.

About November last, in the parish of Spreyton in the county of Devon, there appeared in a field near the dwelling house of Philip Furze, to his servant Francis Fry, being of the age of twenty-one, next August, an aged gentleman with a pole in his hand, and like that he was wont to carry about with him when living, to kill moles withal, who told the young man he should not be afraid of him; but should tell his master, *i. e.* his son, that several legacies that he had bequeathed were unpaid, naming ten shillings to one, ten shillings to another, &c. Fry replied, that the party he last named was dead. The Spectrum replied, he knew that, but said it must be paid to (and named) the next relation. These things being performed, he promised he would trouble him no further. These small legacies were paid accordingly. But the young man having carried twenty shillings ordered by the Spectrum to his sister Mrs. Furze, of the parish of Staverton near Totness, which money the gentlewoman refused to receive, being sent her, as she said, from the Devil. The same night Fry lodging there, the Spectrum appeared to him again, whereupon Fry challenged his promise not to trouble him, and said he had done all he desired him; but that Mrs. Furze would not receive the money. The Spectrum replied, that is true indeed; but bid him ride to Totness and buy a ring of that value, and that she would take. Which was provided for her and received by her. Then Fry rode homewards attended by a servant of Mrs. Furze. But being come into Spreÿton parish, or rather a little before, he seemed to carry an old gentlewoman behind him, that often threw him off his horse, and hurried him with such violence, as astonished all that saw him, or heard how horridly the ground was beaten; and being come into his master's yard, Fry's horse (a mean beast) sprung at once twenty-five feet. The trouble from the man-spectre ceased from this time. But the old gentlewoman, Mrs. Furze, Mr. Furze's second wife, whom the Spectre at his first appearance to Fry, called, that wicked woman my wife, (though I knew her, and took her for a very good woman) presently after appears to several in the house, viz. to Fry, Mrs. Thomasin Gidley, Anne Langdon, born in my parish, and to a little child which was forced to be removed from the house; sometimes in her own shape, sometimes in shapes more horrid, as of a dog belching fire, and of a horse, and seeming to ride out of the window, carrying only one pane of glass away, and a little piece of iron. After this Fry's head was thrust into a narrow space, where a man's fist could not enter, between a bed and a wall; and forced to be taken thence by the strength of men, all bruised and bloody; upon this it was thought fit to bleed him; and after that was done, the binder was removed from his arm, and conveyed about his middle, and presently was drawn so very straight, it had almost killed him, and was cut asunder, making an ugly uncouth noise. Several other times with handkerchiefs, cravats and other things he was near strangled, they were drawn so close upon his throat. He lay one night in his periwig (in his master's chamber, for the more safety) which was torn all to pieces. His best periwig he inclosed in a little box on the inside with a joined-stool, and other weight upon it; the box was snapped asunder, and the wig torn all to flitters. His master saw his buckles fall all to pieces on his feet. But first I should have told you the fate of his shoe strings, one of which a gentlewoman greater than all exception, assured me, that she saw it come out of his shoe, without any visible hand, and fling itself to the farther end of the room; the other was coming out too, but that a maid prevented and helped it out, which crisped and curled about her hand like a living eel. The cloaths worn by Anne Langdon and Fry, (if their own) were torn to pieces on their backs. The same gentlewoman, being the daughter of the minister of the parish, Mr. Roger Specott, showed me one of Fry's gloves, which was torn in his pocket while she was by. I did view it near and narrowly, and do seriously confess that it was torn so very accurately in all the seams and in other places, and laid abroad so artificially, and it is so dexterously tattered, (and all done in the pocket in a minute's time) as nothing human could have done it; no cutler could have made an engine to do it so. Other fantastical freeks have been very frequent, as the marching of a great barrel full of salt out of one room into another; an andiron laying it self over a pan of milk that was scalding on the fire, and two flitches of bacon descending from the chimney where they hung, and laid themselves over that andiron. The appearing of the Spectrum (when in her own shape) in the same cloaths, to seeming, which Mrs. Furze her daughter-in-law has on. The intangling of Fry's face and legs, about his neck, and about the frame of the chairs, so as they have been with great difficulty disengaged.

But the most remarkable of all happened in that day that I passed by the door in my return hither, which was

Easter-eve, when Fry returning from work (that little he can do) he was caught by the woman spectre by the skirts of his doublet, and carried into the air; he was quickly missed by his master and the workmen, and a great enquiry was made for Francis Fry, but no hearing of him; but about half-an-hour after Fry was heard whistling and singing in a kind of a quagmire. He was now affected as he was wont to be in his fits, so that none regarded what he said; but coming to himself an hour after, he solemnly protested, that the dæmon carried him so high that he saw his master's house underneath him no bigger than a hay-cock, that he was in perfect sense, and prayed God not to suffer the Devil to destroy him; that he was suddenly set down in that quagmire. The workmen found one shoe on one side of the house, and the other shoe on the other side; his periwig was espied next morning hanging on the top of a tall tree. It was soon observed, that Fry's part of his body that had laid in the mud, was much benumed, and therefore the next Saturday, which was the eve of Low-Sunday, they carried him to Crediton to be let blood; which being done, and the company having left him for a little while, returning they found him in a fit, with his forehead all bruised and swoln to a great bigness, none able to guess how it came, till he recovered himself, and then he told them, that a bird flew in at the window with a great force, and with a stone in its mouth flew directly against his forehead. The people looked for it, and found on the ground just under where he sat, not a stone, but a weight of brass or copper, which the people were breaking, and parting it among themselves. He was so very ill, that he could ride but one mile or little more that night, since which time I have not heard of him, save that he was ill handled the next day, being Sunday. Indeed Sir, you may wonder that I have not visited that house, and the poor afflicted people; especially, since I was so near, and passed by the very door: but besides that, they have called to their assistance none but nonconforming ministers. I was not qualified to be welcome there, having given Mr. Furze a great deal of trouble the last year about a conventicle in his house, where one of this parish was the preacher. But I am very well assured of the truth of what I have written, and (as more appears) you shall hear from me again.

I had forgot to tell you that Fry's mother came to me, grievously bewailing the miserable condition of her son. She told me, that the day before he had five pins thrust into his side. She asked; and I gave her the best advice I could. Particularly, that her son should declare all that the spectre, especially the woman gave him in charge, for I suspect, there is *aliquid latens;* and that she should remove him thence by all means. But I fear that she will not do it. For I hear that Anne Langdon is come into my parish to her mother, and that she is grievously troubled there. I might have written as much of her, as of Fry, for she had been as ill treated, saving the aerial journey. Her fits and obsessions seem to be greater, for she screeches in a most hellish tone. Thomasin Gidley (though removed) is in trouble I hear.

Sir, this is all my friend wrote. This letter came inclosed in another from a clergyman, my friend, who lives in those parts. He tells me all the relations he receives from divers persons living in Spreyton and the neighbouring parishes, agree with this. He spake with a gentleman of good fashion, that was at Crediton when Fry was blooded, and saw the stone that bruised his forehead; but he did not call it copper or brass, but said it was a strange mineral. That gentleman promised to make a strict inquiry on the place into all particulars, and to give him the result: which my friend also promises me; with hopes that he shall procure for me a piece of that mineral substance, which hurt his forehead.

The occasion of my friend's sending me this narrative, was my entreating him sometime since, to inquire into a thing of this nature, that happened in Barnstable, where he lives. An account was given to me long since, it fills a sheet or two, which I have by me: and to gratify Mr. Glanvil who is collecting histories for his *Sadducismus Triumphatus*. I desired to have it well attested, it being full of very memorable things; but it seems he could meet only a general consent as to the truth of the things; the reports varying in the circumstances.

Sir, Yours.

A Copy of a Letter from a learned Friend of mine in SCOTLAND, *dated March* 25, 1695.

HONOURED SIR,

I RECEIVED yours dated May 24th, 1694, in which you desire me to send you some instances and examples of Transportation by an Invisible Power. The true cause of my delaying so long, to reply to that letter, was not want of kindness; but of fit materials for such a reply.

As soon as I read your letter of May 24, I called to mind, a story which I heard long ago, concerning one of the Lord Duffus, (in the shire of Murray) his predicessors of whom it is reported, that upon a time, when he was walking abroad in the fields near to his own house, he was suddenly carried away, and found the next day at Paris in the French King's cellar, with a silver cup in his hand; that being brought into the King's presence and questioned by him, who he was? and how he came thither? he told his name, his country, and the place of his residence, and that on such a day of the month (which proved to be the day immediately preceding) being in the fields, he heard the noise of a whirl-wind, and of voices crying Horse and Hattock, (this is the word which the fairies are said to use when they remove from any place) whereupon he cried (Horse and Hattock) also, and was immediately caught up, and transported through the air, by the fairies to that place, where after he had drank heartily he fell asleep, and before he awoke, the rest of the company were gone, and had left him in posture wherein he was found. It is said, the King gave him the cup which was found in his hand, and dismissed him.

This story (if it could be sufficiently attested) would be a noble instance for your purpose, for which cause I was at some pains to enquire into the truth of it, and found the means to get the present Lord Duffus's opinion thereof; which shortly is, that there has been, and is such a tradition, but that he thinks it fabulous; this account of it, his Lordship had from his father, who told him that he had it from his father, the present Lord's grandfather; there is yet an old silver cup in his Lordship's possession still, which is called the Fairy Cup; but has nothing engraven upon it, except the arms of the family.

The gentleman, by whose means I came to know the Lord Duffus's sentiment of the foregoing story, being tutor to his Lordship's eldest son, told me another little passage of the same nature, whereof he was an eye witness. He reports, that when he was a boy at school in the town of Forres, yet not so young, but that he had years and capacity, both to observe and remember that which fell out; he and his school-fellows were upon a time whipping their tops in the church-yard before the door of the church; though the day was calm, they heard a noise of a wind, and at some distance saw the small dust begin to arise and turn round, which motion continued, advancing till it came to the place where they were; whereupon they began to bless themselves: but one of their number (being it seems a little more bold and confident than his companions) said,

Horse and Hattock with my top, and immediately they all saw the top lifted up from the ground; but could not see what way it was carried, by reason of a cloud of dust which was raised at the same time: they sought for the top all about the place where it was taken up, but in vain; and it was found afterwards in the church-yard, on the other side of the church. Mr. Steward (so is the gentleman called) declared to me that he had a perfect remembrance of this matter.

The following account I received, November last, from Mr. Alexander Mowat, a person of great integrity and judgment, who being minister at the church at Lesley, in the shire of Aberdene, was turned out for refusing the oath of test, *anno* 1681. He informs, that he heard the late Earl of Caithness, who was married to a daughter of the late Marquis of Argyle, tell the following story, viz. That upon a time, when a vessel which his Lordship kept for bringing home wine and other provisions for his house, was at sea; a common fellow, who was reputed to have the second-sight, being occasionally at his house; the Earl enquired of him, where his men (meaning those in the ship) were at that present time? the fellow replied, at such a place, by name, within four hours sailing of the harbour, which was not far from the place of his Lordship's residence: the Earl asked, what evidence he could give for that? the other replied, that he had lately been at the place, and had brought away with him one of the seamen's caps, which he delivered to his Lordship. At the four hours end, the Earl went down himself to the harbour, where he found the ship newly arrived, and in it one of the seamen without his cap; who being questioned, how he came to lose his cap? answered, that at such a place (the same the second-sighted man had named before) there arose a whirl-wind which endangered the ship, and carried away his cap: the Earl asked, if he would know his cap when he saw it? he said he would; whereupon the Earl produced the cap, and the seaman owned it for that, which was taken from him.

This is all the information which I can give at present concerning Transportation by an Invisible Power. I am sorry that I am able to contribute so little to the publishing of so curious a piece as it seems your collection of Hermetick Philosophy will be. I have given instructions to an acquaintance of mine now living at Kirkwall, and took him engaged when he left this place, to inform him concerning the old stone monuments, the plants and cures in the Orcades, and to send me an account. But I have not heard from him as yet, though I caused a friend that was writing to him, to put him in mind of his promise; the occasions of correspondence betwixt this place and Orkney are very rare.

SIR,

Your faithful affectionate friend
And servant,

J. G.

SIR,

'TIS very likely my Lord Keeper, [North] (if an account of a thing so considerable, hath not been presented to him by another hand) will take it kindly from you. I would transcribe it for Dr. Henry More, to whom, as I remember, I promised some time since an account of the Barnstable apparition; but my hands are full of work. May I beg of you to visit Dr. Whitchcot, minister of St. Laurence church, and to communicate a sight of this letter from Barnstable: probably he will be willing to make his servant transcribe it, and to convey it to Dr. More. Pray present my humble service to him, as also my affectionate service to our friends Mr. Hook and Mr. Lodwick. I ever rest,

Sir,

Your most faithful

And affectionate servant,

Chedzoy. Andrew Paschal.

There was in Scotland one —— (an obsessus) carried in the air several times in the view of several persons, his fellow-soldiers. Major Henton hath seen him carried away from the guard in Scotland, sometimes a mile or two. Sundry persons are living now, (1671) that can attest this story. I had it from Sir Robert Harley (the son) who married Major Henton's widow; as also from E. T. D. D.

A gentleman of my acquaintance, Mr. M. was in Portugal, *anno* 1655, when one was burnt by the inquisition for being brought thither from Goa, in East-India, in the air, in an incredible short time.

VISIONS IN A BERYL OR CRYSTAL.

A BERYL is a kind of Crystal that hath a weal tincture of red; it is one of the twelve stones mentioned in the Revelation. I have heard,* that spectacles were first made of this stone, which is the reason that the Germans do call a spectacle-glass (or pair of spectacles) a Brill.

Dr. Pocock of Oxford, in his Commentary on Hosea, hath a learned discourse of the *Urim* and *Thummim;* as also Dr. Spenser of Cambridge. That the priest had his visions in the stone of the breast plate.

The Prophets had their seers, viz. young youths who were to behold those visions, of whom Mr. Abraham Cowley writes thus.

> With hasty wings, time present they out-fly,
> And tread the doubtful maze of destiny;

* Dr. J. Pell.

There walk and sport among the years to come,
And with quick eye pierce every causes womb.

The magicians now use a crystal sphere, or mineral pearl, as No. 3, for this purpose, which is inspected by a boy, or sometimes by the querent himself.

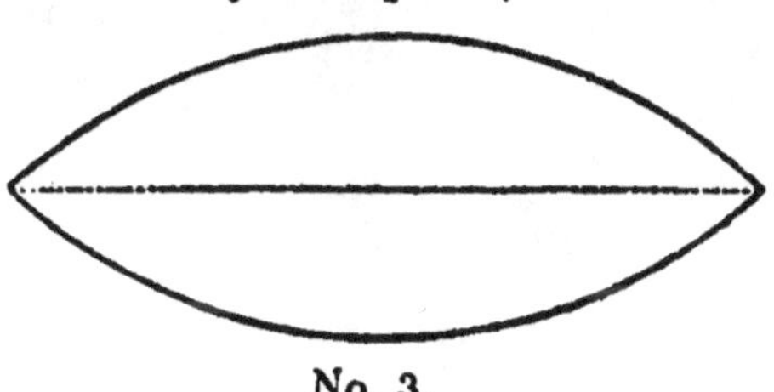

No. 3.

There are certain formulas of prayer to be used, before they make the inspection, which they term a call. In a manuscript of Dr. Forman of Lambeth, (which Mr. Elias Ashmole had) is a discourse of this, and the prayer. Also there is the call which Dr. Nepier did use.

James Harrington (author of Oceana) told me that the Earl of Denbigh, then Ambassador at Venice, did tell him, that one did shew him there several times in a glass, things past and to come.

When Sir Marmaduke Langdale was in Italy, he went to one of those Magi, who did shew him a glass, where he saw himself kneeling before a crucifix: he was then a Protestant; afterwards he became a Roman Catholick. He told Mr. Thomas Henshaw, R.S.S., this himself.

I have here set down the figure of a consecrated Beryl,

No. 4.

as No. 4, now in the possession of Sir Edward Harley, Knight of the Bath, which he keeps in his closet at Brampton-Bryan in Herefordshire, amongst his Cimelia, which I saw there. It came first from Norfolk; a minister had it there, and a call was to be used with it. Afterwards a miller had it, and both did work great cures with it, (if curable) and in the Beryl they did see, either the receipt in writing, or else the herb. To this minister, the spirits or angels would appear openly, and because the miller (who was his familiar friend) one day happened to see them, he gave him the aforesaid Beryl and Call: by these angels the minister was forewarned of his death. This account I had from Mr. Ashmole. Afterwards this Beryl came into somebody's hand in London, who did tell strange things by it; insomuch that at last he was questioned for it, and it was taken away by authority, (it was about 1645).

This Beryl is a perfect sphere, the diameter of it I guess to be something more than an inch : it is set in a ring, or circle of silver resembling the meridian of a globe : the stem of it is about ten inches high, all gilt. At the four quarters of it are the names of four angels, viz. Uriel, Raphael, Michael, Gabriel. On the top is a cross patee.

Sam. Boisardus hath writ a book *de Divinatione per Crystallum.*

A clothier's widow of Pembridge in Herefordshire, desired Dr. Sherborne (one of the canons of the church of Hereford, and Rector of Pembridge) to look over her husband's writings after his decease : among other things he found a call for a crystal. The clothier had his cloths oftentimes stolen from his racks ; and at last obtained this trick to discover the thieves. So when he lost his cloths, he went out about midnight with his crystal and call, and a little boy, or little maid with him (for they say it must be a pure virgin) to look in the crystal, to see the likeness of the person that committed the theft. The doctor did burn the call, 1671.

VISIONS WITHOUT A GLASS OR CRYSTAL.

ABOUT the latter end of the reign of King James I. one —— a taylor in London, had several visions, which he did describe to a painter to paint, and he writ the description himself in an ill taylor-like hand, in false English, but legible: it was at least a quire of paper. I remember one vision is of St. James's park, where is the picture of an altar and crucifix. Mr. Butler of the toy-shop by Ludgate, (one of the masters of Bridewell) had the book in *anno* 1659; the then Earl of Northampton gave five pounds for a copy of it.

CONVERSE WITH ANGELS AND SPIRITS.

DR. RICHARD NEPIER was a person of great abstinence, innocence, and piety: he spent every day two hours in family prayer: when a patient or querent came to him, he presently went to his closet to pray: and told to admiration the recovery, or death of the patient. It appears by his papers, that he did converse with the angel Raphael, who gave him the responses.

Elias Ashmole, Esq. had all his papers, where is contained all his practice for about fifty years; which he, Mr. Ashmole, carefully bound up, according to the year of our Lord, in —— volumes in folio; which are now reposited in the library of the Musæum in Oxford. Before the responses stands this mark, viz. R. Ris. which Mr. Ashmole said was *Responsum Raphælis*.

In these papers are many excellent medicines, or receipts for several diseases that his patients had; and before some of them is the aforesaid mark. Mr. Ashmole took the pains to transcribe fairly with his own hand all the receipts; they are about a quire and a half of paper in folio, which since his death were bought of his relict by E. W. Esq. R.S.S.

The angel told him if the patient were curable or incurable.

There are also several other queries to the angel, as to religion, transubstantiation, &c. which I have forgot. I remember one is, whether the good spirits or the bad be most in number? R. Ris. The good.

It is to be found there, that he told John Prideaux, D.D. *anno* 1621, that twenty years hence (1641) he would be a bishop, and he was so, *sc.* bishop of Worcester.

R. Ris. did resolve him, that Mr. Booth, of —— in Cheshire, should have a son that should inherit three years hence, [*sc.* Sir George Booth, the first Lord Delamere] viz. from 1619, Sir George Booth aforesaid was born, December 18, *anno* 1622.

This I extracted out of Dr. Nepier's Original Diary, then in possession of Mr. Ashmole.

When E. W. Esq. was about eight years old, he was troubled with the worms. His grand father carried him to Dr. Nepier at Lynford. Mr. E. W. peeped in at the closet at the end of the gallery, and saw him upon his knees at prayer. The Doctor told Sir Francis that at fourteen years old his grandson would be freed from that distemper; and he was so. The medicine he prescribed was, to drink a little draught of *Muscadine* in the morning. 'Twas about 1625.

It is impossible that the prediction of Sir George Booth's birth could be found any other way, but by angelical revelation.

This Dr. Richard Nepier was rector of Lynford in Bucks, and did practise physic; but gave most to the poor that he got by it. 'Tis certain he told his own death to a day and hour; he died praying upon his knees, being of a very great age, April 1, 1634. He was nearly related to the learned Lord Nepier, Baron of M—— in Scotland: I have forgot whether his brother. His knees were horny with frequent praying. He left his estate to Sir Richard Nepier, M.D. of the college of physicians, London, from whom Mr. Ashmole had the Doctor's picture, now in the Musæum.

Dr. Richard Nepier, rector of Lynford, was a good astrologer, and so was Mr. Marsh of Dunstable; but Mr. Marsh did seriously confess to a friend of mine, that astrology was but the countenance; and that he did his business by the help of the blessed spirits; with whom only men of great piety, humility and charity, could be acquainted; and such a one he was. He was an hundred years old when my friend was with him; and yet did understand himself very well.

At Ashbridge in Buckinghamshire, near Berkhamsted, was a monastery, (now in the possession of the Earl of Bridgewater) where are excellent good old paintings still to be seen. In this monastery was found an old manuscript entitled *Johannes de Rupescissâ*, since printed, (or part of it) a chymical book, wherein are many receipts; among others, to free a house haunted with evil spirits, by fumes: Mr. Marsh had it, and did cure houses so haunted by it. Ovid in his festivals hath something like it. See *Thesaurus Exorcismorum* writ by —— *è Societate Jesu.* Oct. Wherein are several high physical and medicinal things.

Good spirits are delighted and allured by sweet perfumes, as rich gums, frankincense, salts, &c. which was the reason that priests of the Gentiles, and also the Christians used them in their temples, and sacrifices: and on the contrary, evil spirits are pleased and allured and called up by suffumigations of Henbane, &c. stinking smells, &c. which the witches do use in their conjuration. Toads (saturnine animals) are killed by putting of salt upon them; I have seen the experiment. Magical writers say, that cedar-wood drives away evil spirits; it was, and is much used in magnificent temples.

Plinii Natural Hist. lib. 12, cap. 14.

Alexandro Magno in pueritia sine parsimonia thura ingerenti aris, pœdagogus Leonides dixerat, ut illo modo, cum devicisset thuriferas gentes, supplicaret. At ille Arabia potitus; thure onustam navim misit ei, large exhortatus, ut Deos adoraret.

i.e. As Alexander the great, in the time of his minority, was heaping incense upon the altars, even to a degree of religious prodigality, his preceptor Leonidas told him, that he should prefer his supplications to the Gods after that free manner, when he had subdued the nations, whose produce was frankincense. And he, as soon as he had made himself master of Arabia, sent him accordingly a ship laden with incense, and with it ample exhortations to adore the Gods.

One says, why should one think the intellectual world less peopled than the material? Pliny, in his Natural History, lib. —— cap. —— tells us that in Africa, do sometimes appear multitudes of aerial shapes, which suddenly vanish. Mr. Richard Baxter in his Certainty of the Worlds of Spirits, (the last book he writ, not long before his death) hath a discourse of angels; and wonders they are so little taken notice of; he hath counted in Newman's Concordance of the Bible, the word angel, in above three hundred places.

Hugo Grotius in his Annotations on Jonah, speaking of Niniveh, says, that history has divers examples, that after a great and hearty humiliation, God delivered cities, &c. from their calamities. Some did observe in the late civil wars, that the Parliament, after a humiliation, did shortly obtain a victory. And as a three-fold chord is not easily broken, so when a whole nation shall conjoin in fervent prayer and supplication, it shall produce wonderful effects. William Laud, Arch-Bishop of Canterbury, in a sermon preached before the Parliament, about the beginning of the reign of King Charles I. affirms the power of prayer to be so great, that though there be a conjunction or opposition of Saturn or Mars, (as there was one of them then) it will overcome the malignity of it. In the life of Vavasor Powel, is a memorable account of the effect of fervent prayer, after an exceeding drought: and Mr. Baxter (in his book aforementioned) hath several instances of that kind, which see.

St. Michael and all Angels.

The Collect.

O everlasting God, who hast ordered and constituted the services of men and angels, after a wonderful manner: mercifully grant, that as thy holy angels always do thee service in Heaven: so by thy appointment, they may succour and defend us, through Jesus Christ our Lord. *Amen.*

CORPS-CANDLES IN WALES.

Part of a Letter to MR. BAXTER.

SIR,

I AM to give you the best satisfaction I can touching those fiery apparitions* (Corps Candles) which do as it were mark out the way for corpses to their κοιμητηριον and sometimes before the parties themselves fall sick, and sometimes in their sickness. I could never hear in England of these, they are common in these three counties, viz. Cardigan, Carmarthen, and Pembroke, and as I hear in some other parts of Wales.†

These φαντάσματα in our language, we call Canhwyllan Cyrph, (*i.e.*) Corps Candles; and candles we call them, not that we see any thing besides the light; but because that light doth as much resemble a material candle-light as eggs do eggs, saving, that in their journey these candles be *modo apparentes, modo disparentes*, especially, when one comes near them; and if one come in the way against them, unto whom they vanish; but presently appear be-

---

* Mr. *Baxter's* Certainty of the Worlds of Spirits, p. 137.

† And Radnor.

hind and hold on their course. If it be a little candle pale or bluish, then follows the corps either of an abortive or some infant; if a big one, then the corps of some one come to age: if there be seen two, or three, or more, some big, some small together, then so many and such corpses together. If two candles come from divers places, and be seen to meet, the corpses will the like; if any of these candles are seen to turn, sometimes a little out of the way, or path, that leadeth to the church, the following corps will be forced to turn in that very place, for the avoiding some dirty lane or plash, &c. Now let us fall to evidence. Being about the age of fifteen, dwelling at Lanylar, late at night, some neighbour saw one of these candles hovering up and down along the river bank, until they were weary in beholding it, at last they left it so, and went to bed. A few weeks after came a proper damsel from Montgomeryshire, to see her friends, who dwelt on the other side of that river Istwith, and thought to ford the river at that very place where the light was seen; being dissuaded by some lookers on (some it is most likely of those that saw the light) to adventure on the water, which was high by reason of a flood: she walked up and down along the river bank, even where, and even as the aforesaid candle did, waiting for the falling of the water; which at last she took, but too soon for her, for she was drowned therein. Of late my sexton's wife, an aged understanding woman, saw from her bed, a little bluish candle on her tables-end; within two or three days after, came a fellow enquiring for her husband, and taking something from under his cloak, claped it down upon the tables-end; it was a dead born child.

Another time, the same woman saw such another candle upon the end of the self same table; within a few days after a weak child newly christened by me, was brought to the sexton's house, where presently he died: and when the sexton's wife, who was then abroad, came home, she found the child on the other end of the table, where she had seen the candle.

Some thirty or forty years since, my wife's sister, being nurse to Baronet Rudd's three eldest children, and (the Lady mistress being dead) the Lady comptroller of the house going late into the chamber where the maid servants lay, saw no less than five of these lights together. It happened a while after, that the chamber being newly plaistered, and a grate of coal fire therein kindled to hasten the drying of the plaister, that five of the maid servants went to bed as they were wont (but as it fell out) too soon; for in the morning they were all dead, being suffocated in their sleep with the steam of the new tempered lime and coal. This was at Langathen in Carmarthenshire.—*Jo. Davis.* See more.—

Generglyn, March 1656.

To this account of Mr. Davis, I will subjoin what my worthy friend and neighbour Randal Caldicot, D.D. hath affirmed to me many years since, viz. When any Christian is drowned in the river Dee, there will appear over the water where the corps is, a light, by which means they do find the body: and it is therefore called the Holy Dee. The doctor's father was Mr. Caldicot, of Caldicot in Cheshire, which lies on the river.

ORACLES.

HIERONIMUS *Cardanus*, lib. 3, *Synesiorum Somniorum*, cap. 15, treats of this subject, which see. Johannes Scotus Erigena, when he was in Greece, did go to an Oracle to enquire for a Treatise of Aristotle, and found it, by the response of the oracle. This he mentions in his works lately printed at Oxford; and is quoted by Mr. *Anthony á Wood* in his Antiquities of Oxon, in his life. He lived before the conquest, and taught Greek at the Abby in Malmesbury, where his scholars stabbed him with their penknives for his severity to them. Leland mentions that his statue was in the choir there.

ECSTACY.

Cardanus, lib. 2. Synes. Somniorum, cap. 8.

IN Ecstasin multis modis dilabuntur homines, aut per Syncopen, aut animi deliquium, aut etiam proprie abducto omni sensu externo, absque alia Causa. Id vero contingit consuetis plerunque, & nimio affectu alicujus rei laborantibus; —— Ecstasis medium est inter vigiliam & somnium, sicut somnus inter mortem & vigiliam seuvitam——Visa in Ecstasi certiora insomniis: Clariora & evidentiora —— Ecstasi deprehensi audire possunt, qui dormiunt non possunt.

Men fall into an Ecstacy many ways, either by a syncope, by a vanishing and absence of the spirits, or else by the withdrawing of every external sense without any other cause. It most commonly happens to those who are over sollicitous or fix their whole minds upon doing any one particular thing. An Ecstacy is a kind of medium between sleeping and waking, as sleep is a kind of middle state between life and death. Things seen in an Ecstacy are more certain than those we behold in dreams: they are much more clear, and far more evident. Those seized with an Ecstacy can hear, those who sleep cannot.

Anno 1670, a poor widow's daughter in Herefordshire, went to service not far from Harwood (the seat of Sir John Hoskins, Bart. R.S.S.) She was aged near about twenty; fell very ill, even to the point of death; her mother was old and feeble, and her daughter was the comfort of her life; if she should die, she knew not what to do: she besought God upon her knees in prayer, that he would be pleased to spare her daughter's life, and take her to him: at this very time, the daughter fell into a trance, which continued about an hour: they thought she had been dead: when she recovered out of it, she declared the vision she had in this fit, viz. that one in black habit came to her, whose face was so bright and glorious she could not behold it; and also he had such brightness upon his breast, and (if I forget not) upon his arms. And told her, that her mother's prayers were heard, and that her mother should shortly die, and she should suddenly recover; and she did so, and her mother died. She hath the character of a modest, humble, virtuous maid. Had this been in some Catholick country, it would have made a great noise.

'Tis certain, there was one in the Strand, who lay in a trance a few hours before he departed. And in his trance had a vision of the death of King Charles II. It was at the very day of his apoplectick fit.

There is a sheet of paper printed 16 . . . concerning Ecstacies, that James Usher, late Lord Primate of Ireland, once had: but I have been assured from my hon. friend James Tyrrell, Esq. (his Lordship's grandson) that this was not an ecstacy; but that his Lordship upon reading the 12, 13, 14, &c. chapters of the Revelation, and farther reflecting upon the great increase of the sectaries in England, supposed that they would let in popery, which consideration put him into a great transport, at the time when his daughter (the Lady Tyrrel) came into the room; when he discoursed to her divers things (tho' not all) contained in the said printed paper.

GLANCES OF LOVE AND MALICE.

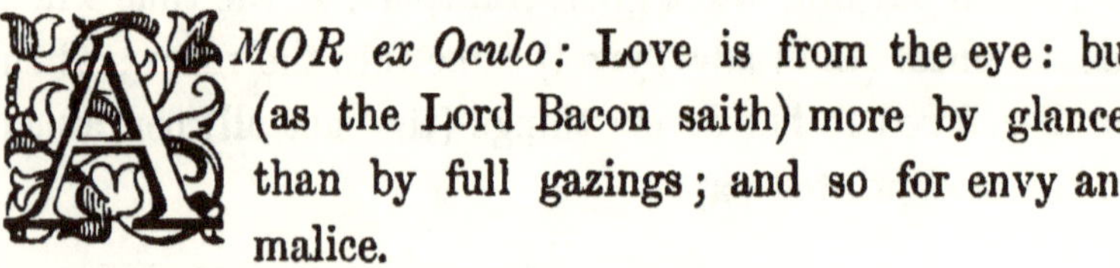

A*MOR ex Oculo:* Love is from the eye: but (as the Lord Bacon saith) more by glances than by full gazings; and so for envy and malice.

Tell me dearest, what is Love?
'Tis a Lightning from above:
'Tis an Arrow, 'tis a Fire,
'Tis a Boy they call Desire.*

'Tis something divine and inexplicable. It is strange, that as one walks the streets sometimes one shall meet with an aspect (of male or female) that pleases our souls; and whose natural sweetness of nature, we could boldly rely upon. One never saw the other before, and so could neither oblige or disoblige each other. Gaze not on a maid, saith Ecclus. 9, 5.

The Glances of envy and malice do shoot also subtilly; the eye of the malicious person, does really infect and make sick the spirit of the other. The Lord Bacon saith

---

* Mr. *Fletcher* in Cupid's Revenge.

it hath been observed, that after triumphs, the triumphants have been sick in spirit.

The chymist can draw subtile spirits, that will work upon one another at some distance, viz. spirits of alkalies and acids, *e.g.* spirits cœlestial (sal armoniac and spirits of C. C. will work on each other at half a yard distance, and smoke;) but the spirits above mentioned are more subtile than they.

Non amo te Sabati, nec possum dicere quare,
Hoc tantum possum dicere, non amo te.

Fellow, I love thee not, I can't tell why,
But this, I'll tell thee, I could sooner die.

But if an astrologer had their nativities, he would find a great disagreement in the schemes. These are hyperphysical opticks, and drawn from the heavens.

Infants are very sensible of these irradiations of the eyes. In Spain, France, &c. southern countries, the nurses and parents are very shy to let people look upon their young children, for fear of fascination. In Spain, they take it ill if one looks on a child, and make one say, God bless it. They talk of *mal dè ojos.* We usually say, witches have evil eyes.

AN
ACCURATE ACCOUNT OF SECOND-SIGHTED MEN IN SCOTLAND.

In Two Letters from a learned friend of mine in Scotland.

I.

To Mr. John Aubrey, *Fellow of the Royal Society.*

Sir,

FOR your satisfaction I drew up some queries about the second-sighted men, and having sent them to the northern parts of this kingdom, some while ago, I received answers to them from two different hands, whereof I am now to give you an account, viz.

Query 1.

If some few credible, well attested instances of such a knowledge as is commonly called the second-sight, can, be given?

Answer.

Many instances of such knowledge can be given, by the confession of such who are skilled in that faculty: for instances I refer you to the fourth query.

Query 2.

If it consists in the discovery of present or past events only? or if it extend to such as are to come?

Answer.

The second-sight relates only to things future, which will shortly come to pass. Past events I learn nothing of it.

Query 3.

If the objects of this knowledge be sad and dismal events only; such as deaths and murders? or, joyful and prosperous also?

Answer.

Sad and dismal events, are the objects of this knowledge: as sudden deaths, dismal accidents. That they are prosperous, or joyful, I cannot learn. Only one instance I have from a person worthy of credit, and thereby judge of the joyfulness, or prosperity of it, and it is this. Near forty years ago, Maclean and his Lady, sister to my Lord Seaforth, were walking about their own house, and in their return both came into the nurse's chamber, where their young child was on the breast: at their coming into the room, the nurse falls a weeping; they asked the cause, dreading the child was sick, or that she was scarce of milk: the nurse replied, the child was well, and she had abundance of milk; yet she still wept; and being pressed to tell what ailed her; she at last said Maclean would die, and the Lady would shortly be married to another man. Being enquired how she knew that event, she told them plainly, that as they both came into the room, she saw a man with a scarlet cloak and a white hat betwixt them, giving the Lady a kiss over the shoulder; and this was the cause of weeping. All which came to pass after Maclean's death; the tutor of Lovet married the Lady in the same habit the woman saw him. Now by this instance, judge if it be prosperous to one, it is as dismal to another.

Query 4.

If these events which second-sighted men discover, or foretel, be visibly represented to them, and acted, as it were before their eyes?

Answer.

Affirmatively, they see those things visibly; but none sees but themselves; for instance, if a man's fatal end be hanging, they will see a gibbet, or a rope about his neck: if beheaded, they will see the man without a head; if drowned, they will see water up to his throat; if unexpected death, they will see a winding sheet about his head: all which are represented to their view. One instance I had from a gentleman here, of a Highland gentleman of the Macdonalds, who having a brother that came to visit him, saw him coming in, wanting a head; yet told not his brother he saw any such thing; but within twenty-four hours thereafter, his brother was taken, (being a murderer) and his head cut off, and sent to Edinburgh. Many such instances might be given.

Query 5.

If the second-sight be a thing that is troublesome and uneasy to those that have it, and such as they would gladly be rid of?

Answer.

It is commonly talked by all I spoke with, that it is troublesome; and they would gladly be freed from it, but cannot: only I heard lately of a man very much troubled in his soul therewith, and by serious begging of God deliverance from it, at length lost the faculty of the second-sight.

Query 6.

If any person, or persons, truly godly, who may justly be presumed to be such, have been known to have had this gift or faculty?

Answer.

Negatively, not any godly, but such as are virtuous.

Query 7.

If it descends by succession from parents to children? or if not, whether those that have it can tell how they came by it?

Answer.

That it is by succession, I cannot learn; how they came by it, it is hard to know, neither will they tell; which if they did, they are sure of their strokes from an invisible hand. One instance I heard of one Allen Miller, being in company with some gentlemen, having gotten a little more than ordinary of that strong liquor they were drinking, began to tell stories and strange passages he had been at: but the said Allen was suddenly removed to the farther end of the house, and was there almost strangled; recovering a little, and coming to the place where he was before, they asked him, what it was that troubled him so? He answered he durst not tell; for he had told too much already.

Query 8.

How came they by it?

Answer.

Some say by compact with the Devil; some say by converse with those dæmons we call fairies. I have heard, that those that have this faculty of the second-sight, have offered to teach it to such as were curious to know it; upon such and such conditions they would teach them; but their proffers were rejected.

This is all I could learn by tradition of that faculty, from knowing and intelligent men. If this satisfy not these queries aforesaid, acquaint me, and what can be known of it shall be transmitted.

I cannot pass by an instance I have from a very honest man in the next parish, who told me it himself. That his wife being big with child near her delivery, he buys half a dozen of boards to make her a bed against the time she lay in. The boards lying at the door of his house, there comes an old fisher-woman, yet alive, and asked him, whose were those boards? He told her they were his own; she asked again, for what use he had them? He replied, for a bed; she again said, I intend them for what use you please, she saw a dead corps lying upon them, and that they would be a coffin: which struck the honest man to the heart, fearing the death of his wife. But when the old woman went off, he calls presently for a carpenter to make the bed, which was accordingly done; but shortly after the honest man had a child died, whose coffin was made of the ends of those boards.

Sir, the original, whereof this that I have writ, is a true copy, was sent by a minister, living within some few miles of Inverness, to a friend of mine whom I employed to get information for me; as I insinuated before: I have other answers to these queries from another hand, which I purposed to have communicated to you at this time; but I find there will not be room enough for them in this sheet; howbeit, in case you think it fit, they shall be sent you afterward.

In the mean time, I shall tell you what I have had from one of the masters of our college here (a north country man both by birth and education, in his younger years) who made a journey in the harvest time into the shire of Ross, and at my desire, made some enquiry there, concerning the second-sight. He reports, that there they told him many instances of this knowledge, which he had forgotten, except two. The first, one of his sisters, a young gentlewoman, staying with a friend, at some thirty miles distance from her father's house, and the ordinary place of her residence; one who had the second-sight in the family where she was, saw a young man attending her as she went up and down the house, and this was about three months before her marriage. The second is of a woman in that country who is reputed to have the second-sight, and declared, that eight days before the death of a gentleman there, she saw a bier or coffin covered with a cloth which she knew, carried as it were, to the place of burial, and attended with a great company, one of which told her it was the corps of such a person, naming that gentleman, who died eight days after. By these instances it appears, that the objects of this knowledge are not sad and dismal events only, but joyful and prosperous ones also: he declares farther, that he was informed there, if I mistake not, by some of those who had the second-sight, that if at any time when they see those strange sights, they set their foot upon the foot of another who hath not the second-sight, that other will for that time see what they are seeing; as also that they offered, if he pleased, to communicate the second-sight to him. I have nothing more to add at present, but that I am,

Sir,

Your faithful friend,

And humble servant.

II.

To Mr. JOHN AUBREY, *Fellow of the Royal-Society at Gresham-College, London.*

Honoured Sir,

SINCE my last to you, I have had the favour of two letters from you: to the first, dated February 6, I had replied sooner, but that I wanted leisure to transcribe some farther accounts of a second-sighted man, sent me from the north, whereof (in obedience to your desire) I give here the doubles.

May the 4th.
1694.

A Copy of an Answer to some Queries concerning Second-sighted Men, sent by a Minister living near Inverness, to a Friend of mine.

Query 1.

THAT there is such an art, commonly called the second-sight, is certain, from these following instances.

First, in a gentleman's house, one night the mistress considering why such persons whom she expected were so late, and so long a coming, the supper being all the while delayed for them; a servant man about the house (finding the mistress anxious) having the second-sight, desires to cover the table, and before all things were put on, those persons she longed for would come in; which happened accordingly.

The second instance, concerning a young Lady of great birth, whom a rich Knight fancied and came in sute of the Lady, but she could not endure to fancy him, being a harsh and unpleasant man: but her friends importuning her daily, she turned melancholy and lean, fasting and weeping continually. A common fellow about the house meeting her one day in the fields, asked her, saying Mrs. Kate, What is that that troubles you, and makes you look so ill? she replied, that the cause is known to many, for my friends would have me marry such a man by name, but I cannot fancy him. Nay, (says the fellow) give over these niceties, for he will be your first husband, and will not live long, and be sure he will leave you a rich dowry, which will procure you a great match, for I see a Lord upon each shoulder of you: all which came to pass in every circumstance; as eye and ear witnesses declare.

A third instance, of a traveller coming in to a certain house, desired some meat: the mistress being something nice and backward to give him victuals; you need not, says he, churle me in a piece of meat; for before an hour and half be over, a young man of such a stature and garb will come in with a great salmon-fish on his back, which I behold yonder on the floor: and it came to pass within the said time.

A fourth instance, of a young woman in a certain house about supper-time, refused to take meat from the steward who was offering in the very time meat to her; being asked why she would not take it? replied, she saw him full of blood, and therefore was afraid to take any thing of his hands. The next morning, the said steward offering to compose a difference between two men, at an ale-house door, got a stroak of a sword on the forehead, and came home full of blood. This was told me by an eye witness.

Query 2.

Those that have this faculty of the second-sight, see only things to come, which are to happen shortly thereafter, and sometimes foretel things which fall out three or four years after. For instance, one told his master, that he saw an arrow in such a man through his body, and yet no blood came out: his master told him, that it was impossible an arrow should stick in a man's body, and no blood come out, and if that came not to pass, he would be deemed an impostor. But about five or six years after the man died, and being brought to his burial-place, there arose a debate anent his grave, and it came to such a height, that they drew arms, and bended their bows; and one letting off an arrow, shot through the dead body upon the bier-trees, and so no blood could issue out at a dead man's wound. Thus his sight could not inform him whether the arrow should be shot in him alive or dead, neither could he condescend whether near or afar off.

Query 3.

They foresee murthers, drownings, weddings, burials, combats, man-slaughters, all of which, many instances might be given. Lately (I believe in August last, 1695) one told there would be drowning in the river Bewly, which come to pass: two pretty men crossing a ford both drowned, which fell out within a month. Another instance; a man that served the Bishop of Catnes, who had five daughters in his house, one of them grudged, that the burthen of the family lay on her wholly: the fellow told her that ere long she should be exonered of that task, for he saw a tall gentleman in black, walking on the Bishop's right-hand, whom she should marry: and this fell out accordingly, within a quarter of a year thereafter. He told also of a covered table, full of varieties of good fare, and their garbs who set about the table.

Query 4.

They see all this visibly acted before their eyes; sometimes within, and sometimes without-doors, as in a glass.

Query 5.

It is a thing very troublesome to them that have it, and would gladly be rid of it. For if the object be a thing that is so terrible, they are seen to sweat and tremble, and shreek at the apparition. At other times they laugh, and tell the thing chearfully, just according as the thing is pleasant or astonishing.

Query 6.

Sure it is, that the persons that have a sense of God and religion, and may be presumed to be godly, are known to have this faculty. This evidently appears, in that they are troubled for having it, judging it a sin, and that it came from the Devil, and not from God; earnestly desiring and wishing to be rid of it, if possible; and to that effect, have made application to their minister, to pray to God for them that they might be exonered from that burden. They have supplicated the presbytery, who judicially appointed publick prayers to be made in several churches, and a sermon preached to that purpose, in their own parish church, by their minister; and they have compeired before the pulpit, after sermon, making confession openly of that sin, with deep sense on their knees; renounced any such gift or faculty which they had to God's dishonour, and earnestly desired the minister to pray for them; and this their recantation recorded; and after this, they were never troubled with such a sight any more.

A Copy of a Letter, written to myself by a Gentleman's Son in Straths-pey in Scotland, being a Student in Divinity, concerning the Second-sight.

Sir,

I am more willing than able to satisfy your desire: as for instances of such a knowledge, I could furnish many. I shall only insert some few attested by several of good credit yet alive.

And, first, Andrew Macpherson, of Clunie in Badenoch, being in sute of Lord of Gareloch's daughter, as he was upon a day going to Gareloch, the Lady Gareloch was going somewhere from her house within kenning to the road which Clunie was coming; the Lady preceiving him, said to her attendants, that yonder was Clunie, going to see his mistress: one that had this second-sight in her company replied, and said, if yon be he, unless he marry within six months, he'll never marry. The Lady asked, how did he know that? he said, very well, for I see him, saith he, all inclosed in his winding-sheet, except his nostrils and his mouth, which will also close up within six months; which happened even as he foretold; within the said space he died, and his brother Duncan Macpherson this present Clunie succeeded. This and the like may satisfy your fourth query, he seeing the man even then covered all over with his dead linens. The event was visibly represented, and as it were acted (before his eyes) and also the last part of your second query, viz. that it was as yet to come. As for the rest of the questions, viz. That they discover present and past events, is also manifest, thus: I have heard of a gentleman, whose son had gone abroad, and being anxious to know how he was, he went to consult one who had this faculty, who told him, that that same day five o'clock in the afternoon his son had married a woman in France, with whom he had got so many thousand crowns, and within two years he should come home to see father and friends, leaving his wife with child of a daughter, and a son of six months age behind him: which accordingly was true. About the same time two years he came home, and verified all that was fore-told.

It is likewise ordinary with persons that lose any thing, to go to some of these men, by whom they are directed; how, what persons, and in what place they shall find it. But all such as profess that skill, are not equally dexterous in it. For instance, two of them were in Mr. Hector Mackenzie, minister of Inverness, his father's house; the one a gentleman, the other a common fellow; and discoursing by the fire side, the fellow suddenly begins to weep, and cry out, alas! alas! such a woman is either dead, or presently expiring. The gentlewoman lived five or six miles from the house, and had been some days before in a fever. The gentleman being somewhat better expert in that faculty, said; no, saith he, she's not dead; nor will she die of this disease. O, saith the fellow, do you not see her all covered with her winding-sheet; ay, saith the gentleman, I see her as well as you; but do you not see her linen all wet, which is her sweat? she being presently cooling of the fever. This story Mr. Hector himself will testify. The most remarkable of this sort, that I hear of now, is one Archibald Mackeanyers, alias Macdonald, living in Ardinmurch, within ten or twenty miles, or thereby, of Glencoe, and I was present myself, where he foretold something which accordingly fell out in 1683; this man being in Strathspey, in John Macdonald of Glencoe his company, told in Balachastell, before the Lord of Grant, his Lady, and several others, and also in my father's house; that Argyle, of whom few or none knew then where he was, at least there was no word of him then here; should within two twelve months thereafter, come to the West-Highlands, and raise a rebellious faction, which would be divided among themselves, and disperse, and he unfortunately be taken and beheaded at Edinburgh, and his head set upon the Talbooth, where his father's head was before him; which proved as true, as he fore-told it, in 1685, thereafter. Likewise in the beginning of May next after the late revolution, as my Lord Dundee returned up Spey-side, after he had followed General Major Mac Kay in his reer down the length of Edinglassie, at the

Milatown of Gartinbeg, the Macleans joined him, and after he had received them, he marched forward, but they remained behind, and fell a plundering: upon which Glencoe and some others, among whom was this Archibald, being in my father's house, and hearing that Mac Leans and others were pillaging some of his lands, went to restrain them, and commanded them to march after the army; after he had cleared the first town, next my father's house of them, and was come to the second, there standing on a hill, this Archibald said, Glencoe, if you take my advice, then make off with your self with all possible haste, ere an hour come and go you'll be put to it as hard as ever you was: some of the company began to droll and say, what shall become of me? whether Glencoe believed him, or no, I cannot tell; but this I am sure of, that whereas before he was of intention to return to my father's house and stay all night, now we took leave, and immediately parted. And indeed, within an hour thereafter, Mac Kay, and his whole forces, appeared at Culnakyle in Abernethie, two miles below the place where we parted, and hearing that Cleaverhouse had marched up the water-side a little before, but that Mac Leans and several other straglers, had stayed behind, commanded Major Æneas Mac Kay, with two troops of horse after them; who finding the said Mac Leans at Kinchardie, in the parish of Luthel, chased them up the Morskaith: in which chase Glencoe happened to be, and was hard put to it, as was foretold. What came of Archibald himself, I am not sure; I have not seen him since, nor can I get a true account of him, only I know he is yet alive, and at that time one of my father's men whom the red-coats meeting, compelled to guide them, within sight of the Mac Leans, found the said Archibald's horse within a mile of the place where I left him. I am also informed, this Archibald said to Glencoe, that he would be murdered in the night time in his own house three months before it happened.

Touching your third query, the objects of this knowledge, are not only sad and dismal; but also joyful and prosperous: thus they foretell of happy marriages, good children, what kind of life men shall live, and in what condition they shall die: and riches, honour, preferment, peace, plenty, and good weather.

Query 7.

What way they pretend to have it? I am informed, that in the Isle of Sky, especially before the gospel came thither, several families had it by succession, descending from parents to children, and as yet there be many there that have it in that way; and the only way to be freed from it is, when a woman hath it herself, and is married to a man that hath it also; if in the very act of delivery, upon the first sight of the child's head, it be baptized, the same is free from it; if not, he hath it all his life; by which, it seems, it is a thing troublesome and uneasy to them that have it, and such as they would fain be rid of. And may satisfy your ninth query. And for your farther contentment in this query, I heard of my father, that there was one John du beg Mac Grigor, a Reanach man born, very expert in this knowledge, and my father coming one day from Inverness, said by the way, that he would go into an ale-house on the road, which then would be about five miles off. This John Mac Grigor being in his company, and taken up a slate stone at his foot, and looking to it, replied; nay, said he, you will not go in there, for there is but a matter of a gallon of ale in it even now, and ere we come to it, it will be all near drunken, and those who are drinking there, are strangers to us, and ere we be hardly past the house, they will discord among themselves: which fell out so; ere we were two pair of butts past the house, those that were drinking there went by the ears, wounded and mischieved one another. My father by this and several other things of this nature, turned curious of this faculty, and being very intimate with the man, told him he would fain learn it: to which he answered, that indeed he could in three days time teach him if he pleased; but yet he would not advise him nor any man to learn it; for had he once learned, he would never be a minute of his life but he would see innumerable men and women night and day round about him; which perhaps he would think wearisome and unpleasant, for which reason my father would not have it. But as skilful as this man was, yet he knew not what should be his own last end; which was hanging: And I am informed, that most, if not all of them, though they can fore-see what shall happen to others: yet they cannot foretell, much less prevent, what shall befal themselves. I am also informed by one who came last summer from the Isle of Sky, that any person that pleases will get it taught him for a pound or two of tobacco.

As for your last query. For my own part, I can hardly

believe they can be justly presumed, much less truly godly. As for this Mac Grigor, several report that he was a very civil discreet man, and some say he was of good deportment, and also unjustly hanged. But Archibald Mackenyere will not deny himself, but once he was one of the most notorious thieves in all the Highlands: but I am informed since I came to this knowledge which was by an accident too long here to relate, that he has turned honester than before.

There was one James Mac Coil-vicalaster alias Grant, in Glenbeum near Kirk-Michael in Strathawin, who had this sight, who I hear of several that were well acquainted with him was a very honest man, and of right blameless conversation. He used ordinarily by looking to the fire, to foretell what strangers would come to his house the next day, or shortly thereafter, by their habit and arms, and sometimes also by their name; and if any of his goods or cattle were missing, he would direct his servants to the very place where to find them, whether in a mire or upon dry ground; he would also tell, if the beast were already dead, or if it would die ere they could come to it; and in winter, if they were thick about the fire-side, he would desire them to make room for some others that stood by, though they did not see them, else some of them would be quickly thrown into the midst of it. But whether this man saw any more than Brownie and Meg Mullach, I am not very sure; some say, he saw more continually, and would often be very angry-like, and something troubled, nothing visibly moving him: others affirm he saw these two continually, and sometimes many more.

They generally term this second-sight in Irish Taishi-taraughk, and such as have it Taishatrin, from Taish, which is properly a shadowy substance, or such naughty, and imperceptible thing, as can only, or rather scarcely be discerned by the eye; but not caught by the hands: for which they assigned it to Bugles or Ghosts, so that Taishtar, is as much as one that converses with ghosts or spirits, or as they commonly call them, the Fairies or Fairy-Folks. Others call these men Phissicin, from Phis, which is properly fore-sight, or fore-knowledge. This is the surest and clearest account of second-sighted men that I can now find, and I have set it down fully, as if I were transiently telling it, in your own presence, being curious for nothing but the verity, so far as I could. What you find improper or superfluous you can best compendise it, *&c.*

Thus far this letter, written in a familiar and homely stile, which I have here set down at length. Meg Mullach, and Brownie mentioned in the end of it, are two ghosts, which (as it is constantly reported) of old, haunted a family in Straths-pey of the name of Grant. They appeared at first in the likeness of a young lass; the second of a young lad.

Dr. Moulin (who presents his service to you) hath no acquaintance in Orkney; but I have just now spoken with one, who not only hath acquaintance in that country, but also entertains some thoughts of going thither himself, to get me an account of the cures usually practised there. The Cortex Winteranus, mentioned by you as an excellent medicine, I have heard it commended as good for the scurvy ; if you know it to be eminent or specific (such as the Peruvian Bark is) for any disease, I shall be well pleased to be informed by you.

Thus, Sir, you have an account of all my informations concerning second-sighted men : I have also briefly touched all the other particulars in both your letters, which needed a reply, except your thanks so liberally and obligingly returned to me for my letters, and the kind sense you express of that small service. The kind reception which you have given to those poor trifles, and the value which you put on them, I consider as effects of your kindness to myself, and as engagements on me to serve you to better purpose when it shall be in the power of

Your faithful friend,

and servant, &c.

ADDITAMENTS OF SECOND-SIGHT.

DIEMERBROECK in his book *de Peste* (*i.e.* of the Plague) gives us a story of Dimmerus de Raet, that being at Delft, where the pestilence then raged, sent then his wife thirty miles off. And when the doctor went to see the gentleman of the house, as soon as he came in, the old chair-woman that washed the cloathes fell a weeping; he asked her why? said she, my mistress is now dead; I saw her apparition but just now without a head, and that it was usual with her when a friend of hers died, to see their apparitions in that manner, though never so far off. His wife died at that time.

Mr. Thomas May in his History, lib. 8, writes, that an old man (like an hermit) second-sighted, took his leave of King James I. when he came into England: he took little notice of Prince Henry, but addressing himself to the Duke of York (since King Charles I.) fell a weeping to think what misfortunes he should undergo; and that he should be one of the miserablest unhappy Princes that ever was.

A Scotch nobleman sent for one of these second-sighted

men out of the Highlands, to give his judgment of the then great favourite, George Villers, Duke of Buckingham ; as soon as ever he saw him, "Pish," said he, he will come to nothing. I see a dagger in his breast ;" and he was stabbed in the breast by Captain Felton.

Sir James Melvil hath several the like stories in his Memoirs. Folio.

A certain old man in South-Wales, told a great man there of the fortune of his family ; and that there should not be a third male generation.

In Spain there are those they call Saludadores, that have this kind of gift. There was a Portugueze Dominican fryar belonging to Queen Katherine Dowager's chapel, who had the second-sight.

FARTHER ADDITAMENTS.

Concerning Predictions, Fatality, Apparitions, &c. From the various History of ÆLIAN. *Rendered out of the Greek Original. By* MR. T. STANLEY.

THE wisdom of the Persian Magi was (besides other things proper to them) conversant in prediction: they foretold the cruelty of Ochus towards his subjects, and his bloody disposition, which they collected from some secret signs. For when Ochus, upon the death of his father Artaxerxes, came to the crown, the Magi charged one of the Eunuchs that were next him, to observe upon what things, when the table was set before him, he first laid hands; who watching intentively, Ochus reached forth both his hands, and with his right, laid hold of a knife that lay by, with the other, took a great loaf, which he laid upon the meat, and did cut and eat greedily. The Magi, hearing this, foretold that there would be plenty during his reign, and much blood shed. In which they erred not.

It is observed, that on the sixth day of the month Thargelion, many good fortunes have befallen not only the Athenians, but divers others. Socrates was born on this day, the Persians vanquished on this day, and the Athenians sacrifice three hundred goats to Agrotera upon this day in pursuit of Miltiades's Vow : on the same day of this month was the fight of Platæa, in which the Grecians had the better ; for the former fight which I mentioned was at Artemisium, neither was the victory which the Greeks obtained at Mycale on any other day ; seeing that the victory at Platæa and Mycale happened on the self-same day. Likewise Alexander the Macedonian, Son of Philip, vanquished many myriads of the Barbarians on the sixth day, when he took Darius prisoner. All which is observed to have happened on this month. It is likewise reported that Alexander was born and died on the same day.

Some Pythian relations affirm, that Hercules, son of Jupiter and Alcmena, was at his birth, named Heraclides ; but that afterwards coming to Delphi to consult the oracle about some business, he obtained that for which he came, and received farther privately from the God, this oracle concerning himself.

Thee Hercules doth Phœbus name,
For thou shalt gain immortal fame.

The Peripateticks assert, that the soul in the day-time is inslaved and involved in the body, so that she cannot behold truth ; but in the night, being freed from this servitude, and gathered together, as it were, in a round about the parts that are in the breast, she is more prophetick, whence proceed dreams.

Socrates said of his dæmon to Theages Demodocus, and

many others, that he many times perceived a voice warning him by divine instinct, which, saith he, when it comes, signifieth a dissuasion from that which I am going to do, but never persuades to do any thing. And when any of my friends, (saith he) impart their business to me, if this voice happens, it dissuades also, giving me the like counsel: whereupon, I dehort him who adviseth with me, and suffer him not to proceed in what he is about, following the divine admonition. He alledged as witness hereof Charmides son of Glauco, who asking his advice, whether he should exercise at the Nemean games; as soon as he began to speak, the voice gave the accustomed sigh. Whereupon Socrates endeavoured to divert Charmides from this purpose, telling him the reason. But he not following the advice, it succeeded ill with him.

Aspacia a Phocian, daughter of Hermotimus, was brought up an orphan, her mother dying in the pains of child-birth. She was bred up in poverty, but modestly and virtuously. She had many times a dream which foretold her that she should be married to an excellent person. Whilst she was yet young, she chanced to have a swelling under her chin, loathsome to sight, whereat both the father and the maid were much afflicted. Her father brought her to a physician: he offered to undertake the cure for three staters; the other said he had not the money. The physician replied, he had then no physic for him. Hereupon Aspasia departed weeping! and holding a looking-glass on her knee, beheld her face in it, which much increased her grief. Going to rest without supping, by the reason of the trouble she was in, she had an opportune dream; a dove seemed to appear to her as she slept, which being changed to a woman, said, "Be of good "courage, and bid a long farewel to physicians and their "medicines: take of the dried rose of Venus garlands, "which being pounded apply to the swelling." After the maid had understood and made trial of this, the tumour was wholly assuaged; and Aspasia recovering her beauty by means of the most beautiful goddess, did once again appear the fairest amongst her virgin-companions, enriched with graces far above any of the rest. Of hair yellow, locks a little curling, she had great eyes, some what hawk-nosed, ears short, skin delicate, complexion like roses; whence the Phocians, whilst she was yet a child called her Milto. Her lips were red, teeth whiter than snow, small insteps, such as of those women whom Homer calls λισφυροῦς. Her voice sweet and smooth, that whosoever heard her might justly say he heard the voice of a Syren. She was averse from womanish curiosity in dressing: such things are to be supplied by wealth. She being poor, and bred up under a poor father, used nothing superfluous or extravagant to advantage her beauty. On a time Aspasia came to Cyrus, son of Darius and Parysatis, brother of Artaxerxes, not willingly nor with the consent of her father, but by compulsion, as it often happens upon the taking of cities, or the violence of tyrants and their officers. One of the officers of Cyrus, brought her with other virgins to Cyrus, who immediately preferred her before all his concubines, for simplicity of behaviour, and modesty; whereto also contributed her beauty without artifice, and her extraordinary discretion, which was such, that Cyrus many times asked her advice in affairs, which he never repented to have followed. When Aspasia came first to Cyrus, it happened that he was newly risen from supper, and was going to drink after the Persian manner: for after they have done eating, they betake themselves to wine, and fall to their cups freely, encountering drink as an adversary. Whilst they were in the midst of their dringing, four Grecian virgins were brought to Cyrus, amongst whom was Aspasia the Phocian. They were finely attired; three of them had their heads neatly drest by their own women which came along with them, and had painted their faces. They had been also instructed by their governesses how to behave themselves towards Cyrus, to gain his favour; not to turn away when he came to them, not to be coy when he touched them, to permit him to kiss them, and many other amatory instructions practised by women who expose their beauty to sale. Each contended to out-vie the other in handsomeness. Only Aspasia would not endure to be clothed with a rich robe, nor to put on a various coloured vest, nor to be washed; but calling upon the Grecian and Eleutherian gods, she cried out upon her father's name, execrating herself to her father. She thought the robe which she should put on was a manifest sign of bondage. At last being compelled with blows she put it on, and was necessitated to behave herself with greater liberty than beseemed a virgin. When they came to Cyrus, the rest smiled, and expressed chearfulness in their looks. But Aspasia looking on the ground, her eyes full of tears, did every way express an extraordinary bashfulness. When he commanded them to sit down by him, the rest instantly obeyed; but the Phocian refused, until the officer caused her to sit down by force. When Cyrus looked upon or touched their eyes, cheeks and fingers, the rest freely permitted him; but she would not suffer it; for if Cyrus did but offer to touch her, she cried out, saying, he should not go unpunished for such actions. Cyrus was herewith extreamly pleased; and when upon his offering to touch her breast, she rose up, and would have run away, Cyrus much taken with her native ingenuity which was not like the Persians, turning to him that brought them, "This maid only saith he, of "those which you have brought me is free and pure; the "rest are adulterate in face, but much more in behaviour." Hereupon Cyrus loved her above all the women he ever had. Afterwards there grew a mutual love between them, and their friendship proceeded to such a height that it almost arrived at parity, not differing from the concord and modesty of Grecian marriage. Hereupon the fame of his affection to Aspasia was spread to Iönia and throughout Greece; Peloponnesus also was filled with discourses of the love betwixt Cyrus and her. The report went even to the great King [of Persia,] for it was conceived that Cyrus, after his acquaintance with her, kept company with no other woman. From these things Aspasia recollected the remembrance of her old apparition, and of the dove, and her words, and what the goddess foretold her. Hence she conceived that she was from the very beginning particularly regarded by her. She therefore offered sacrifice of thanks to Venus. And first caused a great image of gold to be erected to her, which she called the image of Venus, and by it placed the picture of a dove beset with jewels, and every day implored the favour of the goddess with sacrifice and prayer. She sent to Hermotimus her father many rich presents, and made him wealthy. She lived continently all her life, as both the Grecian and Persian women affirm. On a time a neck-lace was sent as a present to Cyrus from Scopas the younger, which had been sent to Scopas out of Sicily. The neck-lace was of extraordinary workmanship, and variety. All therefore to whom Cyrus shewed it admiring it, he was much taken with the jewel, and went immediately to Aspasia, it being about noon, finding her asleep, he lay down gently by her watching quietly while she slept. As soon as she awaked, and saw Cyrus she embraced him after her usual manner. He taking the neck-lace out of a box, said, "this is worthy "either the daughter or the mother of a King." To which she assenting; I will give it you, said he, for your own "use, let me see your neck adorned with it." But she received not the gift, prudently and discreetly answering, "How will Parysatis your mother take it, this being a gift "fit for her that bare you? send it to her, Cyrus, I will "shew you a neck handsome enough without it." Aspasia from the greatness of her mind acted contrary to other royal Queens, who are excessively desirous of rich ornaments. Cyrus being pleased with this answer, kissed Aspasia. All these actions and speeches Cyrus writ in a letter which he sent together with the chain to his mother; and Parysatis receiving the present was no less delighted with the news than with the gold, for which she requited

Aspasia with great and royal gifts; for this pleased her above all things, that though Aspasia were chiefly affected by her son, yet in the love of Cyrus, she desired to be placed beneath his mother. Aspasia praised the gifts, but said she had no need of them; (for there was much money sent with the presents) but sent them to Cyrus, saying, "To you who maintain many men this may be useful: for "me it is enough that you love me and are my ornament." With these things, as it seemeth she much astonished Cyrus. And indeed the woman was without dispute admirable for her personal beauty, but much more for the nobleness of her mind. When Cyrus was slain in the fight against his brother, and his army taken prisoners, with the rest of the prey she was taken, not falling accidentally into the enemies hands, but sought for with much diligence by King Artaxerxes, for he had heard her fame and virtue. When they brought her bound, he was angry, and cast those that did it into prison. He commanded that a rich robe should be given her: which she hearing, intreated with tears and lamentation that she might not put on the garment the King appointed, for she mourned exceedingly for Cyrus. But when she had put it on, she appeared the fairest of all women, and Artaxerxes was immediately surprised and inflamed with love of her. He valued her beyond all the rest of his women, respecting her infinitely. He endeavoured to ingratiate himself into her favour, hoping to make her forget Cyrus, and to love him no less than she had done his brother; but it was long before he could compass it. For the affection of Aspasia to Cyrus had taken so deep impression, that it could not easily be rooted out. Long after this, Teridates, the Eunuch died, who was the most beautiful youth in Asia. He had full surpassed childhood, and was reckoned among the youths. The King was said to have loved him exceedingly: he was infinitely grieved and troubled at his death, and there was an universal mourning throughout Asia, every one endeavouring to gratify the King herein; and none durst venture to come to him and comfort him, for they thought his passion would not admit any consolation. Three days being past, Aspasia taking a mourning robe as the King was going to the bath, stood weeping, her eyes cast on the ground. He seeing her, wondered, and demanded the reason of her coming. She said, "I come, O King, to comfort your "grief and affliction, if you so please; otherwise I shall "go back." The Persian pleased with this care, commanded that she should retire to her chamber, and wait his coming. As soon as he returned, he put the vest of the Eunuch upon Aspasia, which did in a manner fit her; and by this means her beauty appeared with greater splendour to the King's eye, who much affected the youth. And being once pleased herewith, he desired her to come always to him in that dress, until the height of his grief were allayed: which to please him she did. Thus more than all his other women, or his own son and kindred, she comforted Artaxerxes, and relieved his sorrow; the King being pleased with her care, and prudently admitting her consolation.

GEORGE BUCHANAN *in his History of* SCOTLAND, *reciteth of one of their Kings, James IV. the following very remarkable Passages.*

THE presence of this King being required to be with his army, whither he was going, at Linlithgo, whilst he was at Vespers in the church, there entered an old man, the hair of his head being red, inclining to yellow, hanging down on his shoulders; his forehead sleek though baldness, bare-headed, in a long coat of a russet colour, girt with a linen girdle about his loins; in the rest of his aspect, he was very venerable: he pressed through the crowd to come to the King: when he came to him, he leaned upon the chair on which the King sat, with a kind of rustic simplicity, and bespoke him thus; "O King," said he, "I am sent to warn thee, not to proceed in thy intended "design; and if thou neglectest this admonition, neither "thou nor thy followers shall prosper. I am also com-"manded to tell thee, that thou shouldest not use the "familiarity, intimacy, and council of women; which if "thou dost, it will redound to thy ignominy and loss." Having thus spoken, he withdrew himself into the croud; and when the King inquired for him, after prayers were ended, he could not be found; which matter seemed more strange, because none of those who stood next, and observed him, as being desirous to put many questions to him, were sensible how he disappeared; amongst them there was David Lindsey of Mont, a man of approved worth and honesty, (and a great scholar too) for in the whole course of his life, he abhorred lying; and if I had not received this story from him as a certain truth, I had omitted it as a romance of the vulgar.

On Tuesday, July 26, 1720, at a sale of the copies belonging to Mr. Awnsham Churchill, of London, Bookseller, which were sold at the Queen's Head tavern, in Pater Noster Row, there was among them a printed copy of these Miscellanies, corrected for the press by Mr. Aubrey, wherein were many very considerable alterations, corrections, and additions, together with the following letter to Mr. Churchill, written upon the first blank leaf, concerning the then intended second edition.

MR. CHURCHILL,
THERE is a very pretty remark in the Athenian Mercury, concerning Apparitions, which I would have inserted under this head, it is in vol. 17, numb. 25. Tuesday, June 1695.

Mr. Dunton, at the Raven in Jewin-Street, will help you to this Mercury, but yesterday he would not, his wife being newly departed.

J. A.

June 1, 1697.

The Passage referred to by Mr. AUBREY, *in his Letter to Mr.* CHURCHILL.*

Two persons (Ladies) of quality, (both not being long since deceased,) were intimate acquaintance, and loved each other entirely: it so fell out, that one of them fell sick of the small-pox, and desired mightily to see the other, who would not come, fearing the catching of them. The afflicted at last dies of them, and had not been buried very long, but appears at the other's house, in the dress of a widow, and asks for her friend, who was then at cards, but sends down her woman to know her business, who, in short, told her, "she must impart it to none but her "Lady," who, after she had received this answer, bid her woman have her in a room, and desired her to stay while the game was done, and she would wait on her. The game being done, down stairs she came to the apparition, to know her business; "madam," says the ghost, (turning up her veil, and her face appearing full of the small-pox) "You know very well, that you and I, loved entirely; "and your not coming to see me, I took it so ill at your "hands, that I could not rest till I had seen you, and "now I am come to tell you, that you have not long to "live, therefore prepare to die; and when you are at a "feast, and make the thirteenth person in number, then "remember my words;" and so the apparition vanished.

* The passage referred to in this letter is now here inserted: the other additions are incorporated in the text. Ed.

To conclude, she was at a feast, where she made the thirteenth person in number, and was afterwards asked by the deceased's brother, "whether his sister did appear to her "as was reported?" she made him no answer, but fell a weeping, and died in a little time after. The gentleman that told this story, says, that there is hardly any person of quality but what knows it to be true. (From the Athenian Mercury.)

APPENDIX.

AN INTRODUCTION TO THE SURVEY AND NATURAL HISTORY OF THE NORTH DIVISION OF THE COUNTY OF WILTSHIRE.

BY J. AUBREY, Esq.

Printed in "Miscellanies on several curious subjects."
London, E. Curll, 1714.

AT a meeting of gentlemen at the Devizes, for choosing of Knights of the Shire in March 1659, it was wished by some, that this County (wherein are many observable antiquities) was surveyed, in imitation of Mr. Dugdale's illustration of Warwickshire; but it being too great a task for one man, Mr. William Yorke (Councellor at Law, and a lover of this kind of learning) advised to have the labour divided: he himself would undertake the Middle Division; I would undertake the North; T. Gore, Esq., Jeffrey Daniel, Esq., and Sir John Erneley would be assistants. Judge Nicholas was the greatest antiquary, as to evidences, that this County hath had in memory of man, and had taken notes in his *Adversariis* of all the ancient deeds that came to his hands. Mr. York had taken some memorandums in this kind too, both now dead; 'tis pity those papers, falling into the hands of merciless women, should be put under pies. I have since that occasionally made this following Collection, which perhaps may sometime or other fall into some antiquary's hands, to make a handsome Work of it. I hope my worthy friend Mr. Anthony Wood of Oxford will be the man. I am heartily sorry I did not set down the antiquities of these parts sooner, for since the time aforesaid, many things are irrecoverably lost.

In former days the churches and great houses hereabouts did so abound with monuments and things remarkable, that it would have deterred an antiquary from undertaking it. But as Pythagoras did guess at the vastness of Hercules' stature by the length of his foot, so among these ruins are remains enough left for a man to give a guess what noble buildings, &c. were made by the piety, charity, and magnanimity of our forefathers.

And as in prospects, we are there pleased most where something keeps the eye from being lost, and leaves us room to guess; so here the eye and mind is no less affected with these stately ruins, than they would have been when standing and entire. They breed in generous minds a kind of pity, and sets the thoughts a-work to make out their magnifice as they were taken in perfection. These remains are *tanquam Tabulata Naufragii*, that after the revolution of so many years and governments, have escaped the teeth of Time, and (which is more dangerous) the hands of mistaken Zeal. So that the retrieving of these forgotten things from oblivion, in some sort resembles that of a conjurer, who make those walk and appear that have lain in their graves many hundreds of years, and to represent, as it were to the eye, the places, customs, and fashions that were of old time.

Let us imagine then what kind of country this was in the time of the ancient Britains, by the nature of the soil, which is a soure, woodsere land, very natural for the production of oaks especially; one may conclude, that this North-Division was a shady, dismal wood; and the inhabitants almost as salvage as the beasts, whose skins were their only raiment. The language, British (which for the honour of it, was in those days spoken from the Orcades to Italy and Spain). The boats on the Avon (which signifies river) were baskets of twigs covered with an ox-skin, which the poor people in Wales use to this day, and call them curricles.

Within this shire I believe that there were several *Reguli*, which often made war upon one another, and the great ditches which run on the plains and elsewhere so many miles, were (not unlikely) their boundaries, and withall served for defence against the incursion of their enemies, as the Picts' Wall, Offa's Ditch, and that in China; to compare small things to great. Their religion is at large described by Cæsar; their priests were the Druids. Some of their temples I pretend to have restored; as Aubury, Stonehenge, &c., as also British sepulchres. Their way of fighting is livelily set down by Cæsar. Their camps, with those of their antagonists, I have set down in another place. They knew the use of iron; and about

Hedington fields, Bromham, Bowdon, &c. are still ploughed up cinders (*i. e.* the scoria of melted iron). They were two or three degrees I suppose less salvage than the Americans. Till King John's time wolves were in this island; and in our grandfathers' days more foxes than now, and marterns (a beast of brown rich furr) at Stanton Park, &c. the race now extinct thereabout.

The Romans subdued and civilized them; at Lekham (Mr. Camden saith) was a colony of them, as appears there by the Roman coin found there. About 1654, in Weekfield, in the parish of Hedington, digging up the ground deeper than the plough went, they found, for a great way together, foundations of houses, hearths, coals, and a great deal of Roman coin, silver and brass, whereof I had a pint; some little copper-pieces, no bigger than silver half-pence (quære if they were not the Roman Denarii) I have portrayed the pot in which a good deal was found, which pot I presented to the Royal Society's Repository, it resembles an apprentice's earthen Christmas-box.

At Sherston, hath several times been found Roman money in ploughing. I have one silver piece found there (1653) not long since, of Constantine the Great. Among other arts, that of architecture was introduced by them; and no doubt but here, as well as in other parts, were then good buildings, here being so good stone: I know not any *vestigia* now left in this country, except the fragments of the Castle of Sarisbury, which takes its name from Cæsar, Cæsarisburghum, from whence Sarisburgh, whence Salisbury.

At Bath are several Roman inscriptions, which Mr. Camden hath set down, and by the West Gate a piece of a delicate Corinthian freeze, which he calls wreathed leaves, not understanding architecture; and by in a bass relieve of an optriouch. At Bethford, about 1663, was found a grotto paved with Mosaic work, some whereof I have preserved.

The Saxons succeeding them, and driving away to Ireland, Cornwal, &c. these Britains were by Romans left here; for they used the best of them in their wars, (being their best soldiers) here was a mist of ignorance for 600 years. They were so far from knowing arts, that they could not build a wall with stone. They lived sluttishly in poor houses, where they eat a great deal of beef and mutton, and drank good ale in a brown mazard; and their very kings were but a sort of farmers. After the Christian Religion was planted here, it gave a great shoot, and the kings and great men gave vast revenues to the Church, who were ignorant enough in those days. The Normans then came and taught them civility and building; which though it was Gothick (as also their policy *Feudalis Lex)* yet they were magnificent. For the Government, till the time of King Henry VIII. it was like a nest of boxes; for copyholders, (who, till then were villains) held of the lords of the Manor, who held of a superior lord, who perhaps held of another superior lord or duke, who held of the king. Upon any occasion of justing or tournaments in those days, one of these great lords sounded his trumpets (the lords then kept trumpeters, even to King James) and summoned those that held under them. Those again sounded their trumpets, and so downward to the copy-holders. The Court of Wards was a great bridle in those days. A great part of this North Division held of the honour of Trowbridge, where is a ruinated castle of the dukes of Lancaster. No younger brothers then were by the custom and constitution of the realm to betake themselves to trades, but were churchmen or retainers, and servants to great men rid good horses (now and then took a purse) and their blood that was bred of the good tables of their masters, was upon every occasion freely let out in their quarrels; it was then too common among their masters to have feuds with one another, and their servants at market, or where they met (in that slashing age) did commonly bang one another's bucklers. Then an esquire, when he rode to town, was attended by eight or ten men in blue coats with badges. The lords (then lords in deed as well as title) lived in their countries like petty kings, had *jura regalia* belonging to their seigniories, had their castles and boroughs, and sent burgesses to the Lower House; had gallows within their liberties, where they could try, condemn, draw and hang; never went to London but in parliament-time, or once a year to do their homage and duty to the king. The lords of manours kept good houses in their countries, did eat in their great Gothick halls, at the high table; (in Scotland, still the architecture of a lord's house is thus, viz. a great open hall, a kitchen and buttery, a parlour, over which a chamber for my lord and lady; all the rest lye in common, viz. the men-servants in the hall, the women in a common room) or oriele, the folk at the side-tables. (Oriele is an ear, but here it signifies a little room at the upper end of the hall, where stands a square or round table, perhaps in the old time was an oratory; in every old Gothic hall is one, viz. at Dracot, Lekham, Alderton, &c.) The meat was served up by watch-words. Jacks are but an invention of the other age: the poor boys did turn the spits, and licked the dripping-pan, and grew to be hugh lusty knaves. The beds of the servants and retainers were in the great halls, as now in the guard-chamber, &c. The hearth was commonly in the middle, as at most colleges, whence the saying, "Round about our coal-fire." Here in the halls were the mummings, cob-loaf-stealing, and a great number of old Christmas plays performed. Every baron and gentleman of estate kept great horses for a man at arms. Lords had their armories to furnish some hundreds of men. The halls of justices of the peace were dreadful to behold, the skreens were garnished with corslets and helmets, gaping with open mouth, with coats of mail, lances, pikes, halberts, brown bills, batterdashers, bucklers, and the modern colivers and petronils (in King Charles I.'s time) turned into muskets and pistols. Then were entails in fashion, (a good prop for monarchy). Destroying of manors began *temp.* Henry VIII., but now common; whereby the mean people live lawless, nobody to govern them, they care for nobody, having no dependance on anybody. By this method, and by the selling of the church-lands, is the ballance of the Government quite altered, and put into the hands of the common people. No ale-houses, nor yet inns were there then, unless upon great roads: when they had a mind to drink, they went to the fryaries; and when they travelled they had entertainment at the religious houses for three days, if occasion so long required. The meeting of the gentry was not then at tipling-houses, but in the fields or forest, with their hawks and hounds, with their bugle horns in silken bordries. This part very much abounded with forests and parks. Thus were good spirits kept up, and good horses and hides made; whereas now the gentry of the nation are so effeminated by coaches, they are so far from managing great horses, that they know not how to ride hunting-horses, besides the spoiling of several trades dependant. In the last age every yeoman almost kept a sparrow-hawk; and it was a divertisement for young gentlewomen to manage sparrow-hawks and merlins. In King Henry VIII.'s time, one Dame Julian writ *The Art of Hawking* in English verse, which is in Wilton Library. This country was then a lovely champain, as that about Sherston and Cots-wold; very few enclosures, unless near houses: my grandfather Lyte did remember when all between Cromhall (at Eston) and Castle-Comb was so, when Easton, Yatton and Comb did intercommon together. In my remembrance much hath been enclosed, and every year, more and more is taken in. Anciently the Leghs (now corruptly called Slaights) *i. e.* pastures, were noble large grounds, as yet the Demesne Lands at Castle Combe are. So likewise in his remembrance, was all between Kington St. Michael and Dracot-Cerne common fields. Then were a world of labouring people maintained by the plough, as yet in Northamptonshire, &c. There were no rates for the poor in my grandfather's days; but for Kington St. Michael (no small parish) the church-ale at Whitsuntide did the business. In every parish is (or was) a church-house, to which belonged spits, crocks, &c., utensils for dressing provision. Here the housekeepers met, and were merry, and gave their charity. The young people were there too, and had dancing, bowling, shooting at butts, &c., the ancients sitting gravely by and looking on. All things were civil and without scandal. This church-ale is doubtless derived from the *ἀγάπαι*, or love-feast, mentioned in the New Testament. Mr. A. Wood assures me, that there were no alms-houses, at least they were very scarce before the Reformation; that over against Christ Church, Oxon, is one of the ancientest. In every church was a poor man's box, but I never remembered the use of it; nay, there was one at great inns, as I remember it was before the wars. Before the Reformation, at their vigils or revels, sat up all night fasting and praying. The night before the day of the dedication of the church, certain officers were chosen for gathering the money for charitable uses. Old John Wastfield, of Langley, was Peter-man at St. Peter's Chapel there; at which time is one of the greatest revels in these parts, but the chapel is converted into a dwelling-house. Such joy and merriment was every holiday, which days were kept with great solemnity and reverence. These were the days when England was famous for the "grey goose quills." The clerk's was in the Easter holidays for his benefit, and the solace of the neighbourhood.

Since the Reformation, and inclosures aforesaid, these parts have swarmed with poor people. The parish of Caln pays to the poor (1663) £500 per annum; and the parish of Chippenham little less, as appears by the poor's books there. Inclosures are for the private, not for the public, good. For a shepherd and his dog, or a milk-maid, can manage meadow-land, that upon arable, employed the hands of several scores of labourers.

In those times (besides the jollities already mentioned) they had their pilgrimages to Walsingham, Canterbury, &c. to several shrines, as chiefly hereabouts, to St. Joseph's of Arimathea, at his chapel in Glastonbury Abbey. In the roads thither were several houses of entertainment, built purposely for them; among others, was the house called "The Chapel of Playster" near Box; and a great house called . . . . without Lafford's Gate, near Bristol.

Then the Crusado's to the Holy War were most magnificent and glorious, and the rise, I believe, of the adventures of knights errant and romances. The solemnities of processions in and about the churches, and the perambulations in the fields, besides their convenience, were fine pleasing diversions: the priests went before in their formalities, singing the Latin service, and the people came after, making their good-meaning responses. The reverence given to holy men was very great. Then were the churches open all day long, men and women going daily in and out hourly, to and from their devotions. Then were the consciences of the people kept in so great awe by confession, that just dealing and virtue was habitual. Sir Edwyn Sandys observed, in his travels in the Catholic countries, so great use of confession as aforesaid, that though a severe enemy to the Church of Rome, he doth heartily wish it had never been left out by the Church of England, perceiving the great good it does beyond sea. Lent was a dismal time, strictly observed by fasting, prayer, and confessing against Easter. During the forty days, the Fryars preached every day.

This country was very full of religious houses; a man could not have travelled but he must have met monks, fryars, *bonnehommes*, &c. in their several habits, black, white, grey, &c. And the tingle tangle of their convent bells, I fancy, made very pretty musick, like the college bells at Oxford.

Then were there no free-schools; the boys were educated at the monasteries; the young maids, not at Hackney schools, &c. to learn pride and wantonness, but at the nunneries, where they had examples of piety, humility, modesty, and obedience, &c. to imitate and practise. Here they learned needle-work, and the art of confectionary, surgery, physick, writing, drawing, &c.

Old Jaques (who lived where Charles Hadnam did) could see from his house the nuns of the priory of St. Mary's (juxta Kington) come forth into the nymph-hay with their rocks and wheels to spin, and with their sewing work. He would say that he hath told threescore and ten; though of nuns there were not so many, but in all, with lay-sisters, as widows, old maids, and young girls, there might be such a number. This was a fine way of breeding up young women, who are led more by example than precept; and a good retirement for widows and grave single women, to a civil, virtuous, and holy life.

Plato says, that the foundation of government is, the

education of youth; by this means it is most probable that that was a golden age. I have heard Judge Jenkins, Mr. John Latch, and other lawyers, say, that before the Reformation, one shall hardly in a year find an action on the case, as for slander, &c. which was the result of a good government.

It is a sarcasm, more malicious than true, commonly thrown at the church-men, that they had too much land; for their constitution being in truth considered, they were rather administrators of those great revenues to pious and publick uses, than usu-fructuaries. As for themselves, they had only their habit and competent diet, every order according to their prescribed rule; from which they were not to vary. Then for their tenants, their leases were almost as good to them as fee simple, and perchance might longer last in their families. Sir William Button (the father) hath often told me, that Alton farm had been held by his ancestors from the Abbey of Winchester, about four hundred years. The powers of Stanton Quintin held that farm of the Abbey of Cirencester in lease 300 years: and my ancestors, the Danvers, held West Tokenham for many generations, of the Abbey of Broadstock, where one of them was a prior. Memorandum, that in the abbies were several corrodies granted for poor old shiftless men, which Fitzherbert speaks of amongst his writs. In France, to every parish church is more than one priest, (because of the several masses to be said) which fashion, Mr. Dugdale tells me, was used here, and at some churches in London, in near half a dozen.

In many chancels are to be seen three seats with niches

in the wall (most commonly on the south side) rising by degrees, and sometimes only three seats, the first being for the bishop, the second for the priest, and the third for the deacon. Anciently the bishops visited their churches in person. This I had from Mr. Dugdale; as also that in many churches where stalls are, as at cathedrals, (which I mistook for chauntries) and in collegiate churches. This searching after antiquities is a wearisome task. I wish I had gone through all the church-monuments. The Records at London I can search gratis. Though of all studies, I take the least delight in this, yet methinks I am carried on with a kind of *œstrum;* for nobody else hereabout hardly cares for it, but rather makes a scorn of it. But methinks it shows a kind of gratitude and good nature, to revive the memories and memorials of the pious and charitable benefactors long since dead and gone.

Eston Pierse,
April 28, 1670.

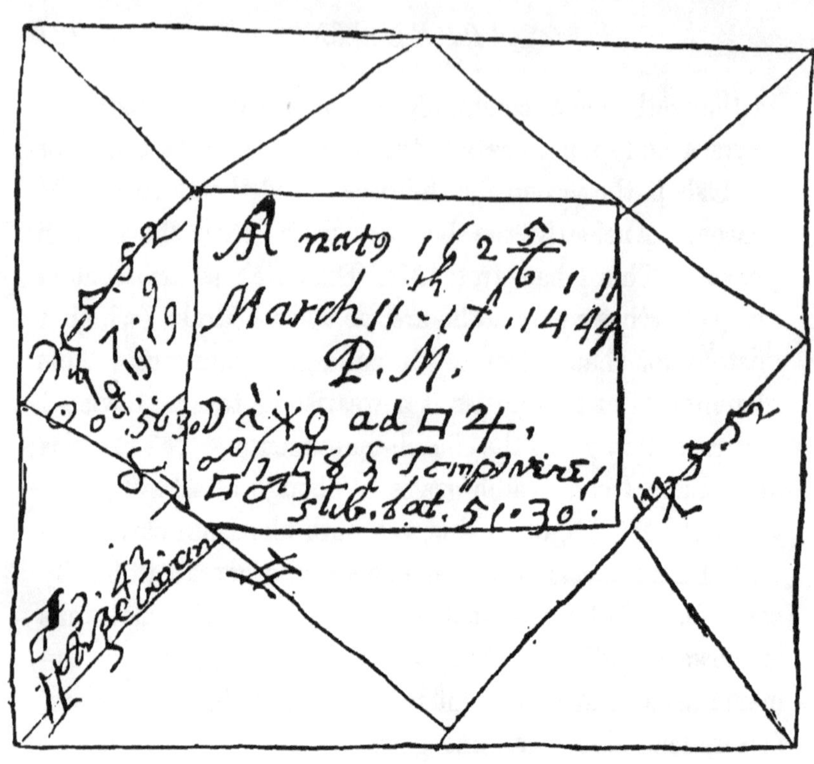

HOROSCOPE OF JOHN AUBREY'S NATIVITY,
from his own Sketch.

HYDRIOTAPHIA.

URN BURIAL; OR, A DISCOURSE OF THE SEPULCHRAL URNS LATELY FOUND IN NORFOLK.

TENTH EDITION.

ORIGINALLY PUBLISHED IN

1658.

En sum quod dicitis quinque levatur onus.—PROPERT.

THE EPISTLE DEDICATORY.

TO MY WORTHY AND HONOURED FRIEND,

THOMAS LE GROS, OF CROSTWICK, ESQUIRE.[1]

WHEN the funeral pyre was out, and the last valediction over, men took a lasting adieu of their interred friends, little expecting the curiosity of future ages should comment upon their ashes; and, having no old experience of the duration of their relicks, held no opinion of such after-considerations.

But who knows the fate of his bones, or how often he is to be buried? Who hath the oracle of his ashes, or whither they are to be scattered? The relicks of many lie like the ruins of Pompey's,* in all parts of the earth;

* *Pompeios juvenes Asia atque Europa, sed ipsum terrâ tegit Libyos.*

[1] *Le Gros, &c.*] Descended from an ancient family of the name (Le Gross, or Groos), settled at Sloly, near Crostwick, so early as the reign of Stephen, and who became possessed of the manor and hall of Crostwick, in the 38th of Henry VIII. His grandfather, Sir Thomas, was knighted by James I. at the Charter-house, in 1603. The property descended to his nephew, Charles Harman, who took the name of Le Gros, but sold the estate to the Walpole family in 1720.

and when they arrive at your hands these may seem to have wandered far, who, in a direct and meridian travel,* have but few miles of known earth between yourself and the pole.

That the bones of Theseus should be seen again in Athens † was not beyond conjecture and hopeful expectation; but that these should arise so opportunely to serve yourself was an hit of fate, and honour beyond prediction.

We cannot but wish these urns might have the effect of theatrical vessels and great Hippodrome urns‡ in Rome, to resound the acclamations and honour due unto you. But these are sad and sepulchral pitchers, which have no joyful voices; silently expressing old mortality, the ruins of forgotten times, and can only speak with life, how long in this corruptible frame some parts may be uncorrupted; yet able to outlast bones long unborn, and noblest pile among us.§

We present not these as any strange sight or spectacle unknown to your eyes, who have beheld the best of urns and noblest variety of ashes; who are yourself no slender master of antiquities, and can daily command the view of so many imperial faces; which raiseth your thoughts unto old things and consideration of times before you, when even living men were antiquities; when the living might

---

* Little directly but sea, between your house and Greenland.[1]

† Brought back by Cimon Plutarch.

‡ The great urns in the Hippodrome at Rome, conceived to resound the voices of people at their shows.

§ Worthily possessed by that true gentleman, Sir Horatio Townshend, my honoured friend.

[1] *Little directly, &c.*] Crostwick-hall is not twenty miles distant from the north coast of Norfolk.

exceed the dead, and to depart this world could not be properly said to go unto the greater number.* And so run up your thoughts upon the ancient of days, the antiquary's truest object, unto whom the eldest parcels are young, and earth itself an infant, and without Egyptian† account makes but small noise in thousands.

We were hinted by the occasion, not catched the opportunity to write of old things, or intrude upon the antiquary. We are coldly drawn unto discourses of antiquities, who have scarce time before us to comprehend new things, or make out learned novelties. But seeing they arose, as they lay almost in silence among us, at least in short account suddenly passed over, we were very unwilling they should die again, and be buried twice among us.

Beside, to preserve the living, and make the dead to live, to keep men out of their urns, and discourse of human fragments in them, is not impertinent unto our profession; whose study is life and death, who daily behold examples of mortality, and of all men least need artificial *mementos*, or coffins by our bedside, to mind us of our graves.

'Tis time to observe occurrences, and let nothing remarkable escape us: the supinity of elder days hath left so much in silence, or time hath so martyred the records, that the most industrious heads‡ do find no easy work to erect a new Britannia.

'Tis opportune to look back upon old times, and contemplate our forefathers. Great examples grow thin, and

---

* *Abiit ad plures.*

† Which makes the world so many years old.

‡ Wherein Mr. Dugdale hath excellently well endeavoured, and worthy to be countenanced by ingenuous and noble persons.

to be fetched from the passed world. Simplicity flies away, and iniquity comes at long strides upon us. We have enough to do to make up ourselves from present and passed times, and the whole stage of things scarce serveth for our instruction. A complete piece of virtue must be made from the Centos of all ages, as all the beauties of Greece could make but one handsome Venus.

When the bones of King Arthur were digged up,* the old race might think they beheld therein some originals of themselves; unto these of our urns none here can pretend relation, and can only behold the relicks of those persons who, in their life giving the laws unto their predecessors, after long obscurity, now lie at their mercies. But, remembering the early civility they brought upon these countries, and forgetting long-passed mischiefs, we mercifully preserve their bones, and piss not upon their ashes.

In the offer of these antiquities we drive not at ancient families, so long outlasted by them. We are far from erecting your worth upon the pillars of your forefathers, whose merits you illustrate. We honour your old virtues, conformable unto times before you, which are the noblest armoury. And, having long experience of your friendly conversation, void of empty formality, full of freedom, constant and generous honesty, I look upon you as a gem of the old rock,† and must profess myself even to urn and ashes,

Your ever faithful Friend and Servant,

THOMAS BROWNE.

Norwich, May 1st.

---

* In the time of Henry the Second.—*Camden.*

† *Adamas de rupe veteri præstantissimus.*

HYDRIOTAPHIA.

CHAPTER I.

IN the deep discovery of the subterranean world, a shallow part would satisfy some enquirers; who, if two or three yards were open about the surface, would not care to rake the bowels of Potosi,* and regions towards the centre. Nature hath furnished one part of the earth, and man another. The treasures of time lie high, in urns, coins, and monuments, scarce below the roots of some vegetables. Time hath endless rarities, and shows of all varieties; which reveals old things in heaven, makes new discoveries in earth, and even earth itself a discovery. That great antiquity America lay buried for thousands of years, and a large part of the earth is still in the urn unto us.

Though if Adam were made out of an extract of the earth, all parts might challenge a restitution, yet few have returned their bones far lower than they might receive

* The rich mountain of Peru.

them; not affecting the graves of giants, under hilly and heavy coverings, but content with less than their own depth, have wished their bones might lie soft, and the earth be light upon them. Even such as hope to rise again, would not be content with central interment, or so desperately to place their relicks as to lie beyond discovery; and in no way to be seen again; which happy contrivance hath made communication with our forefathers, and left unto our view some parts, which they never beheld themselves.

Though earth hath engrossed the name, yet water hath proved the smartest grave; which in forty days swallowed almost mankind, and the living creation; fishes not wholly escaping, except the salt ocean were handsomely contempered by a mixture of the fresh element.

Many have taken voluminous pains to determine the state of the soul upon disunion; but men have been most phantastical in the singular contrivances of their corporal dissolution: whilst the soberest nations have rested in two ways, of simple inhumation and burning.

That carnal interment or burying was of the elder date, the old examples of Abraham and the patriarchs are sufficient to illustrate; and were without competition, if it could be made out that Adam was buried near Damascus, or Mount Calvary, according to some tradition. God himself, that buried but one, was pleased to make choice of this way, collectible from Scripture expression, and the hot contest between Satan and the archangel, about discovering the body of Moses. But the practice of burning was also of great antiquity, and of no slender extent. For (not to derive the same from Hercules) noble descriptions there are hereof in the Grecian funerals of Homer, in the formal obsequies of Patroclus and Achilles; and somewhat elder in the Theban war, and solemn combustion of Meneceus, and Archemorus, contemporary unto Jair the eighth judge of Israel. Confirmable also among the Trojans, from the funeral pyre of Hector, burnt before the gates of Troy: and the burning of Penthesilea the Amazonian queen:* and long continuance of that practice, in the inward countries of Asia; while as low as the reign of Julian, we find that the king of Chionia† burnt the body of his son, and interred the ashes in a silver urn.

The same practice extended also far west;‡ and, besides Herulians, Getes, and Thracians, was in use with most of the Celtæ, Sarmatians, Germans, Gauls, Danes, Swedes, Norwegians; not to omit some use thereof among Carthagenians and Americans. Of greater antiquity among the Romans than most opinion, or Pliny seems to allow: for (beside the old table laws of burning or burying within the city,§ of making the funeral fire with planed wood, or quenching the fire with wine), Manlius the consul burnt the body of his son: Numa, by special clause of his will, was not burnt but buried; and Remus was solemnly burned, according to the description of Ovid.‖

---

* *Q. Calaber.* lib. i.

† Gumbrates, king of *Chionia*, a country near *Persia.—Ammianus Marcellinus.*

‡ *Arnold. Montan. not. in Cæs. Commentar. L. Gyraldus. Kirkmannus.*

§ 12 *Tabul.* part i. *de jure sacro. Hominem mortuum in urbe ne sepelito, neve urito*, tom. 2. *Rogum asciâ ne polito*, tom. 4. *Item Vigeneri Annotat. in Livium, et Alex. cum Tiraquello. Roscinus cum Dempstero.*

‖ *Ultimo prolata subdita flamma rogo. De fast.* lib. iv. *cum Car. Neapol. Anaptyxi.*

Cornelius Sylla was not the first whose body was burned in Rome, but the first of the Cornelian family; which, being indifferently, not frequently used before; from that time spread, and became the prevalent practice. Not totally pursued in the highest run of cremation; for when even crows were funerally burnt, Poppæa the wife of Nero found a peculiar grave interment. Now as all customs were founded upon some bottom of reason, so there wanted not grounds for this; according to several apprehensions of the most rational dissolution. Some being of the opinion of Thales, that water was the original of all things, thought it most equal[1] to submit unto the principle of putrefaction, and conclude in a moist relentment.[2] Others conceived it most natural to end in fire, as due unto the master principle in the composition, according to the doctrine of Heraclitus; and therefore heaped up large piles, more actively to waft them toward that element, whereby they also declined a visible degeneration into worms, and left a lasting parcel of their composition.

Some apprehended a purifying virtue in fire, refining the grosser commixture, and firing out the æthereal particles so deeply immersed in it. And such as by tradition or rational conjecture held any hint of the final pyre of all things; or that this element at last must be too hard for all the rest; might conceive most naturally of the fiery dissolution. Others pretending no natural grounds, politickly declined the malice of enemies upon their buried bodies. Which consideration led Sylla unto this practice; who having thus served the body of Marius, could not but

---

[1] *most equal.*] Most equitable.

[2] *relentment.*] Dissolution: not in Johnson.

fear a retaliation upon his own; entertained after in the civil wars, and revengeful contentions of Rome.

But as many nations embraced, and many left it indifferent, so others too much affected, or strictly declined this practice. The Indian Brachmans seemed too great friends unto fire, who burnt themselves alive, and thought it the noblest way to end their days in fire; according to the expression of the Indian, burning himself at Athens,* in his last words upon the pyre unto the amazed spectators, thus I make myself immortal.

But the Chaldeans, the great idolaters of fire, abhorred the burning of their carcasses, as a pollution of that deity. The Persian magi declined it upon the like scruple, and being only solicitous about their bones, exposed their flesh to the prey of birds and dogs. And the Persees now in India, which expose their bodies unto vultures, and endure not so much as *feretra* or biers of wood, the proper fuel of fire, are led on with such niceties. But whether the ancient Germans, who burned their dead, held any such fear to pollute their deity of Herthus, or the earth, we have no authentic conjecture.

The Egyptians were afraid of fire, not as a deity, but a devouring element, mercilessly consuming their bodies, and leaving too little of them; and therefore by precious embalments, depositure in dry earths, or handsome inclosure in glasses, contrived the notablest ways of integral conservation. And from such Egyptian scruples, imbibed by Pythagoras, it may be conjectured that Numa and the Pythagorical sect first waved the fiery solution.

---

* And therefore the inscription of his tomb was made accordingly.—*Nic. Damasc.*

The Scythians, who swore by wind and sword, that is, by life and death, were so far from burning their bodies, that they declined all interment, and made their graves in the air: and the Ichthyophagi, or fish-eating nations about Egypt, affected the sea for their grave; thereby declining visible corruption, and restoring the debt of their bodies. Whereas the old heroes, in Homer, dreaded nothing more than water or drowning; probably upon the old opinion of the fiery substance of the soul, only extinguishable by that element; and therefore the poet emphatically implieth the total destruction in this kind of death, which happened to Ajax Oileus.*

The old Balearians† had a peculiar mode, for they used great urns and much wood, but no fire in their burials, while they bruised the flesh and bones of the dead, crowded them into urns, and laid heaps of wood upon them. And the Chinese‡ without cremation or urnal interment of their bodies, make use of trees and much burning, while they plant a pine-tree by their grave, and burn great numbers of printed draughts of slaves and horses over it, civilly content with their companies *in effigy*, which barbarous nations exact unto reality.

Christians abhorred this way of obsequies, and though they sticked not to give their bodies to be burnt in their lives, detested that mode after death; affecting rather a depositure than absumption, and properly submitting unto the sentence of God, to return not unto ashes but unto dust again, conformable unto the practice of the patriarchs, the interment of our Saviour, of Peter, Paul, and the

---

* Which *Magius* reads ἐξαπόλωλε. † *Diodorus Siculus.*

‡ *Ramusius* in *Navigat.*

ancient martyrs. And so far at last declining promiscuous interment with Pagans, that some have suffered ecclesiastical censures* for making no scruple thereof.

The Musselman believers will never admit this fiery resolution. For they hold a present trial from their black and white angels in the grave; which they must have made so hollow, that they may rise upon their knees.

The Jewish nation, though they entertained the old way of inhumation, yet sometimes admitted this practice. For the men of Jabesh burnt the body of Saul; and by no prohibited practice, to avoid contagion or pollution, in time of pestilence, burnt the bodies of their friends.† And when they burnt not their dead bodies, yet sometimes used great burnings near and about them, deducible from the expressions concerning Jehoram, Zedechias, and the sumptuous pyre of Asa. And were so little averse from Pagan burning, that the Jews lamenting the death of Cæsar their friend, and revenger on Pompey, frequented the place where his body was burnt for many nights together.‡ And as they raised noble monuments and mausoleums for their own nation,§ so they were not scrupulous in erecting some for others, according to the practice of Daniel, who left that lasting sepulchral pile in Ecbatana, for the Median and Persian kings.||

But even in times of subjection and hottest use, they

---

* *Martialis* the Bishop. *Cyprian.* † Amos vi. 10.

‡ *Sueton. in vita Jul. Cæs.*

§ As that magnificent sepulchral monument erected by *Simon*, 1 Macc. xiii.

|| *Κατασκεύασμα θαυμασίως πεποιημένον*, whereof a Jewish priest had always the custody unto Josephus, his days.—*Jos. Antiq.* lib. x.

conformed not unto the Roman practice of burning; whereby the prophecy was secured concerning the body of Christ, that it should not see corruption, or a bone should not be broken; which we believe was also providentially prevented, from the soldier's spear and nails that passed by the little bones both in his hands and feet; not of ordinary contrivance, that it should not corrupt on the cross, according to the laws of Roman crucifixion, or an hair of his head perish, though observable in Jewish customs, to cut the hairs of malefactors.

Nor in their long cohabitation with Egyptians, crept into a custom of their exact embalming, wherein deeply slashing the muscles, and taking out the brains and entrails, they had broken the subject of so entire a resurrection, nor fully answered the types of Enoch, Elijah, or Jonah, which yet to prevent or restore, was of equal facility unto that rising power, able to break the fasciations and bands of death, to get clear out of the cerecloth, and an hundred pounds of ointment, and out of the sepulchre before the stone was rolled from it.

But though they embraced not this practice of burning, yet entertained they many ceremonies agreeable unto Greek and Roman obsequies. And he that observeth their funeral feasts, their lamentations at the grave, their music, and weeping mourners; how they closed the eyes of their friends, how they washed, anointed, and kissed the dead; may easily conclude these were not mere Pagan civilities. But whether that mournful burthen, and treble calling out after Absalom,* had any reference unto the last conclamation, and triple valediction, used by other nations, we hold but a wavering conjecture.

---

* 2 Sam. xviii. 33.

Civilians make sepulture but of the law of nations, others do naturally found it and discover it also in animals. They that are so thick-skinned as still to credit the story of the Phœnix, may say something for animal burning. More serious conjectures find some examples of sepulture in elephants, cranes, the sepulchral cells of pismires, and practice of bees,—which civil society carrieth out their dead, and hath exequies, if not interments.

CHAPTER II.

THE solemnities, ceremonies, rites of their cremation or interment, so solemnly delivered by authors, we shall not disparage our reader to repeat. Only the last and lasting part in their urns, collected bones and ashes, we cannot wholly omit or decline that subject, which occasion lately presented, in some discovered among us.

In a field of Old Walsingham, not many months past, were digged up between forty and fifty urns, deposited in a dry and sandy soil, not a yard deep, nor far from one another.—Not all strictly of one figure, but most answering these described: some containing two pounds of bones, distinguishable in skulls, ribs, jaws, thigh bones, and teeth, with fresh impressions of their combustion; besides the extraneous substances, like pieces of small boxes, or combs handsomely wrought, handles of small brass instruments, brazen nippers, and in one some kind of opal.*

* In one sent me by my worthy friend, Dr. Thomas Witherly of Walsingham.

Near the same plot of ground, for about six yards com pass, were digged up coals and incinerated substances, which begat conjecture that this was the *ustrina* or place of burning their bodies, or some sacrificing place unto the *manes*, which was properly below the surface of the ground, as the *æra* and altars unto the gods and heroes above it.

That these were the urns of Romans from the common custom and place where they were found, is no obscure conjecture, not far from a Roman garrison, and but five miles from Brancaster, set down by ancient record under the name of Branodunum. And where the adjoining town, containing seven parishes, in no very different sound, but Saxon termination, still retains the name of Burnham, which being an early station, it is not improbable the neighbour parts were filled with habitations, either of Romans themselves, or Britons Romanized, which observed the Roman customs.

Nor is it improbable that the Romans early possessed this country. For though we meet not with such strict particulars of these parts before the new institution of Constantine and military charge of the count of the Saxon shore, and that about the Saxon invasions, the Dalmatian horsemen were in the garrison of Brancaster; yet in the time of Claudius, Vespasian, and Severus, we find no less than three legions dispersed through the province of Britain. And as high as the reign of Claudius a great overthrow was given unto the Iceni, by the Roman lieutenant Ostorius. Not long after, the country was so molested, that, in hope of a better state, Prasutagus bequeathed his kingdom unto Nero and his daughters; and Boadicea, his queen, fought the last decisive battle with Paulinus. After which time, and conquest of Agricola, the lieutenant of Vespasian, probable it is, they wholly possessed this country; ordering it into garrisons or habitations best suitable with their securities. And so some Roman habitations not improbable in these parts, as high as the time of Vespasian, where the Saxons after seated, in whose thin-filled maps we yet find the name of Walsingham. Now if the Iceni were but Gammadims, Anconians, or men that lived in an angle, wedge, or elbow of Britain, according to the original etymology, this country will challenge the emphatical appellation, as most properly making the elbow or *iken* of Icenia.[1]

That Britain was notably populous is undeniable, from that expression of Cæsar.* That the Romans themselves were early in no small numbers (seventy thousand, with their associates), slain by Boadicea, affords a sure account. And though many Roman habitations are now unknown, yet some, by old works, rampiers, coins, and urns, do testify their possessions. Some urns have been found at Castor, some also about Southcreak, and, not many years past, no less than ten in a field at Buxton,† not near any

* *Hominum infinita multitudo est, creberrimaque; ædificia ferè Gallicis consimilia.—Cæs. de Bello Gal.* l. v.

† In the ground of my worthy friend Robert Jegon, Esq.; wherein some things contained were preserved by the most worthy Sir William Paston, Bart.

[1] *Now if the, &c.*] That is to say, *if iken* (as well αγκων) signified an elbow—and thus, the Icenians were but "men that lived in an angle or elbow," then would the inhabitants of Norfolk have the best claim to the appellation, that county being most emphatically the *elbow* of Icenia. But unfortunately, *iken* does *not* signify an elbow; and it appears that the Iceni derived their name from the river Ouse, on whose

recorded garrison. Nor is it strange to find Roman coins of copper and silver among us; of Vespasian, Trajan, Adrian, Commodus, Antoninus, Severus, &c.; but the greater number of Dioclesian, Constantine, Constans, Valens, with many of Victorinus Posthumius, Tetricus, and the thirty tyrants in the reign of Gallienus; and some as high as Adrianus have been found about Thetford, or Sitomagus, mentioned in the *Itinerary* of Antoninus, as the way from Venta or Castor unto London.* But the most frequent discovery is made at the two Castors by Norwich and Yarmouth,† at Burghcastle, and Brancaster.‡

Besides the Norman, Saxon, and Danish pieces of Cuthred, Canutus, William, Matilda,§ and others, some British coins of gold have been dispersedly found, and no small number of silver pieces near Norwich,|| with a rude head upon the obverse, and an ill-formed horse on the

---

* From Castor to Thetford the Romans accounted thirty-two miles, and from thence observed not our common road to London, but passed by *Combretonium ad Ansam*, *Canonium*, *Cæsaromagus*, &c. by Bretenham, Coggeshall, Chelmsford, Brentwood, &c.

† Most at Castor by Yarmouth, found in a place called East-bloudy-burgh Furlong, belonging to Mr. Thomas Wood, a person of civility, industry, and knowledge in this way, who hath made observation of remarkable things about him, and from whom we have received divers silver and copper coins.

‡ Belonging to that noble gentleman, and true example of worth, Sir Ralph Hare, Bart., my honoured friend.

§ A piece of Maud, the empress, said to be found in Buckenham Castle, with this inscription,—*Elle n' a elle.*

|| At Thorpe.

banks they resided,—anciently called Iken, Yken, or Ycin. Whence, also, Ikenild-street, Ikenthorpe, Ikenworth.

reverse, with inscriptions *Ic. Duro. T.;* whether implying Iceni, Durotriges, Tascia, or Trinobantes, we leave to higher conjecture. Vulgar chronology will have Norwich Castle as old as Julius Cæsar; but his distance from these parts, and its gothick form of structure, abridgeth such antiquity. The British coins afford conjecture of early habitation in these parts, though the city of Norwich arose from the ruins of Venta; and though, perhaps, not without some habitation before, was enlarged, builded, and nominated by the Saxons. In what bulk or populosity it stood in the old East-Angle monarchy tradition and history are silent. Considerable it was in the Danish eruptions, when Sueno burnt Thetford and Norwich,* and Ulfketel, the governor thereof, was able to make some resistance, and after endeavoured to burn the Danish navy.

How the Romans left so many coins in countries of their conquests seems of hard resolution; except we consider how they buried them under ground when, upon barbarous invasions, they were fain to desert their habitations in most part of their empire, and the strictness of their laws forbidding to transfer them to any other uses: wherein the Spartans † were singular, who, to make their copper money useless, contempered it with vinegar. That the Britons left any, some wonder, since their money was iron and iron rings before Cæsar; and those of after-stamp by permission, and but small in bulk and bigness. That so few of the Saxons remain, because, overcome by succeeding conquerors upon the place, their coins, by degrees, passed into other stamps and the marks of after-ages.

---

* *Brampton Abbas Journallensis.* † *Plut. in vita Lycurg.*

Than the time of these urns deposited, or precise antiquity of these relicks, nothing of more uncertainty; for since the lieutenant of Claudius seems to have made the first progress into these parts, since Boadicea was overthrown by the forces of Nero, and Agricola put a full end to these conquests, it is not probable the country was fully garrisoned or planted before; and, therefore, however these urns might be of later date, not likely of higher antiquity.

And the succeeding emperors desisted not from their conquests in these and other parts, as testified by history and medal-inscription yet extant:—the province of Britain, in so divided a distance from Rome, beholding the faces of many imperial persons, and in large account; no fewer than Cæsar, Claudius, Britannicus, Vespasian, Titus, Adrian, Severus, Commodus, Geta, and Caracalla.

A great obscurity herein, because no medal or emperor's coin enclosed, which might denote the date of their interments; observable in many urns, and found in those of Spitalfields, by London,* which contained the coins of Claudius, Vespasian, Commodus, Antoninus, attended with lacrymatories, lamps, bottles of liquor, and other appurtenances of affectionate superstition, which in these rural interments were wanting.

Some uncertainty there is from the period or term of burning, or the cessation of that practice. Macrobius affirmeth it was disused in his days; but most agree, though without authentic record, that it ceased with the Antonini,—most safely to be understood after the reign of those emperors which assumed the name of Antoninus,

---

* *Stow's Survey of London.*

extending unto Heliogabalus. Not strictly after Marcus; for about fifty years later, we find the magnificent burning and consecration of Severus; and, if we so fix this period or cessation, these urns will challenge above thirteen hundred years.

But whether this practice was only then left by emperors and great persons, or generally about Rome, and not in other provinces, we hold no authentic account; for after Tertullian, in the days of Minucius, it was obviously objected upon Christians, that they condemned the practice of burning.* And we find a passage in Sidonius,† which asserteth that practice in France unto a lower account. And, perhaps, not fully disused till Christianity fully established, which gave the final extinction to these sepulchral bonfires.

Whether they were the bones of men, or women, or children, no authentic decision from ancient custom in distinct places of burial. Although not improbably conjectured, that the double sepulture, or burying place of Abraham,‡ had in it such intention. But from exility of bones, thinness of skulls, smallness of teeth, ribs, and thigh bones, not improbable that many thereof were persons of minor age, or women. Confirmable also from things contained in them. In most were found substances resembling combs, plates like boxes, fastened with iron pins, and handsomely overwrought like the necks or bridges of musical instruments, long brass plates overwrought like the handles of neat implements, brazen nip-

---

* *Execrantur rogos, et damnant ignium sepulturam.—Min. in Oct.*

† *Sidon. Apollinaris.*

‡ Gen. xxiii. 4.

pers, to pull away hair, and in one a kind of opal, yet maintaining a bluish colour.

Now that they accustomed to burn or bury with them, things wherein they excelled, delighted, or which were dear unto them, either as farewells unto all pleasure, or vain apprehension that they might use them in the other world, is testified by all antiquity, observable from the gem or beryl ring upon the finger of Cynthia, the mistress of Propertius, when after her funeral pyre her ghost appeared unto him; and notably illustrated from the contents of that Roman urn preserved by Cardinal Farnese,* wherein besides great number of gems with heads of gods and goddesses, were found an ape of agath, a grasshopper, an elephant of amber, a crystal ball, three glasses, two spoons, and six nuts of crystal; and beyond the content of urns, in the monument of Childerick the first,† and fourth king from Pharamond, casually discovered three years past at Tournay, restoring unto the world much gold richly adorning his sword, two hundred rubies, many hundred imperial coins, three hundred golden bees, the bones and horse shoes of his horse interred with him, according to the barbarous magnificence of those days in their sepulchral obsequies. Although, if we steer by the conjecture of many and septuagint expression, some trace thereof may be found even with the ancient Hebrews, not only from the sepulchral treasure of David, but the circumcision knives which Joshua also buried.

Some men, considering the contents of these urns, lasting pieces and toys included in them, and the custom of burning with many other nations, might somewhat doubt

---

* *Vigeneri Annot. in* 4. *Liv.* † *Chifflet. in Anast. Childer.*

whether all urns found among us, were properly Roman relicks, or some not belonging unto our British, Saxon, or Danish forefathers.

In the form of burial among the ancient Britons, the large discourses of Cæsar, Tacitus, and Strabo are silent. For the discovery whereof, with other particulars, we much deplore the loss of that letter which Cicero expected or received from his brother Quintus, as a resolution of British customs; or the account which might have been made by Scribonius Largus the physician, accompanying the Emperor Claudius, who might have also discovered that frugal bit of the old Britons,* which in the bigness of a bean could satisfy their thirst and hunger.

But that the Druids and ruling priests used to burn and bury, is expressed by Pomponius, that Bellinus the brother of Brennus, and king of the Britons, was burnt, is acknowledged by Polydorus, as also by Amandus Zierexensis in *Historia*, and Pineda in his *Universa Historia*, (Spanish.) That they held that practice in Gallia, Cæsar expressly delivereth. Whether the Britons (probably descended from them, of like religion, language, and manners) did not sometimes make use of burning, or whether at least such as were after civilized unto the Roman life and manners, conformed not unto this practice, we have no historical assertion or denial. But since, from the account of Tacitus, the Romans early wrought so much civility upon the British stock, that they brought them to build temples, to wear the gown, and study the Roman laws and language, that they conformed also unto

---

* *Dionis excerpta per Xiphilin. in Severo.*

their religious rites and customs in burials, seems no improbable conjecture.

That burning the dead was used in Sarmatia is affirmed by Gaguinus, that the Sueons and Gothlanders used to burn their princes and great persons, is delivered by Saxo and Olaus; that this was the old German practice, is also asserted by Tacitus. And though we are bare in historical particulars of such obsequies in this island, or that the Saxons, Jutes, and Angles burnt their dead, yet came they from parts where 'twas of ancient practice; the Germans using it, from whom they were descended. And even in Jutland and Sleswick in Anglia Cymbrica, urns with bones were found not many years before us.

But the Danish and northern nations have raised an era or point of compute from their custom of burning their dead:* some deriving it from Unguinus, some from Frotho the great, who ordained by law, that princes and chief commanders should be committed unto the fire, though the common sort had the common grave interment. So Starkatterus, that old hero, was burnt, and Ringo royally burnt the body of Harold the king slain by him.

What time this custom generally expired in that nation, we discern no assured period; whether it ceased before Christianity, or upon their conversion, by Ausgurius the Gaul, in the time of Ludovicus Pius, the son of Charles the Great, according to good computes; or whether it might not be used by some persons, while for an hundred and eighty years Paganism and Christianity were promiscuously embraced among them, there is no assured con-

* *Roisold, Brendetyde. Ild tyde.*

clusion. About which times the Danes were busy in England, and particularly infested this county; where many castles and strongholds were built by them, or against them, and great number of names and families still derived from them. But since this custom was probably disused before their invasion or conquest, and the Romans confessedly practised the same since their possession of this island, the most assured account will fall upon the Romans, or Britons Romanized.

However, certain it is, that urns conceived of no Roman original, are often digged up both in Norway and Denmark, handsomely described, and graphically represented by the learned physician Wormius.* And in some parts of Denmark in no ordinary number, as stands delivered by authors exactly describing those countries.† And they contained not only bones, but many other substances in them, as knives, pieces of iron, brass, and wood, and one of Norway a brass gilded jew's-harp.

Nor were they confused or careless in disposing the noblest sort, while they placed large stones in circle about the urns or bodies which they interred: somewhat answerable unto the monument of Rollrich stones in England,‡ or sepulchral monument probably erected by Rollo, who after conquered Normandy; where 'tis not improbable somewhat might be discovered. Meanwhile to what nation or person belonged that large urn found at Ashbury,§ containing mighty bones, and a buckler; what those large

* *Olai Wormii Monumenta et Antiquitat. Dan.*

† *Adolphus Cyprius in Annal. Slesvic. urnis adeo abundabat collis, etc.*

‡ In Oxfordshire, *Camden.*

§ In Cheshire, *Twinus de rebus Albionicis.*

urns found at Little Massingham;* or why the Anglesea urns are placed with their mouths downward, remains yet undiscovered.

CHAPTER III.

PLAISTERED and whited sepulchres were anciently affected in cadaverous and corrupted burials; and the rigid Jews were wont to garnish the sepulchres of the righteous.† Ulysses, in Hecuba, cared not how meanly he lived, so he might find a noble tomb after death.‡ Great princes affected great monuments; and the fair and larger urns contained no vulgar ashes, which makes that disparity in those which time discovereth among us. The present urns were not of one capacity, the largest containing above a gallon, some not much above half that measure; nor all of one figure, wherein there is no strict conformity in the same or different countries; observable from those represented by Casalius, Bosio, and others, though all found in Italy; while many have handles, ears, and long necks, but most imitate a circular figure, in a spherical and round composure; whether from any mystery, best duration, or capacity, were but a conjecture. But the common form with necks was a proper figure, making our last bed like our first; nor much unlike the urns of our nativity, while

---

* In Norfolk, *Hollingshead.* † Matt. xxiii. ‡ *Euripides.*

we lay in the nether part of the earth,* and inward vault of our microcosm. Many urns are red, these but of a black colour, somewhat smooth, and dully sounding, which begat some doubt, whether they were burnt, or only baked in oven or sun, according to the ancient way, in many bricks, tiles, pots, and testaceous works; and as the word *testa* is properly to be taken, when occurring without addition and chiefly intended by Pliny, when he commendeth bricks and tiles of two years old, and to make them in the spring. Nor only these concealed pieces, but the open magnificence of antiquity, ran much in the artifice of clay. Hereof the house of Mausolus was built, thus old Jupiter stood in the Capitol, and the statua of Hercules, made in the reign of Tarquinius Priscus, was extant in Pliny's days. And such as declined burning or funeral urns, affected coffins of clay, according to the mode of Pythagoras, a way preferred by Varro. But the spirit of great ones was above these circumscriptions, affecting copper, silver, gold, and porphyry urns, wherein Severus lay, after a serious view and sentence on that which should contain him.† Some of these urns were thought to have been silvered over, from sparklings in several pots, with small tinsel parcels; uncertain whether from the earth, or the first mixture in them.

Among these urns we could obtain no good account of their coverings; only one seemed arched over with some kind of brick-work. Of those found at Buxton, some were covered with flints, some, in other parts, with tiles; those at Yarmouth Caster were closed with Roman bricks, and

* Psal. lxiii.

† *Χωρήσεις τὸν ἄνθρωπον, ὃν ἡ οἰκουμένη οὐκ ἐχώρησεν.—Dion.*

some have proper earthen covers adapted and fitted to them. But in the Homerical urn of Patroclus, whatever was the solid tegument, we find the immediate covering to be a purple piece of silk: and such as had no covers might have the earth closely pressed into them, after which disposure were probably some of these, wherein we found the bones and ashes half mortared unto the sand and sides of the urn, and some long roots of quich, or dog's-grass, wreathed about the bones.

No lamps, included liquors, lacrymatories, or tear bottles, attended these rural urns, either as sacred unto the *manes*, or passionate expressions of their surviving friends. While with rich flames, and hired tears, they solemnized their obsequies, and in the most lamented monuments made one part of their inscriptions.* Some find sepulchral vessels containing liquors, which time hath incrassated into jellies. For, besides these lacrymatories, notable lamps, with vessels of oils, and aromatical liquors, attended noble ossuaries; and some yet retaining a vinosity† and spirit in them, which, if any have tasted, they have far exceeded the palates of antiquity. Liquors not to be computed by years of annual magistrates, but by great conjunctions and the fatal periods of kingdoms.‡ The draughts of consulary date were but crude unto these, and Opimian wine§ but in the must unto them.

In sundry graves and sepulchres we meet with rings, coins, and chalices. Ancient frugality was so severe, that they allowed no gold to attend the corpse, but only that

---

* *Cum lacrymis posuêre.* † *Lazius.*

‡ About five hundred years.—*Plato.*

§ *Vinum Opiminianum annorum centum.*—*Petron.*

which served to fasten their teeth.* Whether the Opaline stone in this were burnt upon the finger of the dead, or cast into the fire by some affectionate friend, it will consist with either custom. But other incinerable substances were found so fresh, that they could feel no singe from fire. These, upon view, were judged to be wood; but, sinking in water, and tried by the fire, we found them to be bone or ivory. In their hardness and yellow colour they most resembled box, which, in old expressions, found the epithet of eternal,† and perhaps in such conservatories might have passed uncorrupted.

That bay leaves were found green in the tomb of S. Humbert,‡ after an hundred and fifty years, was looked upon as miraculous. Remarkable it was unto old spectators, that the cypress of the temple of Diana lasted so many hundred years. The wood of the ark, and olive-rod of Aaron, were older at the captivity; but the cypress of the ark of Noah was the greatest vegetable of antiquity, if Josephus were not deceived by some fragments of it in his days: to omit the moor logs and fir trees found underground in many parts of England; the undated ruins of winds, floods, or earthquakes, and which in Flanders still show from what quarter they fell, as generally lying in a north-east position.§

But though we found not these pieces to be wood, according to first apprehensions, yet we missed not altoge-

---

* 12 *Tabul.* l. xi. *De Jure Sacro. Neve aurum adito ast quoi auro dentes vincti escunt im cum ilo sepelire urereve, se fraude esto.*

† *Plin.* l. xvi. *Inter ξύλα ἀσαπῆ numerat Theophrastus.*

‡ *Surius.*

§ *Gorop. Becanus in Niloscopio.*

ther of some woody substance; for the bones were not so clearly picked but some coals were found amongst them; a way to make wood perpetual, and a fit associate for metal, whereon was laid the foundation of the great Ephesian temple, and which were made the lasting tests of old boundaries and land-marks. Whilst we look on these, we admire not observations of coals found fresh after four hundred years.* In a long-deserted habitation† even egg-shells have been found fresh, not tending to corruption.

In the monument of King Childerick the iron relicks were found all rusty and crumbling into pieces; but our little iron pins, which fastened the ivory works held well together, and lost not their magnetical quality, though wanting a tenacious moisture for the firmer union of parts; although it be hardly drawn into fusion, yet that metal soon submitteth unto rust and dissolution. In the brazen pieces we admired not the duration, but the freedom from rust, and ill savour, upon the hardest attrition; but now exposed unto the piercing atoms of air, in the space of a few months, they begin to spot and betray their green entrails. We conceive not these urns to have descended thus naked as they appear, or to have entered their graves without the old habit of flowers. The urn of Philopœmen was so laden with flowers and ribbons, that it afforded no sight of itself. The rigid Lycurgus allowed olive and myrtle. The Athenians might fairly except against the practice of Democritus, to be buried up in honey, as fearing to embezzle a great commodity of their country, and the best of that kind in Europe. But Plato seemed too frugally politick, who allowed no larger monument than

---

* Of *Beringuccio nella pyrotechnia.* † At Elmham.

would contain four heroick verses, and designed the most barren ground for sepulture: though we cannot commend the goodness of that sepulchral ground which was set at no higher rate than the mean salary of Judas. Though the earth had confounded the ashes of these ossuaries, yet the bones were so smartly burnt, that some thin plates of brass were found half melted among them. Whereby we apprehend they were not of the meanest carcases, perfunctorily fired, as sometimes in military, and commonly in pestilence, burnings; or after the manner of abject corpses, huddled forth and carelessly burnt, without the Esquiline Port at Rome; which was an affront continued upon Tiberius, while they but half burnt his body,* and in the amphitheatre, according to the custom in notable malefactors; whereas Nero seemed not so much to fear his death as that his head should be cut off and his body not burnt entire.

Some, finding many fragments of skulls in these urns, suspected a mixture of bones; in none we searched was there cause of such conjecture, though sometimes they declined not that practice. The ashes of Domitian† were mingled with those of Julia; of Achilles with those of Patroclus. All urns contained not single ashes; without confused burnings they affectionately compounded their bones; passionately endeavouring to continue their living unions. And when distance of death denied such conjunctions, unsatisfied affections conceived some satisfaction to be neighbours in the grave, to lie urn by urn, and touch but in their manes. And many were so curious to

* *Sueton. in vita Tib. Et in amphitheatro semiustulandum,* not. *Casaub.*

† *Sueton. in vitâ Domitian.*

continue their living relations, that they contrived large and family urns, wherein the ashes of their nearest friends and kindred might successively be received,* at least some parcels thereof, while their collateral memorials lay in minor vessels about them.

Antiquity held too light thoughts from objects of mortality, while some drew provocatives of mirth from anatomies,† and jugglers shewed tricks with skeletons. When fiddlers made not so pleasant mirth as fencers, and men could sit with quiet stomachs, while hanging was played before them.‡ Old considerations made few mementos by skulls and bones upon their monuments. In the Egyptian obelisks and hieroglyphical figures it is not easy to meet with bones. The sepulchral lamps speak nothing less than sepulture, and in their literal draughts prove often obscene and antick pieces. Where we find *D. M.*§ it is obvious to meet with sacrificing *pateras* and vessels of libation upon old sepulchral monuments. In the Jewish hypogæum‖ and subterranean cell at Rome, was little observable beside the variety of lamps and frequent draughts of the holy candlestick. In authentick draughts of Anthony and Jerome we meet with thigh bones and death's-heads; but the cemeterial cells of ancient Christians and martyrs were filled with draughts of Scripture stories;

---

* See the most learned and worthy Mr. M. Casaubon upon Antoninus.

† *Sic erimus cuncti, &c. Ergo dum vivimus vivamus.*

‡ Ἀγώνον παίζειν. A barbarous pastime at feasts, when men stood upon a rolling globe, with their necks in a rope and a knife in their hands, ready to cut it when the stone was rolled away; wherein if they failed, they lost their lives, to the laughter of their spectators.—*Athenæus.*

§ *Diis manibus.*

‖ *Bosio.*

not declining the flourishes of cypress, palms, and olive, and the mystical figures of peacocks, doves, and cocks; but iterately affecting the portraits of Enoch, Lazarus, Jonas, and the vision of Ezekiel, as hopeful draughts, and hinting imagery of the resurrection, which is the life of the grave, and sweetens our habitations in the land of moles and pismires.

Gentile inscriptions precisely delivered the extent of men's lives, seldom the manner of their deaths, which history itself so often leaves obscure in the records of memorable persons. There is scarce any philosopher but dies twice or thrice in Laertius; nor almost any life without two or three deaths in Plutarch; which makes the tragical ends of noble persons more favourably resented by compassionate readers who find some relief in the election of such differences.

The certainty of death is attended with uncertainties, in time, manner, places. The variety of monuments hath often obscured true graves; and cenotaphs confounded sepulchres. For beside their real tombs, many have found honorary and empty sepulchres. The variety of Homer's monuments made him of various countries. Euripides* had his tomb in Africa, but his sepulture in Macedonia. And Severus† found his real sepulchre in Rome, but his empty grave in Gallia.

He that lay in a golden urn‡ eminently above the earth, was not like to find the quiet of his bones. Many of these urns were broke by a vulgar discoverer in hope of inclosed treasure. The ashes of Marcellus§ were lost

* *Pausan. in Atticis.* † *Lamprid. in vit. Alexand. Severi.*

‡ *Trajanus.—Dion.*

§ *Plut. in vit. Marcelli.* The commission of the Gothish King above ground, upon the like account. Where profit hath prompted, no age hath wanted such miners. For which the most barbarous expilators found the most civil rhetorick. Gold once out of the earth is no more due unto it; what was unreasonably committed to the ground, is reasonably resumed from it; let monuments and rich fabricks, not riches adorn men's ashes. The commerce of the living is not to be transferred unto the dead; it is not injustice to take that which none complains to lose, and no man is wronged where no man is possessor.

What virtue yet sleeps in this *terra damnata* and aged cinders, were petty magic to experiment. These crumbling relicks and long fired particles superannuate such expectations; bones, hairs, nails, and teeth of the dead, were the treasures of old sorcerers. In vain we revive such practices; present superstition too visibly perpetuates the folly of our forefathers, wherein unto old observation* this island was so complete, that it might have instructed Persia.

Plato's historian of the other world lies twelve days incorrupted, while his soul was viewing the large stations of the dead. How to keep the corpse seven days from corruption by anointing and washing, without exenteration, were an hazardable piece of art, in our choicest practice. How they made distinct separation of bones and ashes from fiery admixture, hath found no historical solution; though they seemed to make a distinct collection, and overlooked not Pyrrhus his toe which could not

Theodoric for finding out sepulchral treasure.—*Cassiodor. var.* I. 4.

* *Britannia hodie eam attonitè celebrat tantis ceremoniis ut dedisse Persis videri possit.—Plin.* I. 29.

be burnt. Some provision they might make by fictile vessels, coverings, tiles, or flat stones, upon and about the body, (and in the same field, not far from these urns, many stones were found under ground,) as also by careful separation of extraneous matter, composing and raking up the burnt bones with forks, observable in that notable lamp of [Joan.] Galvanus.* Martianus, who had the sight of the *vas ustrinum*† or vessel wherein they burnt the dead, found in the Esquiline field at Rome, might have afforded clearer solution. But their insatisfaction herein begat that remarkable invention in the funeral pyres of some princes, by incombustible sheets made with a texture of asbestos, incremable flax, or Salamander's wool, which preserved their bones and ashes incommixed.

How the bulk of a man should sink into so few pounds of bones and ashes, may seem strange unto any who considers not its constitution, and how slender a mass will remain upon an open and urging fire of the carnal composition. Even bones themselves, reduced into ashes, do abate a notable proportion. And consisting much of a volatile salt, when that is fired out, make a light kind of cinders. Although their bulk be disproportionable to their weight, when the heavy principle of salt is fired out, and the earth almost only remaineth; observable in sallow, which makes more ashes than oak, and discovers the common fraud of selling ashes by measure, and not by ponderation.

---

* To be seen *in Licet. de reconditis veterum lucernis.* [p. 599, fol. 1653.]

† *Typograph. Roma ex Martiano. Erat et vas ustrinum appellatum, quod in eo cadavera comburerentur. Cap. de Campo Esquilino.*

Some bones make best skeletons,* some bodies quick and speediest ashes. Who would expect a quick flame from hydropical Heraclitus? The poisoned soldier when his belly brake, put out two pyres in Plutarch† But in the plague of Athens,‡ one private pyre served two or three intruders; and the Saracens burnt in large heaps, by the king of Castile,§ shewed how little fuel sufficeth. Though the funeral pyre of Patroclus took up an hundred foot,|| a piece of an old boat burnt Pompey; and if the burthen of Isaac were sufficient for an holocaust, a man may carry his own pyre.

From animals are drawn good burning lights, and good medicines against burning.¶ Though the seminal humour seems of a contrary nature to fire, yet the body completed proves a combustible lump, wherein fire finds flame even from bones, and some fuel almost from all parts; though the metropolis of humidity** seems least disposed unto it, which might render the skulls of these urns less burned than other bones. But all flies or sinks before fire almost in all bodies: when the common ligament is dissolved, the attenuable parts ascend, the rest subside in coal, calx, or ashes.

To burn the bones of the king of Edom for lime,†† seems no irrational ferity; but to drink of the ashes of dead relations,‡‡ a passionate prodigality. He that hath the ashes of his friend, hath an everlasting treasure;

---

* Old bones according to Lyserus. Those of young persons not tall nor fat according to Columbus.

† *In vitâ Gracc.* ‡ *Thucydides.* § *Laurent. Valla.*

|| Ἑκατόμπεδον ἔνθα ἢ ἔνθα.

¶ *Alb. Ovor.* ** The brain. *Hippocrates.*

†† Amos ii. 1. ‡‡ As Artemisia of her husband Mausolus.

where fire taketh leave, corruption slowly enters. In bones well burnt, fire makes a wall against itself; experimented in cupels,[1] and tests of metals, which consist of such ingredients. What the sun compoundeth, fire analyseth, not transmuteth. That devouring agent leaves almost always a morsel for the earth, whereof all things are but a colony; and which, if time permits, the mother element will have in their primitive mass again.

He that looks for urns and old sepulchral relicks, must not seek them in the ruins of temples, where no religion anciently placed them. These were found in a field, according to ancient custom, in noble or private burial; the old practice of the Canaanites, the family of Abraham, and the burying-place of Joshua, in the borders of his possessions; and also agreeable unto Roman practice to bury by high-ways, whereby their monuments were under eye;—memorials of themselves, and mementos of mortality unto living passengers; whom the epitaphs of great ones were fain to beg to stay and look upon them,—a language though sometimes used, not so proper in church inscriptions.* The sensible rhetorick of the dead, to exemplarity of good life, first admitted the bones of pious men and martyrs within church walls, which in succeeding ages crept into promiscuous practice: while Constantine was peculiarly favoured to be admitted into the church porch, and the first thus buried in England, was in the days of Cuthred.

---

[1] *cupels.*] "A chemical vessel, made of earth, ashes, or burnt bones, and in which assay-masters try metals. It suffers all baser ores, when fused and mixed with lead, to pass off, and retains only gold and silver."

* *Siste viator.*

Christians dispute how their bodies should lie in the grave.* In urnal interment they clearly escaped this controversy. Though we decline the religious consideration, yet in cemeterial and narrower burying-places, to avoid confusion and cross-position, a certain posture were to be admitted; which even Pagan civility observed. The Persians lay north and south; the Megarians and Phœnicians placed their heads to the east; the Athenians, some think, towards the west, which Christians still retain. And Beda will have it to be the posture of our Saviour. That he was crucified with his face toward the west, we will not contend with tradition and probable account; but we applaud not the hand of the painter, in exalting his cross so high above those on either side: since hereof we find no authentic account in history, and even the crosses found by Helena, pretend no such distinction from longitude or dimension.

To be gnawed out of our graves, to have our skulls made drinking bowls, and our bones turned into pipes, to delight and sport our enemies, are tragical abominations escaped in burning burials.

Urnal interments and burnt relicks lie not in fear of worms, or to be an heritage for serpents. In carnal sepulture, corruptions seem peculiar unto parts; and some speak of snakes out of the spinal-marrow. But while we suppose common worms in graves, it is not easy to find any there; few in churchyards above a foot deep, fewer or none in churches though in fresh decayed bodies. Teeth, bones, and hair, give the most lasting defiance to corruption.[1] In an hydropical body, ten years buried in

---

* *Kirkmannus de funer.*

[1] *hair, &c.*] This assertion of the durability of human hair

the churchyard, we met with a fat concretion, where the nitre of the earth, and the salt and lixivious liquor of the body, had coagulated large lumps of fat into the consistence of the hardest Castile soap, whereof part remaineth with us.[1] After a battle with the Persians, the Roman corpses decayed in few days, while the Persian bodies remained dry and uncorrupted. Bodies in the same ground do not uniformly dissolve, nor bones equally moulder; whereof, in the opprobrious disease, we expect no long duration. The body of the Marquis of Dorset seemed sound and handsomely cereclothed, that after seventy-eight years was found uncorrupted.* Common tombs preserve not beyond powder: a firmer consistence and compage of parts might be expected from arefaction, deep

---

has been corroborated by modern experiment. M. Pictet, of Geneva, instituted a comparison between recent human hair and that from a mummy brought from Teneriffe, with reference to the constancy of those properties which render hair important as a hygrometrick substance. For this purpose, hygrometers, constructed according to the principles of Saussure were used; one with a fresh hair, the other from the mummy. The results of the experiments were, that the hygrometrick quality of the Guanche hair is sensibly the same as that of recent hair.—*Edin. Phil. Journal*, xiii. 196.

[1] *In an hydropical body, &c.*] This substance was afterwards found in the cemetery of the Innocents at Paris, by Fourcroy, and became known to the French chemists under the name of *adipo-cire.* Sir Thomas is admitted to have been the first discoverer of it.

* Of Thomas, Marquis of Dorset, whose body being buried 1530, was 1608, upon the cutting open of the cerecloth, found perfect and nothing corrupted, the flesh not hardened, but in colour, proportion, and softness like an ordinary corpse newly to be interred.—*Burton's Descript. of Leicestershire.*

burial, or charcoal. The greatest antiquities of mortal bodies may remain in putrefied bones, whereof, though we take not in the pillar of Lot's wife, or metamorphosis of Ortelius,*[1] some may be older than pyramids, in the putrefied relicks of the general inundation. When Alexander opened the tomb of Cyrus, the remaining bones discovered his proportion, whereof urnal fragments afford but a bad conjecture, and have this disadvantage of grave interments, that they leave us ignorant of most personal discoveries. For since bones afford not only rectitude and stability but figure unto the body, it is no impossible physiognomy to conjecture at fleshy appendencies, and after what shape the muscles and carnous parts might hang in their full consistencies. A full spread *cariola*† shews a well-shaped horse behind; handsome formed skulls give some analogy to fleshy resemblance. A critical view of bones makes a good distinction of sexes. Even colour is not beyond conjecture, since it is hard to

---

* In his map of Russia.

† That part in the skeleton of a horse, which is made by the haunch-bones.

[1] *metamorphosis, &c.*] His map of Russia (*Theatrum orbis Terrarum*, fol. Lond. 1606) exhibits but one "metamorphosis,"—a vignette of some figures kneeling before a figure seated in a tree, who is sprinkling something upon his audience. On other trees in the distance hang several figures. This is the legend beneath:—"*Kergessi gens catervatim degit, id est in hordis; habetque ritum hujusmodi. Cum rem divinam ipsorum sacerdos peragit, sanguinem, lac et fimum jumentorum accipit, ac terræ miscet, inque vas quoddam infundit eoque arborem scandit, atque concione habita, in populum spargit, atque* hæc aspersio pro Deo habetur et colitur. *Cum quis diem inter illos obit, loco sepulturæ arboribus suspendit.*"

be deceived in the distinction of Negroes' skulls.* Dante's† characters are to be found in skulls as well as faces. Hercules is not only known by his foot. Other parts make out their comproportions and inferences upon whole or parts. And since the dimensions of the head measure the whole body, and the figure thereof gives conjecture of the principal faculties, physiognomy outlives ourselves, and ends not in our graves.

Severe contemplators, observing these lasting relicks, may think them good monuments of persons past, little advantage to future beings; and, considering that power which subdueth all things unto itself, that can resume the scattered atoms, or identify out of any thing, conceive it superfluous to expect a resurrection out of relicks: but the soul subsisting, other matter, clothed with due accidents, may solve the individuality. Yet the saints, we observe, arose from graves and monuments about the holy city. Some think the ancient patriarchs so earnestly de-

---

* For their extraordinary thickness.[1]

† The poet Dante, in his view of Purgatory, found gluttons so meagre, and extenuated, that he conceited them to have been in the siege of Jerusalem, and that it was easy to have discovered *Homo* or *Omo* in their faces: M being made by the two lines of their cheeks, arching over the eye-brows to the nose, and their sunk eyes making O O which makes up *Omo*.

Parén l'occhiaje anella senza gemme:
Chi, nel viso degli uomini legge OMO,
Bene avria quivi conosciuto l'emme.—Purgat. xxiii. 31.

[1] The remark in the text is more correct than the explanation given of it in the note. The configuration of the skull (more particularly with reference to the *facial angle*) affords a criterion by which the various races of mankind may, with sufficient certainty, be discriminated.

sired to lay their bones in Canaan, as hoping to make a part of that resurrection; and, though thirty miles from Mount Calvary, at least to lie in that region which should produce the first fruits of the dead. And if, according to learned conjecture, the bodies of men shall rise where their greatest relicks remain, many are not like to err in the topography of their resurrection, though their bones or bodies be after translated by angels into the field of Ezekiel's vision, or as some will order it, into the valley of judgment, or Jehosaphat.*

CHAPTER IV.

CHRISTIANS have handsomely glossed the deformity of death by careful consideration of the body, and civil rites which take off brutal terminations: and though they conceived all reparable by a resurrection, cast not off all care of interment. And since the ashes of sacrifices burnt upon the altar of God, were carefully carried out by the priests, and deposed in a clean field; since they acknowledged their bodies to be the lodging of Christ, and temples of the Holy Ghost, they devolved not all upon the sufficiency of soul existence; and therefore with long services and full solemnities, concluded their last exequies, wherein to all distinctions the Greek devotion seems most pathetically ceremonious.†

* *Tirin.* in Ezek.

† *Rituale Græcum, operâ J. Goar, in officio exequiarum.*

Christian invention hath chiefly driven at rites, which speak hopes of another life, and hints of a resurrection. And if the ancient Gentiles held not the immortality of their better part, and some subsistence after death, in several rites, customs, actions, and expressions, they contradicted their own opinions: wherein Democritus went high, even to the thought of a resurrection, as scoffingly recorded by Pliny.* What can be more express than the expression of Phocylides?† Or who would expect from Lucretius‡ a sentence of Ecclesiastes? Before Plato could speak, the soul had wings in Homer, which fell not, but flew out of the body into the mansions of the dead; who also observed that handsome distinction of Demas and Soma, for the body conjoined to the soul, and body separated from it. Lucian spoke much truth in jest, when he said, that part of Hercules which proceeded from Alcmena perished, that from Jupiter remained immortal. Thus Socrates§ was content that his friends should bury his body, so they would not think they buried Socrates; and, regarding only his immortal part, was indifferent to be burnt or buried. From such considerations, Diogenes might contemn sepulture, and, being satisfied that the soul could not perish, grow careless of corporal interment. The Stoicks, who thought the souls of wise men had their

---

* *Similis * * * * reviviscendi promissa Democrito vanitas, qui non revixit ipse. Quæ (malum) ista dementia est, iterari vitam morte?*—Plin. l. vii. c. 58.

† Καὶ τάχα δ' ἐκ γαίης ἐλπίζομεν ἐς φάος ἐλθεῖν λεῖψαν ἀποιχομένων, *et deinceps.*

‡ *Cedit enim retro de terrâ quod fuit ante in terram, &c.—Lucret.*

§ *Plato in Phæd.*

habitation about the moon, might make slight account of subterraneous deposition; whereas the Pythagoreans and transcorporating philosophers, who were to be often buried, held great care of their interment. And the Platonicks rejected not a due care of the grave, though they put their ashes to unreasonable expectations, in their tedious term of return and long set revolution.

Men have lost their reason in nothing so much as their religion, wherein stones and clouts make martyrs; and, since the religion of one seems madness unto another, to afford an account or rational of old rites requires no rigid reader. That they kindled the pyre aversely, or turning their face from it was an handsome symbol of unwilling ministration. That they washed their bones with wine and milk; that the mother wrapt them in linen, and dried them in her bosom, the first fostering part and place of their nourishment; that they opened their eyes towards heaven before they kindled the fire, as the place of their hopes or original, were no improper ceremonies. Their last valediction,* thrice uttered by the attendants, was also very solemn, and somewhat answered by Christians, who thought it too little, if they threw not the earth thrice upon the interred body. That, in strewing their tombs, the Romans affected the rose; the Greeks amaranthus and myrtle: that the funeral pyre consisted of sweet fuel, cypress, fir, larix, yew, and trees perpetually verdant, lay silent expressions of their surviving hopes. Wherein Christians, who deck their coffins with bays, have found a more elegant emblem; for that it, seeming dead, will restore itself from the root, and its dry and

---

* *Vale, vale, nos te ordine quo natura permittet sequamur.*

exsuccous leaves resume their verdure again; which, if we mistake not, we have also observed in furze. Whether the planting of yew in churchyards hold not its original from ancient funeral rites, or as an emblem of resurrection, from its perpetual verdure, may also admit conjecture.

They made use of musick to excite or quiet the affections of their friends, according to different harmonies. But the secret and symbolical hint was the harmonical nature of the soul; which, delivered from the body, went again to enjoy the primitive harmony of heaven, from whence it first descended; which, according to its progress traced by antiquity, came down by Cancer, and ascended by Capricornus.

They burnt not children before their teeth appeared, as apprehending their bodies too tender a morsel for fire, and that their gristly bones would scarce leave separable relicks after the pyral combustion. That they kindled not fire in their houses for some days after, was a strict memorial of the late afflicting fire. And mourning without hope, they had an happy fraud against excessive lamentation, by a common opinion that deep sorrows disturb their ghosts.*

That they buried their dead on their backs, or in a supine position, seems agreeable unto profound sleep, and common posture of dying; contrary to the most natural way of birth; nor unlike our pendulous posture, in the doubtful state of the womb. Diogenes was singular, who preferred a prone situation in the grave; and some Christians† like neither, who decline the figure of rest, and make choice of an erect posture.

---

* *Tu manes ne læde meos.*

† Russians, &c.

That they carried them out of the world with their feet forward, not inconsonant unto reason, as contrary unto the native posture of man, and his production first into it; and also agreeable unto their opinions, while they bid adieu unto the world, not to look again upon it; whereas Mahometans who think to return to a delightful life again, are carried forth with their heads forward, and looking toward their houses.

They closed their eyes, as parts which first die, or first discover the sad effects of death. But their iterated clamations to excitate their dying or dead friends, or revoke them unto life again, was a vanity of affection; as not presumably ignorant of the critical tests of death, by apposition of feathers, glasses, and reflection of figures, which dead eyes represent not: which, however not strictly verifiable in fresh and warm *cadavers*, could hardly elude the test, in corpses of four or five days.*

That they sucked in the last breath of their expiring friends, was surely a practice of no medical institution, but a loose opinion that the soul passed out that way, and a fondness of affection, from some Pythagorical foundation,† that the spirit of one body passed into another, which they wished might be their own.

That they poured oil upon the pyre, was a tolerable practice, while the intention rested in facilitating the accension. But to place good omens in the quick and speedy burning, to sacrifice unto the winds for a dispatch in this office, was a low form of superstition.

The archimime, or jester, attending the funeral train,

---

* At least by some difference from living eyes.

† *Francesco Perucci, Pompe funebri.*

and imitating the speeches, gesture, and manners of the deceased, was too light for such solemnities, contradicting their funeral orations and doleful rites of the grave.

That they buried a piece of money with them as a fee of the Elysian ferryman, was a practice full of folly. But the ancient custom of placing coins in considerable urns, and the present practice of burying medals in the noble foundations of Europe, are laudable ways of historical discoveries, in actions, persons, chronologies; and posterity will applaud them.

We examine not the old laws of sepulture, exempting certain persons from burial or burning. But hereby we apprehend that these were not the bones of persons planet-struck or burnt with fire from heaven; no relicks of traitors to their country, self-killers, or sacrilegious malefactors; persons in old apprehension unworthy of the earth; condemned unto the Tartarus of hell, and bottomless pit of Pluto, from whence there was no redemption.

Nor were only many customs questionable in order to their obsequies, but also sundry practices, fictions, and conceptions, discordant or obscure, of their state and future beings. Whether unto eight or ten bodies of men to add one of a woman, as being more inflammable, and unctuously constituted for the better pyral combustion, were any rational practice: or whether the complaint of Periander's wife be tolerable, that wanting her funeral burning, she suffered intolerable cold in hell, according to the constitution of the infernal house of Pluto, wherein cold makes a great part of their tortures; it cannot pass without some question.

Why the female ghosts appear unto Ulysses, before the heroes and masculine spirits,—why the Psyche or soul of

Tiresias is of the masculine gender,* who being blind on earth, sees more than all the rest in hell; why the funeral suppers consisted of eggs, beans, smallage, and lettuce, since the dead are made to eat asphodels† about the Elysian meadows,—why, since there is no sacrifice acceptable, nor any propitiation for the covenant of the grave, men set up the deity of Morta, and fruitlessly adored divinities without ears, it cannot escape some doubt.

The dead seem all alive in the human Hades of Homer, yet cannot well speak, prophesy, or know the living, except they drink blood, wherein is the life of man. And therefore the souls of Penelope's paramours, conducted by Mercury, chirped like bats, and those which followed Hèrcules, made a noise but like a flock of birds.

The departed spirits know things past and to come; yet are ignorant of things present. Agamemnon foretells what should happen unto Ulysses; yet ignorantly enquires what is become of his own son. The ghosts are afraid of swords in Homer; yet Sibylla tells Æneas in Virgil, the thin habit of spirits was beyond the force of weapons. The spirits put off their malice with their bodies, and Cæsar and Pompey accord in Latin hell; yet Ajax, in Homer, endures not a conference with Ulysses: and Deiphobus appears all mangled in Virgil's ghosts, yet we meet with perfect shadows among the wounded ghosts of Homer.

Since Charon in Lucian applauds his condition among the dead, whether it be handsomely said of Achilles, that living contemner of death, that he had rather be a plough-

---

* In Homer:—*Ψυχὴ Θηβαίου Τειρεσίαο σκῆπτρον ἔχων.*

† In Lucian.

man's servant, than emperor of the dead? How Hercules his soul is in hell, and yet in heaven; and Julius his soul in a star, yet seen by Æneas in hell?—except the ghosts were but images and shadows of the soul, received in higher mansions, according to the ancient division of body, soul, and image, or *simulachrum* of them both. The particulars of future beings must needs be dark unto ancient theories, which Christian philosophy yet determines but in a cloud of opinions. A dialogue between two infants in the womb concerning the state of this world,* might handsomely illustrate our ignorance of the next, whereof methinks we yet discourse in Plato's den, and are but embryo philosophers.

Pythagoras escapes in the fabulous hell of Dante,* among that swarm of philosophers, wherein, whilst we meet with Plato and Socrates, Cato is to be found in no lower place than purgatory. Among all the set, Epicurus is most considerable, whom men make honest without an Elysium, who contemned life without encouragement of immortality, and making nothing after death, yet made nothing of the king of terrors.

Were the happiness of the next world as closely apprehended as the felicities of this, it were a martyrdom to

---

* *Del Inferno*, cant. 4.

[1] *A dialogue, &c.*] In one of Sir Thomas's Common-place Books occurs this sentence, apparently as a memorandum to write such a dialogue. And from "*A Catalogue MSS. written by, and in the possession of, Sir Thomas Browne, M.D., late of Norwich, and of his son Dr. Edward Browne, late President of the College of Physicians, London,*" in the Bodleian Library (*MSS. Rawlinson*, 390, xi.), it appears that he actually did write such a Dialogue. I have searched, hitherto in vain, for it, as I have elsewhere lamented.

live; and unto such as consider none hereafter, it must be more than death to die, which makes us amazed at those audacities that durst be nothing and return into their chaos again. Certainly such spirits as could contemn death, when they expected no better being after, would have scorned to live, had they known any. And therefore we applaud not the judgment of Machiavel, that Christianity makes men cowards, or that with the confidence of but half dying, the despised virtues of patience and humility have abased the spirits of men, which Pagan principles exalted; but rather regulated the wildness of audacities, in the attempts, grounds, and eternal sequels of death; wherein men of the boldest spirits are often prodigiously temerarious. Nor can we extenuate the valour of ancient martyrs, who contemned death in the uncomfortable scene of their lives, and in their decrepit martyrdoms did probably lose not many months of their days, or parted with life when it was scarce worth the living. For (beside that long time past holds no consideration unto a slender time to come) they had no small disadvantage from the constitution of old age, which naturally makes men fearful, and complexionally superannuated from the bold and courageous thoughts of youth and fervent years. But the contempt of death from corporal animosity, promoteth not our felicity. They may sit in the orchestra, and noblest seats of heaven, who have held up shaking hands in the fire, and humanly contended for glory.

Mean while Epicurus lies deep in Dante's hell, wherein we meet with tombs enclosing souls, which denied their immortalities. But whether the virtuous heathen, who lived better than he spake, or erring in the principles of himself, yet lived above philosophers of more specious maxims, lie so deep as he is placed, at least so low as not to rise against Christians, who believing or knowing that truth, have lastingly denied it in their practice and conversation—were a query too sad to insist on.

But all or most apprehensions rested in opinions of some future being, which, ignorantly or coldly believed, begat those perverted conceptions, ceremonies, sayings, which Christians pity or laugh at. Happy are they, which live not in that disadvantage of time, when men could say little for futurity, but from reason: whereby the noblest minds fell often upon doubtful deaths, and melancholy dissolutions. With these hopes, Socrates warmed his doubtful spirits against that cold potion; and Cato, before he durst give the fatal stroke, spent part of the night in reading the Immortality of Plato, thereby confirming his wavering hand unto the animosity of that attempt.

It is the heaviest stone that melancholy can throw at a man, to tell him he is at the end of his nature; or that there is no further state to come, unto which this seems progressional, and otherwise made in vain. Without this accomplishment, the natural expectation and desire of such a state, were but a fallacy in nature; unsatisfied considerators would quarrel the justice of their constitutions, and rest content that Adam had fallen lower; whereby, by knowing no other original, and deeper ignorance of themselves, they might have enjoyed the happiness of inferior creatures, who in tranquillity possess their constitutions, as having not the apprehension to deplore their own natures, and, being framed below the circumference of these hopes, or cognition of better being, the wisdom of God hath necessitated their contentment: but the superior ingredient and obscured part of ourselves, whereto all present felicities afford no resting contentment, will be able at last to tell us, we are more than our present selves, and evacuate such hopes in the fruition of their own accomplishments.

CHAPTER V.

Now since these dead bones have already out-lasted the living ones of Methuselah, and in a yard under ground, and thin walls of clay, out-worn all the strong and specious buildings above it; and quietly rested under the drums and tramplings of three conquests: what prince can promise such diuturnity unto his relicks, or might not gladly say,

*Sic ego componi versus in ossa velim?**

Time, which antiquates antiquities, and hath an art to make dust of all things, hath yet spared these minor monuments. In vain we hope to be known by open and visible conservatories, when to be unknown was the means of their continuation, and obscurity their protection. If they died by violent hands, and were thrust into their

* *Tibullus.*

urns, these bones become considerable, and some old philosophers would honour them,* whose souls they conceived most pure, which were thus snatched from their bodies, and to retain a stronger propension unto them; whereas they weariedly left a languishing corpse, and with faint desires of re-union. If they fell by long and aged decay, yet wrapt up in the bundle of time, they fall into indistinction, and make but one blot with infants. If we begin to die when we live, and long life be but a prolongation of death, our life is a sad composition; we live with death, and die not in a moment. How many pulses made up the life of Methuselah, were work for Archimedes: common counters sum up the life of Moses his man.† Our days become considerable, like petty sums, by minute accumulations; where numerous fractions make up but small round numbers; and our days of a span long, make not one little finger.‡

If the nearness of our last necessity brought a nearer conformity into it, there were a happiness in hoary hairs, and no calamity in half senses. But the long habit of living indisposeth us for dying: when avarice makes us the sport of death, when even David grew politickly cruel, and Solomon could hardly be said to be the wisest of men. But many are too early old, and before the date of age. Adversity stretcheth our days, misery makes

---

* *Oracula Chaldaica cum scholiis Pselli et Phethonis.* Βίῃ λιπόντων σῶμα ψυχαὶ καθαρώταται. *Vi corpus relinquentium animæ purissimæ.*

† In the Psalm of Moses.

‡ According to the ancient arithmetick of the hand, wherein the little finger of the right hand contracted, signified an hundred.—*Pierius in Hieroglyph.*

Alcmena's nights,* and time hath no wings unto it. But the most tedious being is that which can unwish itself, content to be nothing, or never to have been, which was beyond the mal-content of Job, who cursed not the day of his life, but his nativity; content to have so far been, as to have a title to future being, although he had lived here but in an hidden state of life, and as it were an abortion.

What song the Syrens sang, or what name Achilles assumed when he hid himself among women, though puzzling questions,† are not beyond all conjecture. What time the persons of these ossuaries entered the famous nations of the dead,‡ and slept with princes and counsellors, might admit a wide solution. But who were the proprietaries of these bones, or what bodies these ashes made up, were a question above antiquarism; not to be resolved by man, nor easily perhaps by spirits, except we consult the provincial guardians, or tutelary observators. Had they made as good provision for their names, as they have done for their relicks, they had not so grossly erred in the art of perpetuation. But to subsist in bones, and be but pyramidally extant, is a fallacy in duration. Vain ashes which in the oblivion of names, persons, times, and sexes, have found unto themselves a fruitless continuation, and only arise unto late posterity, as emblems of mortal vanities, antidotes against pride, vain-glory, and madding vices. Pagan vain-glories which thought the world might last for ever, had encouragement for ambition; and, finding no *atropos* unto the immortality of

---

* One night as long as three.

† The puzzling questions of Tiberius unto grammarians.—*Marcel. Donatus in Suet.*

‡ Κλυτὰ ἔθνεα νεκρῶν.—*Hom. Job.*

their names, were never dampt with the necessity of oblivion. Even old ambitions had the advantage of ours, in the attempts of their vain-glories, who acting early, and before the probable meridian of time, have by this time found great accomplishment of their designs, whereby the ancient heroes have already out-lasted their monuments, and mechanical preservations. But in this latter scene of time, we cannot expect such mummies unto our memories, when ambition may fear the prophecy of Elias,* and Charles the Fifth can never hope to live within two Methuselahs of Hector.†

And therefore, restless inquietude for the diuturnity of our memories unto present considerations seems a vanity almost out of date, and superannuated piece of folly. We cannot hope to live so long in our names, as some have done in their persons. One face of Janus holds no proportion unto the other. It is too late to be ambitious. The great mutations of the world are acted, or time may be too short for our designs. To extend our memories by monuments, whose death we daily pray for, and whose duration we cannot hope, without injury to our expectations in the advent of the last day, were a contradiction to our beliefs. We whose generations are ordained in this setting part of time, are providentially taken off from such imaginations; and, being necessitated to eye the remaining particle of futurity, are naturally constituted unto thoughts of the next world, and cannot excusably decline the consideration of that duration, which maketh pyramids pillars of snow, and all that is past a moment.

* That the world may last but six thousand years.

† Hector's fame lasting above two lives of Methuselah, before that famous prince was extant.

Circles and right lines limit and close all bodies, and the mortal right lined circle* must conclude and shut up all. There is no antidote against the opium of time, which temporally considereth all things: our fathers find their graves in our short memories, and sadly tell us how we may be buried in our survivors. Grave-stones tell truth scarce forty years.† Generations pass while some trees stand, and old families last not three oaks. To be read like bare inscriptions like many in Gruter,‡ to hope for eternity by enigmatical epithets or first letters of our names, to be studied by antiquaries, who we were, and have new names given us like many of the mummies,§ are cold consolations unto the students of perpetuity, even by everlasting languages.

To be content that times to come should only know there was such a man, not caring whether they knew more of him, was a frigid ambition in Cardan;‖ disparaging his horoscopal inclination and judgment of himself. Who cares to subsist like Hippocrates's patients, or Achilles's horses in Homer, under naked nominations, without deserts and noble acts, which are the balsam of our memories, the *entelechia* and soul of our subsistencies? To be nameless in worthy deeds, exceeds an infa-

---

* The character of death.

† Old ones being taken up, and other bodies laid under them.

‡ *Gruteri Inscriptiones Antiquæ.*

§ Which men show in several countries, giving them what names they please; and unto some the names of the old Egyptian kings, out of Herodotus.

‖ *Cuperem notum esse quod sim, non opto ut sciatur qualis sim.—Card. in vita propria.*

mous history. The Canaanitish woman lives more happily without a name, than Herodias with one. And who had not rather have been the good thief, than Pilate?

But the iniquity of oblivion blindly scattereth her poppy, and deals with the memory of men without distinction to merit of perpetuity. Who can but pity the founder of the pyramids? Herostratus lives that burnt the temple of Diana, he is almost lost that built it. Time hath spared the epitaph of Adrian's horse, confounded that of himself. In vain we compute our felicities by the advantage of our good names, since bad have equal durations, and Thersites is like to live as long as Agamemnon. Who knows whether the best of men be known, or whether there be not more remarkable persons forgot, than any that stand remembered in the known account of time? Without the favour of the everlasting register, the first man had been as unknown as the last, and Methuselah's long life had been his only chronicle.

Oblivion is not to be hired. The greater part must be content to be as though they had not been, to be found in the register of God, not in the record of man. Twenty-seven names make up the first story before the flood, and the recorded names ever since contain not one living century. The number of the dead long exceedeth all that shall live. The night of time far surpasseth the day, and who knows when was the equinox? Every hour adds unto that current arithmetick, which scarce stands one moment. And since death must be the *Lucina* of life, and even Pagans* could doubt, whether thus to live were to die; since our longest sun sets at right descensions,

---

* Euripides.

and makes but winter arches, and therefore it cannot be long before we lie down in darkness, and have our light in ashes;* since the brother of death[1] daily haunts us with dying mementos, and time that grows old in itself, bids us hope no long duration;—diuturnity is a dream and folly of expectation.[2]

Darkness and light divide the course of time, and oblivion shares with memory a great part even of our living beings; we slightly remember our felicities, and the smartest strokes of affliction leave but short smart upon

---

* According to the custom of the Jews, who place a lighted wax-candle in a pot of ashes by the corpse.—*Leo.*

[1] *the brother of death.*] That is, *sleep.* See a Fragment *On Dreams*, *post.*

[2] *Diuturnity*, *&c.*] Here may properly be noticed a similar passage which I find in *MS. Sloan.* 1848, fol. 194.

"Large are the treasures of oblivion, and heaps of things in a state next to nothing almost numberless; much more is buried in silence than recorded, and the largest volumes are but epitomes of what hath been. The account of time began with night, and darkness still attendeth it. Some things never come to light; many have been delivered; but more have been swallowed in obscurity and the caverns of oblivion. How much is as it were *in vacuo*, and will never be cleared up, of those long living times when men could scarce remember themselves young; and men seem to us not ancient but antiquities, when they [lived] longer in their lives than we can now hope to do in our memories; when men feared not apoplexies and palsies after seven or eight hundred years; when living was so lasting that homicide might admit of distinctive qualifications from the age of the person, and it might seem a lesser injury to kill a man at eight hundred than at forty, and when life was so well worth the living that few or none would kill themselves."

us. Sense endureth no extremities, and sorrows destroy us or themselves. To weep into stones are fables. Afflictions induce callosities; miseries are slippery, or fall like snow upon us, which notwithstanding is no unhappy stupidity. To be ignorant of evils to come, and forgetful of evils past, is a merciful provision in nature, whereby we digest the mixture of our few and evil days, and, our delivered senses not relapsing into cutting remembrances, our sorrows are not kept raw by the edge of repetitions. A great part of antiquity contented their hopes of subsistency with a transmigration of their souls,—a good way to continue their memories, while, having the advantage of plural successions, they could not but act something remarkable in such variety of beings, and enjoying the fame of their passed selves, make accumulation of glory unto their last durations. Others, rather than be lost in the uncomfortable night of nothing, were content to recede into the common being, and make one particle of the public soul of all things, which was no more than to return into their unknown and divine original again. Egyptian ingenuity was more unsatisfied, contriving their bodies in sweet consistencies, to attend the return of their souls. But all was vanity,* feeding the wind, and folly. The Egyptian mummies, which Cambyses or time hath spared, avarice now consumeth. Mummy is become merchandise, Mizraim cures wounds, and Pharaoh is sold for balsams.

In vain do individuals hope for immortality, or any patent from oblivion, in preservations below the moon:

---

* *Omnia vanitas et pastio venti, νομὴ ἀνέμου καὶ βόσκησις, ut olim Aquila et Symmachus. v. Drus. Eccles.*

men have been deceived even in their flatteries, above the sun, and studied conceits to perpetuate their names in heaven. The various cosmography of that part hath already varied the names of contrived constellations; Nimrod is lost in Orion, and Osyris in the Dog-star. While we look for incorruption in the heavens, we find they are but like the earth;—durable in their main bodies, alterable in their parts; whereof, beside comets and new stars, perspectives begin to tell tales, and the spots that wander about the sun, with Phaeton's favour, would make clear conviction.

There is nothing strictly immortal but immortality. Whatever hath no beginning, may be confident of no end; —which is the peculiar of that necessary essence that cannot destroy itself;—and the highest strain of omnipotency, to be so powerfully constituted as not to suffer even from the power of itself: all others have a dependent being and within the reach of destruction. But the sufficiency of Christian immortality frustrates all earthly glory, and the quality of either state after death, makes a folly of posthumous memory. God who can only destroy our souls, and hath assured our resurrection, either of our bodies or names, hath directly promised no duration. Wherein there is so much of chance, that the boldest expectants have found unhappy frustration; and to hold long subsistence, seems but a scape in oblivion. But man is a noble animal, splendid in ashes, and pompous in the grave, solemnizing nativities and deaths with equal lustre, nor omitting ceremonies of bravery in the infamy of his nature.[1]

---

[1] *Man is a noble animal, &c.*] Southey quotes this striking

Life is a pure flame, and we live by an invisible sun within us. A small fire sufficeth for life, great flames seemed too little after death, while men vainly affected precious pyres, and to burn like Sardanapalus; but the wisdom of funeral laws found the folly of prodigal blazes, and reduced undoing fires unto the rule of sober obsequies, wherein few could be so mean as not to provide wood, pitch, a mourner, and an urn.*

Five languages secured not the epitaph of Gordianus.† The man of God lives longer without a tomb than any by one, invisibly interred by angels, and adjudged to obscurity, though not without some marks directing human discovery. Enoch and Elias, without either tomb or burial, in an anomalous state of being, are the great examples of perpetuity, in their long and living memory, in strict account being still on this side death, and having a late part yet to act upon this stage of earth. If in the decretory term of the world we shall not all die but be changed, according to received translation, the last day will make but few graves; at least quick resurrections will anticipate lasting sepultures. Some graves will be opened before they be quite closed, and Lazarus be no

---

passage in the opening of his *Colloquies*,—but in a note he conjectures that Browne wrote *infimy* instead of *infamy*.

* According to the epitaph of Rufus and Beronica, in Gruterus.

> nec ex
> Eorum bonis plus inventum est, quam
> Quod sufficeret ad emendam pyram
> Et picem quibus corpora cremarentur,
> Et præfica conducta, et olla empta.

† In Greek, Latin, Hebrew, Egyptian, Arabic; defaced by Licinius the emperor.

wonder. When many that feared to die, shall groan that they can die but once, the dismal state is the second and living death, when life puts despair on the damned; when men shall wish the coverings of mountains, not of monuments, and annihilation shall be courted.

While some have studied monuments, others have studiously declined them,[1] and some have been so vainly boisterous, that they durst not acknowledge their graves; wherein Alaricus* seems most subtle, who had a river turned to hide his bones at the bottom. Even Sylla, that thought himself safe in his urn, could not prevent revenging tongues, and stones thrown at his monument. Happy are they whom privacy makes innocent, who deal so with men in this world, that they are not afraid to meet them in the next; who, when they die, make no commotion among the dead, and are not touched with that poetical taunt of Isaiah.†

Pyramids, arches, obelisks, were but the irregularities of vain-glory, and wild enormities of ancient magnanimity. But the most magnanimous resolution rests in the Christian religion, which trampleth upon pride, and sits on the neck of ambition, humbly pursuing that infallible perpetuity, unto which all others must diminish their diameters, and be poorly seen in angles of contingency.‡

---

1 *others have studiously declined them.*] In a work entitled ΠΕΡΙΑΜΜΑ ΕΝΔΗΜΙΟΝ, *or Vulgar Errours in Practice censured*, is a chapter on Decent Sepulture, the greater part of which is devoted to a censure against "the affectation of epitaphs," which, the author observes, are of Pagan origin, and are not even once mentioned in the whole book of God.

* *Jornandes de rebus Geticis.*

† Isa. xiv. 16, &c. ‡ *Angulus contingentiæ*, the least of angles.

Pious spirits who passed their days in raptures of futurity, made little more of this world, than the world that was before it, while they lay obscure in the chaos of pre-ordination, and night of their fore-beings. And if any have been so happy as truly to understand Christian annihilation, ecstacies, exolution, liquefaction, transformation, the kiss of the spouse, gustation of God, and ingression into the divine shadow, they have already had an handsome anticipation of heaven ; the glory of the world is surely over, and the earth in ashes unto them.

To subsist in lasting monuments, to live in their productions, to exist in their names and predicament of chimæras, was large satisfaction unto old expectations, and made one part of their Elysiums. But all this is nothing in the metaphysicks of true belief. To live indeed, is to be again ourselves, which being not only an hope, but an evidence in noble believers, it is all one to lie in St. Innocent's* church-yard, as in the sands of Egypt. Ready to be any thing, in the ecstacy of being ever, and as content with six foot as the *moles* of Adrianus.†

tabésne cadavera solvat,
An rogus, haud refert.—LUCAN.

---

* In Paris, where bodies soon consume.

† A stately mausoleum or sepulchral pile, built by Adrianus in Rome, where now standeth the castle of St. Angelo.

"A Roman urn drawn with a coal taken out of it, and found among the burnt bones, and is now in the possession of Dr. Hans Sloane, to whom this plate is most humbly inscribed."—First Edition.

BRAMPTON URNS.

PARTICULARS

OF SOME URNS FOUND IN BRAMPTON FIELD,

FEBRUARY, 1667-8.

CORRECTED FROM THREE MS. COPIES IN THE BRITISH MUSEUM

AND THE BODLEIAN LIBRARY.

ORIGINALLY PUBLISHED IN 1712.

BRAMPTON URNS.

I THOUGHT I had taken leave of Urns, when I had some years past given a short account of those found at Walsingham,* but a new discovery being made, I readily obey your commands in a brief description thereof.

In a large arable field, lying between Buxton and Brampton, but belonging to Brampton, and not much more than a furlong from Oxnead-park, divers urns were found. A part of the field being designed to be inclosed, the workmen digged a ditch from north to south, and another from east to west, in both which they fell upon divers urns; but earnestly and carelessly digging, they broke all they met with, and finding nothing but ashes and burnt bones, they scattered what they found. Upon notice given unto me, I went myself to observe the same, and to have obtained a whole one; and though I met with two in the side of the ditch, and used all care I could with the workmen, yet they were broken. Some advantage there was from the wet season alone that day, the earth not readily falling from about them, as in the summer. When some were digging the north and south ditch, and others at a good distance the east and west one, those at this latter upon every stroke which was made at the other ditch, heard a hollow sound near to them, as though the ground had been arched, vaulted, or hollow, about them. It is very probable there are very

* See *Hydriotaphia, Urn Burial: or, a Discourse of the Sepulchral Urns lately found in Norfolk.* 8vo, London, printed 1658.

many urns about this place, for they were found in both ditches, which were one hundred yards from each other; and this very sounding of the earth, which might be caused by hollow vessels in the earth, might make the same probable. There was nothing in them but fragments of burnt bones; not any such implements and extraneous substances as I found in the Walsingham urns: some pieces of skulls and teeth were easily discernible. Some were very large, some small, some had coverings, most none.

Of these pots none were found above three-quarters of a yard in the ground; whereby it appeareth, that in all this time the earth hath little varied its surface, though this ground hath been ploughed to the utmost memory of man. Whereby it may be also conjectured, that this hath never been a wood-land, as some conceive all this open part to have been; for in such places they made no common burying-places in old time, except for some special persons in groves: and likewise that there hath been an ancient habitation about these parts; for at Buxton also, not a mile off, urns have been found in my memory; but in their magnitude, figure, colour, posture, &c., there was no small variety; some were large and capacious, able to contain above two gallons, some of a middle, others of a smaller size. The great ones probably belonging to greater persons, or might be family urns, fit to receive the ashes successively of their kindred and relations, and therefore, of these, some had coverings of the same matter, either fitted to them, or a thin flat stone, like a grey slate, laid over them; and therefore also great ones were but thinly found, but others in good number. Some were of large wide mouths, and bellies proportionable, with short necks, and bottoms of three inches diameter, and near an inch thick; some small, with necks like jugs, and about that bigness; the mouths of some few were not round, but after the figure of a circle compressed, not ordinarily to be imitated; though some had small, yet none had pointed bottoms, according to the figures of those which are to be seen in Roma Soteranea, Viginerus, or Mascardus.

In the colours also there was great variety; some were whitish, some blackish, and inclining to a blue, others yellowish, or dark red, arguing the variety of their materials.[1] Some fragments, and especially bottoms of vessels, which seemed to be handsome neat pans, were also found of a fine coral-like red, somewhat like Portugal vessels, as though they had been made out of some fine Bolary earth, and very smooth; but the like had been found in diverse places, as Dr. Casaubon hath observed about the pots found at Newington, in Kent, and as other pieces do yet testify, which are to be found at Burrow Castle, an old Roman station, not far from Yarmouth.

Of the urns, those of the larger sort, such as had coverings, were found with their mouths placed upwards; but great numbers of the others were, as they informed me, (and one I saw myself,) placed with their mouths downward, which were probably such as were not to be opened again, or receive the ashes of any other person. Though some wondered at this position, yet I saw no inconveniency in it; for the earth being closely pressed, and especially in minor mouthed pots, they stand in a posture as like to continue as the other, as being less

[1] *arguing the variety of their materials.*] More probably, perhaps, their being more or less thoroughly burned.

subject to have the earth fall in, or the rain to soak into them. And the same posture has been observed in some found in other places, as Holingshead delivers of divers found in Anglesea.

Some had inscriptions, the greatest part none; those with inscriptions, were of the largest sort, which were upon the reverted verges thereof. The greatest part of those which I could obtain were somewhat obliterated; yet some of the letters to be made out: the letters were between lines, either single or double, and the letters of some few, after a fair Roman stroke, others more rudely and illegibly drawn, wherein there seemed no great variety; "NUON" being upon very many of them; only upon the inside of the bottom of a small red pan-like vessel, with a glaze, or varnish, like pots which come from Portugal, but finer, were legibly set down in embossed letters, *CRACUNA F.* which might imply *Cracuna figulus*, or *Cracuna fecit*, the name of the manufactor; for inscriptions commonly signified the name of the person interred, the names of servants official to such provisions, or the name of the artificer, or manufactor of such vessels; all which are particularly exemplified by the learned Licetus,* where the same inscription is often found, it is probably of the artificer, or where the name also is in the genitive case, as he also observeth.

Out of one was brought unto me a silver denarius, with the head of Diva Faustina on the obverse side, and with this inscription, *Diva Augusta Faustina*, and on the reverse the figures of the Emperor and Empress joining their right hands, with this inscription, *Concordia;* the

---

* Vid. *Licet. de Lucernis.*

same is to be seen in Augustino, and must be coined after the death of Faustina, (who lived three years wife unto Antoninus Pius,) from the title of Diva, which was not given them before their deification. I also received from some men and women then present, coins of Posthumus and Tetricus, two of the thirty tyrants in the reign of Galienus, which being of much later date, begat an inference that burning of the dead and urn-burial lasted longer, at least in this country, than is commonly supposed. Good authors conceive, that this custom ended with the reign of the Antonini, whereof the last was Antoninus Heliogabalus, yet these coins extend about fourscore years lower; and since the head of Tetricus is made with a radiated crown, it must be conceived to have been made after his death, and not before his consecration, which, as the learned Tristan conjectures, was most probably in the reign of the Emperor Tacitus, and the coin not made, or at least not issued abroad, before the time of the Emperor Probus, for Tacitus reigned but six months and a half, his brother Florianus but two months, unto whom Probus succeeding, reigned five years.

In the digging they brake divers glasses and finer vessels, which might contain such liquors as they often buried, in or by the urns; the pieces of glass were fine and clear, though thick; and a piece of one was finely streaked with smooth white streaks upon it. There were also found divers pieces of brass, of several figures; and one piece which seemed to be of bell metal. And in one urn was found a nail two inches long; whether to declare the trade or occupation of the person is uncertain. But upon the monuments of smiths, in Gruter, we meet with the figures of hammers, pincers, and the like; and we find the figure of a cobler's awl on the tomb of one of that trade, which was in the custody of Berini, as Argulus hath set it down in his notes upon *Onuphrius, of the antiquities of Verona.*

Now though urns have been often discovered in former ages, many think it strange there should be many still found, yet assuredly there may be great numbers still concealed. For,—though we should not reckon upon any who were thus buried before the time of the Romans, (although that the Druids were thus buried it may be probable, and we read of the urn of Chindonactes, a Druid, found near Dijon in Burgundy, largely discoursed by Licetus,) and though I say, we take not in any infant which was *minor igne rogi*, before seven months, or appearance of teeth, nor should account this practice of burning among the Britons higher than Vespasian, when it is said by Tacitus, that they conformed unto the manners and customs of the Romans, and so both nations might have one way of burial;—yet from his days, to the dates of these urns, were about two hundred years. And therefore if we fall so low, as to conceive there were buried in this nation yearly but twenty thousand persons, the account of the buried persons would amount unto four millions, and consequently so great a number of urns dispersed through the land, as may still satisfy the curiosity of succeeding times, and arise unto all ages.

The bodies whose reliques these urns contained, seemed thoroughly burned; for beside pieces of teeth, there were found few fragments of bones, but rather ashes in hard lumps and pieces of coals, which were often so fresh, that one sufficed to make a good draught of its urn, which still remaineth with me.

Some persons digging at a little distance from the urn places, in hopes to find something of value, after they had digged about three quarters of a yard deep, fell upon an observable piece of work, whose description [hereupon followeth.] The work was square, about two yards and a quarter on each side. The wall, or outward part, a foot thick, in colour red, and looked like brick; but it was solid, without any mortar, or cement, or figured brick in it, but of an whole piece, so that it seemed to be framed and burnt in the same place where it was found. In this kind of brick-work were thirty-two holes, of about two inches and a half diameter, and two above a quarter of a circle in the east and west sides. Upon two of these holes on the east side, were placed two pots, with their mouths downward; putting in their arms they found the work hollow below, and the earth being cleared off, much water was found below them, to the quantity of a barrel, which was conceived to have been the rain-water which soaked in through the earth above them.

The upper part of the work being broke, and opened, they found a floor about two foot below, and then digging onward, three floors successively under one another, at the distance of a foot and half, the floors being of a slaty, not bricky substance; in these partitions some pots were found, but broke by the workmen, being necessitated to use hard blows for the breaking of the floors; and in the last partition but one, a large pot was found of a very narrow mouth, short ears, of the capacity of fourteen pints, which lay in an inclining posture, close by, and somewhat under a kind of arch in the solid wall, and by the great care of my worthy friend, Mr. William Marsham, who employed the workmen, was taken up whole, almost full of water, clean, and without smell, and insipid, which being poured out, there still remains in the pot a great lump of an heavy crusty substance. What work this was we must as yet reserve unto better conjecture. Mean while we find in Gruter that some monuments of the dead had divers holes successively to let in the ashes of their relations; but holes in such a great number to that intent, we have not any where met with.

About three months after, my noble and honoured friend, Sir Robert Paston, had the curiosity to open a piece of ground in his park at Oxnead, which adjoined unto the former field, where fragments of pots were found, and upon one the figure of a well-made face; and there was also found an unusual coin of the Emperor Volusianus, having on the obverse the head of the Emperor, with a radiated crown, and this inscription, *Imp. Cæs. C. Vib. Volusiano Aug.* that is *Imperatori Cæsari Caio Vibio Volusiano Augusto.* On the reverse an human figure, with the arms somewhat extended, and at the right foot an altar, with the inscription, *Pietas.* This Emperor was son unto Caius Vibius Tribonianus Gallus, with whom he jointly reigned after the Decii, about the year 254; both he himself, and his father, were slain by the Emperor Æmilianus. By the radiated crown this piece should be coined after his death and consecration, but in whose time it is not clear in history. But probably this ground had been opened and digged before, though out of the memory of man, for we found divers small pieces of pots, sheeps' bones, sometimes an oyster-shell a yard deep in the earth.

INDEX.

www.ingramcontent.com/pod-product-compliance
Lightning Source LLC
Chambersburg PA
CBHW020241290326
41929CB00045B/1175

* 9 7 8 3 3 3 7 3 0 3 5 8 7 *